Florida

GARDEN GUIDE

TOP 10

By Robert E. Bowden and the Editors of Sunset Books

MENLO PARK · CALIFORNIA

SUNSET BOOKS

VICE PRESIDENT, GENERAL MANAGER: Richard A. Smeby
VICE PRESIDENT, EDITORIAL DIRECTOR: Bob Doyle
PRODUCTION DIRECTOR: Lory Day
OPERATIONS DIRECTOR: Rosann Sutherland
MARKETING MANAGER: Linda Barker
ART DIRECTOR: Vasken Guiragossian
SPECIAL SALES: Brad Moses

AUTHOR

ROBERT BOWDEN is an avid, hands-on gardener and the Executive Director of Harry P. Leu Gardens in Orlando, Florida. He contributes gardening articles monthly to several southeastern magazines; appears regularly on HGTV, PBS, and NPR; and has twice been featured as a "Great American Gardener" at Walt Disney World's EPCOT Flower Festival."

STAFF FOR THIS BOOK

PROJECT EDITORS: Lynn Ocone and Michael MacCaskey
COPY EDITOR: Vicky Congdon
CONSULTANT: Eric Schmidt, Harry P. Leu Gardens
PHOTO RESEARCH: Lois Chaplin, Lisa Love
DESIGN & PRODUCTION: Linda M. Bouchard
ILLUSTRATORS: Erin O'Toole, Lois Lovejoy, Jenny Speckels
MAP DESIGN AND CARTOGRAPHY:
Reineck & Reineck, San Francisco
PREPRESS COORDINATOR: Eligio Hernandez
PROOFREADER: Michelle Pollace
INDEXER: Mary Pelletier-Hunyadi

ACKNOWLEDGEMENT: *Blueberry Gardener's Guide*, Jeff Williamson and Paul Lyrene, University of Florida

COVER: Photograph by Susan A. Roth.
Design by Vasken Guiragossian.

Library of Congress Control Number: 2005929634.
ISBN 13: 978-0-376-03182-2.
ISBN 10: 0-376-03182-4.

Printed in the United States.

PHOTOGRAPHERS

WILLIAM D. ADAMS: 46R, 47C, 65L, 142, 143, 220, 249B; JEAN ALLSOPP/SPC PHOTO COLLECTION: 221T, 251B; ROBERT BOWDEN/HARRY P. LEU GARDENS: 19, 45B, 83B, 182; KAREN BUSSOLINI: 45B; ROB CARDILLO: 190C, 251T; DAVID CAVAGNARO: 36T, 210, 219BL/BR, 237; VAN CHAPLIN/SPC PHOTO COLLECTION: 13, 54, 108, 109, 141R, 151, 163, 170, 176, 189R, 192, 194, 206, 208, 231T, 247L, 248, 267; CLAIRE CURRAN: 215L; ROBIN B. CUSHMAN: 5; ROGER FOLEY: 1, 4, 6T/B, 7, 8, 9T, 49B, 50, 55R, 77B, 112, 113T/C, 115B, 133T, 146C, 147B, 149, 152, 155B, 158, 172, 176B, 185T, 191, 196, 198, 203B, 263, 264; FREDERICA GEORGIA/SPC PHOTO COLLECTION: 93R; DAVID GOLDBERG/SUSAN A. ROTH & CO.: 230; SAXON HOLT: 144, 165B, 167T/B, 173T, 212T, 213T, 231B, 256; MARY-GRAY HUNTER/SPC PHOTO COLLECTION: 44, 241R; EMILY JENKINS/SPC PHOTO COLLECTION: 249T; ANDREA JONES: 228; JUDYWHITE/GARDENPHOTOS.COM: 27C, 34, 35B, 45T, 47R, 56, 72, 78, 122T, 123R, 125, 130, 147T, 179B, 199L/R, 215R, 255T; DENCY KANE: 14C, 17B, 27B, 31L, 33TR, 35T, 38, 41R, 53T, 62, 63TL/BL, 69B, 73R, 76, 77TL/TR, 87B, 97TL, 97B, 99, 121B, 131B, 166, 181L, 185B, 187T, 221B, 245T, 254; MICHAEL MACCASKEY: 12B, 105, 145, 146T, 154, 157B, 229L; IAN MAGUIRE: 9B, 213B, 216, 217T/B, 222, 223, 226, 227L/R, 232, 233T/B; SYLVIA MARTIN/SPC PHOTO COLLECTION: 28, 73L, 96, 104, 116, 162, 204, 218, 235; STEPHEN G. PATEGAS: 25B, 29TL, 29TR, 42, 58C, 65R, 68T, 133B, 139L, 150, 153T/B, 155T, 156, 157T, 159T, 160, 161T/B, 165T, 180, 183, 195T/B, 202, 209B, 224; JERRY PAVIA: 39T/B, 45T, 107B, 117B, 135B, 141L, 171L/R, 197B, 203T, 211L/R, 214, 219TR, 225B, 229R; PAMELA K. PEIRCE: 57; PAM PEIRCE/SUSAN A. ROTH & CO.: 213C, 219TL, 242, 243T/B; MARY CAROLYN PINDAR/SPC PHOTO COLLECTION: 225T; GRAHAM RICE/GARDENPHOTOS.COM: 17T, 21B, 30; ROBERT RIFFLE: 69T, 164; SUSAN A. ROTH: 10, 11T/B, 12T, 16, 18, 20, 21T, 22, 23T/B, 25T, 26, 27T, 31R, 32, 33TL, 33B, 36C, 37, 40, 41L, 46L, 48, 49T/C, 51, 52, 53B, 55L, 59, 60, 61T/B, 63R, 64, 66, 67T/B, 70, 71T/B, 74, 75T/C/B, 79TL/TR/B, 80T, 81, 84, 85T/B, 86, 87T, 88, 89T/C/B, 90L/R, 91, 92T/C/B, 93L, 94, 95, 97TR, 98, 100, 101T/B, 102T/C, 106, 107T, 110, 111, 113B, 114, 115T, 117T, 118, 119, 120, 121T, 122B, 123L, 124B, 126, 127T/B, 129T/B, 131T, 132, 134, 135T, 136, 137, 138, 139R, 140, 148, 159B, 168, 169, 174, 175T/B, 176T, 178, 179T, 181R, 184, 186, 187B, 188, 189L, 193B, 197T, 200, 201TL/TR/B, 207T/B, 209T, 212, 234, 236, 238, 239L/R, 240, 241L, 244, 245B, 246, 247R, 250, 252, 253T, 255B, 261, 263, 265B, 266L/R; G. MICHAEL SHOUP: 82T/B, 83T; SPC PHOTO COLLECTION: 14T, 24, 29B, 80C, 103, 128, 193T, 205, 253T; PATRICK STAMILE: 47L; DARROW M. WATT: 234T; TOM WOODWARD: 58T, 124T, 190T

GARDEN DESIGNERS

BILL HARRIS: 49B; KAI HINKATY: 10, 36; KRISTIN HORNE: 263; RAYMOND JUNGLES: 1, 4, 7, 147B, 155B, 158, 191, 196, 198, 203B, 263, 264; LANDCRAFT ENVIRONMENTS LTD.: 48, 52; LEE LINK: 110; AUGUST MOORE: 50; BEN PAGE & ASSOCIATES: 169; TOM PELLET: 188; DOUGLAS RUHREN: 11B; BUNNY WILLIAMS: 246

For additional copies of *Florida Top 10 Garden Guide* or any other Sunset book, call 1-800-526-5111 or visit our web site at *www.sunsetbooks.com*.

Contents

Gardening in Florida

The word itself—*Florida*—speaks volumes in the imaginations of gardeners and tourists around the world. The mystique of the Sunshine State began way back, with legends of a "fountain of youth," which, five centuries ago, were widely believed to have at least a grain of truth in them. In a way, the legends are true, although not in the magical way imagined. The beaches and the climate here do inspire youthfulness.

Much of Florida's image as a paradise is thanks to its native and exotic plants: swaying palm trees, tropical fruits, and brightly colored flowers and foliage, summer and winter. Imagine picking a ripe banana from a nearby tree for your morning breakfast, or snacking on a fresh, ripe star fruit. Imagine, too, never having to store your garden tools for the winter—consider instead being able to garden 12 months of the year in sandy, warm soil without clay or rocks.

Florida is different. We plant snapdragons in October, not in spring like most of the rest of the country. Even more contrarian, tomatoes grow in the fall and spring here, not summer. In many areas of the state, fall is determined simply by a change in the direction of the wind, not by the arrival of temperatures below freezing or the first snowfall.

OPPOSITE PAGE: *Innumerable varieties of flowers, outdoor orchids, and bold-leaved foliage plants (such as bromeliads, ti plant, and palms), combined with the opportunity for homeowners to enjoy their gardens nearly year-round, is both the promise and the reality of gardening in Florida.*

In North Florida, winter frosts knock back pests so they have to start over again in spring. Not so in the south. There gardeners have to live with them, and I emphasize *live with them*. Forget the concept of eliminating pests. Trying to do so will only bring frustration.

So what is it about Florida? Ample rain, warm temperatures, and plenty of sun add up to the perfect recipe for growing plants. What's more, many of the plants grown indoors by northern gardeners are outdoor landscape plants in Florida. Landscapes here often include trees, shrubs, and perennials from tropical regions throughout the world.

ABOVE: *Showy and exotic plants such as lobster-claw* (Heliconia 'Pedro Ortiz') *are among the signature plants of tropical Florida.*
BELOW LEFT: *A common houseplant elsewhere, croton* (Codiaeum) *is a landscape shrub in South Florida.*
OPPOSITE PAGE: *A water feature is anchored at both ends by cabada palms* (Dypsis cabadae). *Hibiscus, yellow firecracker flower* (Crossandra), *and ti plant complete the picture.*

In Florida, we grow plants with exotic names—bat plants, crocodile ferns, angel's trumpets, lobster-claw, and elephant's ears come to mind. If you have a passion for growing plants that are out of the ordinary, or simply the desire to be surrounded by natural beauty outdoors, Florida is your paradise.

Choosing the top plants for Florida, given the scope of what's available and the range of climates here, is an admittedly subjective process. My intention here is not to expand the number of choices you have to make, but to simplify things by narrowing them down. To do so, I offer my experience, based on both 20 years of gardening here and, as director of the Harry P. Leu Gardens in Orlando, my many visits to and conversations with home gardeners throughout this state.

If you're new to Florida, the following pages will serve as an introduction to the three main sections of the state, all from a gardener's perspective, of course. Then, for a more specific delineation of Florida's gardening regions, refer to the zone map on pages 268 and 269. There you'll find the key to the zone recommendations that I've used throughout this book.

SOUTH FLORIDA

With the mildest temperatures of any location in the continental United States, the southern end of Florida is a gardener's dream. Most areas are nearly frost free, though occasionally temperatures drop down into the upper twenties (around −2°C). Key West, on the other hand, has never recorded a temperature below 41°F (5°C). Humidity and warm temperatures create a haven for an incredible range of plants, although lilacs, delphinium, and tulips are out. Take solace instead from the knowledge that mangoes, oranges, bananas, and even coconuts can grow just a few steps from your living room.

Plan on getting wet if you live in South Florida. Rainfall often exceeds 55 inches per year here, most of it coming in the summer and fall. The rain, in combination with the warm temperatures, spurs plants to grow at an incredible rate. Banana leaves can grow to 10 feet long in a single year. and bamboo can grow up to 8 inches a day.

South Florida is a tropical paradise, and gardeners can choose from a smorgasbord that includes tropical plants from all corners of the world. Most popular in landscapes are the flowering trees, shrubs, and vines. Noteworthy shrubs include the glamorous hibiscus, the royal-looking princess flower, and the fragrant plumeria (frangipani). Tropical flowering trees and vines are available in virtually every description. Some are covered with imposing dinosaur-like thorns, while others bear loads of flowers with fragrances that can fill the entire neighborhood with aromatic perfume.

But perhaps the most enjoyable aspect of gardening in South Florida is the ease with which you can grow rare and interesting fruits. If you have read about the luscious flavors of carambolas or sapodilla, or enjoyed these tropical fruits when they appeared in the exotic produce section of the supermarket, imagine the pleasure of growing them in your own garden.

Anyone new to gardening in South Florida needs to be mindful that the alkaline soil here is quite different from the typical, slightly acid soil of central and North Florida. Growing plants that are accustomed to alkaline soil is standard practice here, although many gardeners choose to grow favorite plants that are not adapted to this type of soil. They must add supplements to make the soil more neutral for those plants that prefer it that way. Many gardeners can be seen going so far as to remove

native soils and replace them with muck soils, or add heavy layers of mulch. Given the warm temperatures and plentiful rain, it is a never-ending process.

The trick to growing plants in the intense heat of South Florida is to garden smart. Make lists of those projects best completed during the cooler parts of the day and those for the warm periods. Get out into the garden early in the morning when the air is cool and moist. Besides, it's often just after sunrise that the fragrances from the surrounding flowers are strongest. Do any hard physical work in the morning. Once the sun rises up over the tops of the trees, retreat to the shade and attend to any jobs that can be taken care of there. Once it gets too hot—and it will—head for the air-conditioning until after dinner. Finally, the evening hours are the perfect time to stroll about and enjoy the fruits of your labor (and make lists of things to do tomorrow).

CENTRAL FLORIDA

If you can't make up your mind whether you want to grow temperate or tropical plants, central Florida is your dream come true. Mild winters, hot summers, and plenty of rainfall summer through winter create a unique situation in which pines and palms grow side by side. Temperate black-eyed Susans grow next to Brazilian plume flower, and subtropical fruits like papaya flourish next to nectarines. Although occasional freezes will damage the tenderest tropical plants, that doesn't stop gardeners in this region from regularly pushing the limits.

here range from 15°F (−9°C) at the north end of the zone to 27°F (−3°C) at the southern end. Heavier frosts do occur every five years or so, knocking many plants to the ground. But most bounce back, and with gusto. Every 100 years or so, temperatures in the southern end plummet down into the upper teens, wreaking havoc among home gardeners and commercial growers alike. Regardless of the severity, you can always count on the weather to improve and regain its greenhouse-like quality in a few days.

Humidity in Central Florida is always high, usually in the 80 to 95 percent range spring through fall. And rain is plentiful, sometimes as high as 60 inches in the southern reaches of this region and 45 inches in the northern section. If you think *you're* hot and sticky in the summer and fall months, think of how the plants feel.

Soils in central Florida are mostly sandy, well drained, and infertile. Adding a 2- to 3-inch layer of leaf litter, pine straw, or pine bark nuggets to the soil adds to the already slightly acidic makeup. Mulch also moderates soil temperatures, keeps the weeds down (because weed seeds need light to germinate), and helps keep the soil moist. In fact, gardening in this part of Florida is a lot like gardening hydroponically. Given the sandy soil, plants

Gardeners here enjoy the best of two horticultural worlds. While they can grow many of the tropical trees, shrubs, and fruits that thrive farther south, they can also grow plants that are staples up north. Normally cold-loving grapes grow right alongside subtropical flowering trees in Orlando. Camellias thrive down into Tampa, but call it quits by Sarasota.

Florida's interior regions are usually at least touched by frost. Light frosts occur up to six times a year in Orlando and extend all the way down to Fort Myers and Palm Beach on the coasts perhaps one or two times a year. Lows

need a diluted but steady supply of nutrients for proper growth. The bottom line: Fertilize frequently and water deeply once or twice a week. For the gardener, straw hats, sunscreen, plenty of drinking water, and periodic rest periods are the order of the day.

Exactly when to plant flowers and vegetables can be a bit tricky, especially if you've recently moved here from up north. Until you get the hang of it, the easiest way to learn is to visit nearby botanical gardens with an eye to what they plant, and when. Another way to quickly pick up the timing of central Florida gardening is to talk with your neighbors, especially the ones who have the better-looking gardens.

ABOVE: *Graced with hanging Spanish moss, wide-spreading live oaks are icons of North Florida and the Old South.*
LEFT: *Lavender azalea blooms frame a soft gray garden statue.*
OPPOSITE PAGE: *A stone-edged flower border is filled with hibiscus, castor bean, coleus, and fountain grass.*

NORTH FLORIDA

Large live oak trees draped in Spanish moss, arching over meandering roads, are northern Florida's trademarks. Slight, rounded hills are common here and complement the wide array of evergreen and deciduous trees and shrubs found growing in abundance. If you are searching for an unhurried, mannerly lifestyle, then North Florida is for you. Gardeners here share their secrets of growing award–winning plants, willingly give cuttings and "snips" of plants to neighbors, and even wave a friendly "hello" across the fence. It's North Florida, yes, but in tradition, it is the Deep South.

Gardening here is a joy. Ample rainfall, coupled with a variety of soils ranging from rich sandy loam to clay, provide the perfect growing conditions for many favorite plants. From palms in the south of the region to mountain laurel and native rhododendrons in the north, gardening is full of rewards. Camellia, the queen of the southern garden, grows here as in no other place in the United States. Azaleas of nearly every color of the rainbow perform exceedingly well with little attention. Other traditional southern plants, including magnolias, old garden roses, sweet olive, and gardenias, outperform themselves every year despite frequent light frosts. Unlike the stiff lawn grasses of central and southern Florida, North Florida has grass you want to wiggle your toes in. Soft, supple grasses like bermudagrass are virtually trouble free in this climate.

Vegetable gardening here is more in sync with the rest of the country. Tomatoes, squash, cucumbers, and peppers grow in summer, and in the winter, hardy pansies provide a little color. Corn is planted so that it's "knee-high by the Fourth of July," and potatoes and peas are planted on Valentine's Day. Plant a few extra rows of beans and sweet potatoes so you and the deer, raccoons, and possums will get along.

Cold down into the midteens during winter is not uncommon. Rainfall rarely exceeds 50 inches a year. Summertime highs of 90°F (32°C), combined with the canopy of tall trees that is common here, make gardening a much more pleasant task than farther south. This is

not flashy, flamboyant Florida. Here, life is quiet and peaceful. In its own right, this region, by declaration of many gardeners, may be the prettiest part of the state.

North Florida gardening is a four-step process: work hard in the morning, have a belt-unbuckling lunch, then take a nap in the hammock hung between two century-old loblolly pines. Later in the afternoon, try a tall glass of iced sun tea, perhaps with a smidgen of sippin' whiskey (for medicinal purposes, of course), and putter about the yard, enjoying the sights, colors, flavors, and fragrances of your little piece of paradise. Come to think of it, this is pretty much the gardening formula I recommend for the entire state!

Annuals

Annuals fill the landscape with quick, dependable color in every imaginable hue. These are plants that germinate, flower profusely, set seed, and die, all in a single growing season. Bringing showy color to an otherwise quiet corner of the landscape, annuals create drama. Use them to fill spaces between shrubs in mixed borders, set them out for temporary color in a newly planted rose garden or perennial flower border, and put them in pots or window boxes where you want continuous color.

For a dramatic effect in beds and borders, use annuals to create broad sheets of color. It's an incomparable effect, and the kind that annuals do best.

Plant an annual of a single variety and single color. A long, sweeping bed of pink petunias or bright red salvias, for example, is a major attention-getter in front of an evergreen hedge or along a brick patio. Certain annuals, however, seem to look most natural in a confetti-like mix of colors—pastel cosmos and the Climax hybrid marigolds, for example.

The best time to plant annuals in Florida depends on the plant. Annuals are cool season or warm season, based on their hardiness and ability to grow in cool soils.

Cool-season annuals, such as calendula (page 16), pansy (page 26), and snapdragon (page 30), grow best in the cool soils and mild temperatures of spring and fall. When the weather turns hot, they set seed and deteriorate. The best time to plant these annuals is early fall. They'll start blooming in a month or two and continue until the hot weather of the following summer.

Warm-season annuals include impatiens (page 20), marigold (page 22), and verbena (page 34). They grow and flower best in the warm months of late spring, summer, and early fall. Plant them just before the onset of hot weather (as long as frost no longer threatens).

Careful soil preparation helps get annuals off to a good start and keeps them growing well all season. Dig out any weeds and add a 3-inch layer of compost or other organic amendment. It's also a good idea to add a complete fertilizer; follow the package directions for amounts. Dig or till amendments and fertilizer into the soil, and then rake the bed smooth.

OPPOSITE PAGE: *'Homestead Purple' verbena and silver licorice plant (Helichrysum) combine perfectly.*
ABOVE: *Montgomery (left) and thatch palms shelter impatiens.*

For best results, choose nursery plants that are relatively small but with healthy foliage. Plants with yellowing leaves and those that are leggy, root-bound, or too big for their pots will establish slowly in your garden, and they'll usually bloom poorly.

After planting, water thoroughly. Apply a 2- to 4-inch layer of mulch (such as compost, ground bark, or pine needles) to conserve moisture and help prevent weeds from becoming established.

Calendula, Pot Marigold
Calendula officinalis

The bright yellow and orange flowers of calendula, or pot marigold, brighten Florida gardens through the cool months from fall into spring. Where it's native and blooms year-round (the Mediterranean and southern Europe), it is normally in bloom on the first day of every month, hence the origin of its name: *Calendula* comes from the Latin *calendae,* meaning the first day of the month. Calendula also serves as a clock of sorts because its flowers open in the morning, around 9 A.M., and close at sunset.

Europeans have grown this flowering plant in their gardens for at least 1,000 years, and used it during most of that time as a food and a healing herb to treat wounds, bruises, and ulcers, among other ailments. It was the Elizabethans of England who began calling it marigold, which creates confusion today with another orange and yellow member of the daisy family, the common marigold *(Tagetes),* from Mexico (page 22).

Few annual flowers are as easy to grow as pot marigolds. They are excellent in flower beds or in containers, and they make long-lasting cut flowers.

Calendula are irrepressible flower machines through the cooler months. Use them in containers, to edge beds and paths, and in mass plantings.

PEAK SEASON

Fall through spring

MY FAVORITES

'Indian Prince' flashes crimson in its center and on the backs of petals, and orange elsewhere. The result is a striking bicolor effect.

'Orange Prince' is a bright orange double-flowered type with strong stems that reach 18 inches in height.

'Pacific Beauty Mix', a long-time favorite, is a good calendula to start with. Superior heat tolerance allows these plants to last longer into spring. They grow about 2 feet tall and have 2- to 3-inch orange, yellow, apricot, or cream-colored blooms.

'Pink Surprise' has ruffled, orange, 3-inch flowers with a tinge of pink on a compact 15-inch-tall and 10-inch-wide plant.

'Red Splash' is a collection of several calendula colors, from orange and yellow to more unusual hues of peach, apricot, and ivory with red petal backs and burnt orange tips.

GARDEN COMPANIONS

Grow pot marigold as a border plant, especially in the winter garden, with other cool-season annuals, including snapdragons, statice, pansies, dianthus, and wax begonia.

ABOVE: *Orange-apricot flowers of 'Pink Surprise' are tinged with pink.*
RIGHT: *Two-tone petals of 'Indian Prince' stand out in the garden.*

When Seeds sown outdoors in August will bloom well before the end of December and provide color all winter.

Where Plant in full sun and in moderately fertile soil. Sow seeds directly where you want them to grow, in borders or containers, throughout fall.

How The plants are very easy to grow from seed sown directly into the garden. Keep well watered and transplant into the garden when the third set of leaves appears. Add compost to the garden bed first, if necessary. When transplanting calendulas, it is important not to damage the long, thin taproots.

TLC Water deeply during dry spells. Pot marigolds can tolerate light frosts but should be protected from hard freezes. For cut-flower use, pick the blooms in bud or when they are just beginning to open.

Coleus

Solenostemon scutellarioides

Coleus is an old-fashioned annual that is being rediscovered by a new generation of gardeners, and for a very simple reason. It is one of the most colorful and reliable plants to grow in a shade garden, where often only variations of green prevail. While coleus has been grown in Florida shade gardens for many years, in recent years breeders have begun to develop varieties that are suitable for growing in full sun.

A good, modern coleus variety for Florida has robust heat and sun tolerance, and it branches readily without being pinched back. It also has good disease and pest resistance, and produces few flowers, if any, and then only late in the season. In addition to a high degree of color variation in leaves, look for varieties that have highly serrated, frilled, or cupped leaves.

Coleus ranges in habit from full-sized, 3-foot-tall shrublike plants to low-growing ground-cover types that never exceed 12 inches in height.

Tiny, deeply fingered leaves of 'India Frills' are chartreuse with purple blotches. It's combined here with 'Tapien Blue' verbena.

These are trouble-free, easy-to-grow foliage plants that come in enough sizes, shapes, and shades to please almost anybody.

When Plant in spring just in advance of warmest weather. In northern Florida, plant after the danger of frost has passed.

Where Dappled shade is best for most varieties, but newer varieties are more tolerant of sun. Too much shade results in spindly growth, and too much sun will burn the leaves. Coleus grows best if planted in a well-drained, fertile, moist soil. The low-growing and trailing types also perform well in patio containers mixed with other shade-tolerant plants, in window boxes, and in hanging baskets.

How Buy plants in cell-packs or 4-inch pots, or grow your own from cuttings. (The latter is notoriously easy—coleus will root in a glass of water on the windowsill. Or, stick 3- to 4-inch cuttings in builder's sand, and keep moist. Plants will usually form roots within 2 weeks.) Plant outdoors at the same level that the plant was growing in the pot, being careful not to get soil in the crown (where the stems and roots meet) of the plant. Firm the soil around the root ball and water well to eliminate air pockets.

TLC Water well and fertilize every 3 weeks with water-soluble fertilizer. Remove the flower spikes as they develop and keep the plant pinched back to encourage branching.

Bred in Florida for Florida gardens, 'Astatula' coleus features a crimson red edge surrounding a yellow-green leaf.

PEAK SEASON
Spring through first frost

MY FAVORITES
I recommend any of the Florida City series, which are bred for naturally compact growth and sun tolerance. Varieties include 'Astatula', 'Elfers', 'Micanopy', 'Two Egg', and 'Yulee'. Colors vary, but all grow 12 to 24 inches high.

Other good varieties that have performed well in Florida include (by height):

To 12 inches high: 'Black Sun', 'Green and Gold', 'Red Trailing Queen', and 'Tell Tale Heart'.

12 to 24 inches high: 'Butter Cutter', 'Charlie McCarthy', 'Dark Frills', and 'India Frills'.

24 to 36 inches high: 'Grace Ann', 'Kiwi Fern', and 'Tilt-a-Whirl'.

36 inches high or more: 'Fack', 'Hurricane Louise', 'Inky Fingers', and 'Yada, Yada, Yada'.

GARDEN COMPANIONS
Combine with other summer annuals that prefer dappled shade, including begonia, common heliotrope, globe amaranth (*Gomphrena*), Madagascar periwinkle (*Catharanthus*), sweet alyssum (*Lobularia*), and wishbone flower (*Torenia*).

Impatiens
Impatiens walleriana

Impatiens are just about the easiest plants to grow and are among the most reliable annuals for summer color in deep to partial shade, and even in full sun if given enough water. They bloom constantly without deadheading, will double in size if fertilized, and never seem to get any diseases. Blooms are so prolific that the structure of the plant is obscured by the canopy of flowers from early summer to a heavy frost. In mildest areas of the Sunshine State, impatiens will reseed themselves year after year. It's not uncommon to have them last 4 to 5 years in the garden.

Native to the tropical forests of east Africa, impatiens welcome Florida's heat. They are so easy to grow that they make the least experienced gardener feel like a pro.

In general, impatiens work best in simple designs, though one guideline is to use lighter-colored flowers in heavier shade; they'll show up better. Classic uses include edging a shady bed or filling in between other plants. Impatiens grow equally well in garden beds and containers, thriving in tubs, hanging baskets, pots, window boxes, and stone troughs.

'Deco Red' makes a summer-long display of blazing red flowers.

PEAK SEASON

Year-round in most of Florida; at least spring through late fall in frost-prone areas.

MY FAVORITES

Hundreds of varieties are now available, but in my experience the following are the best in Florida:

Single-flowered types

'Accent Apricot', 'Accent Orange', and 'Accent White'; 'Dazzler Orange'; any of the Deco series; 'Violet Star', 'Red Star', and 'Coral Star'; 'Stardust Salmon' and 'Infinity Salmon'; 'Impact Orange'; 'Formula Mix'; any of the Tempo series; and 'Carnival Deep Pink.'

Double-flowered types

'Tutu Natural Rose', 'Fanciful Orchid Rose' and 'Salmon' have good repeat bloom and disease resistance.

GARDEN COMPANIONS

For seasonal color, plant with other annuals, including cool-season plants such as calendula, California poppy, delphinium, lobelia, foxglove, lupines, monkey flower, pansy, petunia, snapdragon, stock, and sweet William. Warm-season annuals that combine well include begonia, coleus, cosmos, flowering tobacco (Nicotiana), lantana, Mexican sunflower (Tithonia), moss rose, spider flower (Cleome), strawflower (Helichrysum), verbena, and torenia.

When Plant in the fall in the warmer southern areas of the state, plant in spring elsewhere.

Where Most impatiens grow best in deep shade to partial sun, and fertile, well-drained soil that is never soggy. Exposure to full sun is okay as long as plants receive at least some shade during the day as well as plenty of water and water-soluble fertilizer.

How Starting with plants in cell-packs or 4-inch pots, space them 6 to 12 inches apart. To increase the survival rate of your impatiens plants during the hot summer months, enrich the garden soil with compost or other organic matter to maintain adequate soil moisture and to reduce the number of round-worms (nematodes). When planting, be certain to keep the crown of the plant (where roots and stems meet) well above the garden soil level. Lightly fertilize with a controlled-release fertilizer after planting.

TLC Plants require no deadheading or pinching. They do need plenty of water, especially during the heat of summer, and they will respond well to regular fertilizing. Although home gardeners typically plant impatiens purchased at nurseries, you can root 4-inch-long tips of favorite varieties in a good potting soil. Keep well watered and the individual cuttings will be ready for planting out into the garden in 45 days.

TOP: *'Accent White'*
BOTTOM: *'Tutu Natural Rose'*

Marigold
Tagetes

'Little Hero Yellow' takes Florida's hot summers in stride. It's combined here with creeping zinnia.

Sunshine-bright marigolds are an all-American summer staple, right up there with corn on the cob, barbecues, and baseball. In Florida, marigolds are the backbone of any garden of summer annuals, with their bright yellow and gold flowers that contrast attractively with the finely divided dark green foliage.

Wild marigolds are native to Mexico and Central America (despite common names referencing "African" and "French"). From these, breeders have fashioned an array of choices from ankle-high to 4-foot plants in colors ranging from cream, yellow, and orange to bronzy red and maroon. The flowers actually are daisies, and some types show that familiar circular petal arrangement around a center tuft of stamens. The majority of available kinds, though, are full of petals—like pompoms on sticks. All have finely cut, dark green leaves, usually with a strong, distinctive aroma.

African marigolds *(Tagetes erecta)* feature the tallest plants (to 4 feet) and the largest flowers (3 to 5 inches across). But this group also offers shorter-growing strains that retain the large blossom size. These larger marigolds often require staking to help them stand erect in the garden. French marigolds *(T. patula)* give you front-of-the-border plants—dense and bushy with small bright flowers in yellow or orange, often combined with bronze or maroon. Signet marigolds *(T. tenuifolia)* are quite different from most marigolds. These plants are bushy with fine, lacy foliage. The small, 1-inch single flowers literally cover the plants in summer.

PEAK SEASON

Summer

MY FAVORITES

African marigolds (*Tagetes erecta*) are by far the most popular and the best varieties for growing in the heat of summer: 'Climax Hybrid'—yellow and gold, 3 feet; 'Flagstaff'—orange, 4 feet; 'Inca Gold'—12 inches; 'Simba'—gold, ruffled, 30 inches; 'Sunset Giants'—yellow, gold, orange, 30 inches; and 'Yellow Climax'—3 feet.

Copper canyon daisy (*T. lemmonii*) grows to 3 feet tall and wide, and the fine lacy foliage has a spicy fragrance.

French marigolds (*T. patula*) varieties include: 'Disco Flame'—red-gold, 8 inches; 'Hero Flame'—orange-red, 10 inches; 'Janie Gold'—8 inches; 'Little Hero Yellow'—8 inches; 'Royal Orange'—12 inches; 'Yellow Boy'—10 inches.

Mexican mint marigold (*T. lucida*) is a small shrub that grows 18 to 30 inches tall. The foliage has a licorice fragrance.

Signet marigold (*T. tenuifolia*): 'Luna Lemon Yellow' is the best cultivar.

GARDEN COMPANIONS

Plant with other heat-tolerant annuals, including floss flower (*Ageratum*), creeping zinnia (*Sanvitalia*), blanket flower (*Gaillardia*), lantana, moss rose, petunia, verbena, and zinnia.

When Plant marigolds outdoors at the beginning of the warm season, or after the danger of frost has passed.

Where Plant marigolds in full sun and well-drained soil.

How Grow from seeds sown in place. Or, transplant plants from the nursery or grown from seeds sown indoors 6 to 8 weeks before the outside planting date. To enhance the plants' vigor during the hot summer months, enrich the garden soil with compost or other organic matter to maintain adequate moisture. Dig a planting hole just as deep as the plant's root ball and twice as wide. Remove the marigold from its cell-pack or pot, loosen the root ball's sides, and cut or pull off any matted roots at the bottom. Place the root ball in the hole, making sure its surface is even with the soil level; fill in with soil around the root ball, firming with your fingers, then water gently. Plant tallest varieties deep: Strip leaves from the bottom inch or two of the stem, then set the root ball into the hole up to the plant's leaves.

TLC Remove spent blooms to prevent the plants from setting seed, which diverts energy from bloom production. French marigolds can help suppress nematodes. Till them into the soil in fall or winter instead of pulling them out.

RIGHT: *'Inca Gold', an African marigold*
BELOW: *The French marigold 'Disco Flame'*

Moss Rose, Portulaca
Portulaca grandiflora

If you are looking for a colorful annual that's very easy to grow in a variety of soil and moisture conditions, moss rose is an excellent choice.

This low-growing, fleshy plant, with brightly colored, almost cactus-like flowers, thrives in high temperatures and intense light. Moss rose, also called portulaca, can grow in ordinary soil and is very drought resistant. Little fazes it.

Originally from South America, it grows 6 inches high and spreads to 18 inches wide. Trailing, branching reddish stems are set with narrow, cylindrical, pointed leaves up to 1 inch long.

The 1-inch-wide, lustrous flowers are shaped like tiny roses. Flowers come in white, as well as in many shades of red, cerise, rose pink, orange, and yellow, and these blooms attract both resident and migrating butterflies. These flowers will cover the plant from early spring through the first frost, where there is one. Flowers of the species close on cloudy days and in early evening, but newer varieties like the Sundial strain don't.

Candy-colored flowers of moss rose bask and thrive in Florida's summer sunshine.

PEAK SEASON
Summer

MY FAVORITES
'Fairytales Snow White' has pincushion-like 1-inch flowers and 'Fairytales Cinderella' has interesting yellow–hot pink double blooms on maintenance-free, drought-resistant plants.

'Sundial Fuchsia', 'Sundial Peach', 'Sundial Peppermint', and 'Sundial Cream' have large, 2-inch-wide, double flowers on 4- to 5-inch mounds of needle-like leaves. A key advantage of these varieties is that, in my experience, slugs don't bother them.

GARDEN COMPANIONS
Plant moss rose with other warm-season annuals, including *Angelonia*, cuphea, begonia, *Evolvulus glomeratus* 'Blue Daze', cockscomb (*Celosia*), cosmos, fanflower (*Scaevola*), floss flower, flowering tobacco (*Nicotiana*), heliotrope, impatiens, blanket flower (*Gaillardia*), lantana, Madagascar periwinkle (*Catharanthus*), sunflower (*Helianthus*), nasturtium, petunia, spider flower (*Cleome*), strawflower (*Helichrysum*), alyssum, verbena, torenia, and zinnia.

TOP RIGHT: *'Sundial Peppermint' flowers are a rich purple-pink on a pink background.*
BOTTOM RIGHT: *'Sundial Fuchsia' consistently excels in Florida trials.*

When Set out nursery transplants in early spring, or just after any threat of frost has passed. Or sow seeds indoors 8 to 10 weeks before the anticipated outdoor planting date.

Where Moss rose loves sun. It will take as much as we can give it, and must have at least 8 hours of full sun a day. Growth and flowering is best in fertile, well-drained soil; soggy soil will kill plants. Ideal spots include rock gardens, in between pavers, and along driveways or sidewalks.

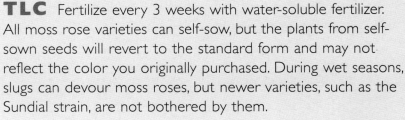

How Plant from cell-packs or 4-inch pots into well-prepared, fertile garden soil. Plant at the same level in the soil that the plant was growing in the pot, being careful not to get soil in the crown (where roots and stems meet) of the plant. Firm the soil around the root ball and water well to eliminate air pockets.

TLC Fertilize every 3 weeks with water-soluble fertilizer. All moss rose varieties can self-sow, but the plants from self-sown seeds will revert to the standard form and may not reflect the color you originally purchased. During wet seasons, slugs can devour moss roses, but newer varieties, such as the Sundial strain, are not bothered by them.

Pansy
Viola

ABOVE: *'Penny Yellow' is more heat tolerant than typical pansies.*
OPPOSITE BOTTOM: *Flowers of 'Bingo Mix' are more upright than other pansies.*

Who can resist pansies? After all, they have such friendly faces—those blotches of color that suggest eyes, nose, and mouth.

A typical pansy flower features two or three colors, from a total color range that includes practically any hue you can imagine: white, cream, yellow, orange, red, bronze, violet, black, purple, pink, lavender, and blue. In addition to the familiar "pansy face" pattern, you can get flowers with "fresh-scrubbed faces," in which the trademark blotches or lines are totally missing. Flower size is 2 to 4 inches across, depending on the strain, with blossoms borne on low, bushy plants that grow to nearly a foot high and spread a bit wider.

Pansies are short-lived perennials that love cool weather. Excellent in containers, they're often set out in pots in early spring, and replaced in the heat of summer by marigolds or other heat-loving plants.

26

PEAK SEASON

Fall through winter in most of Florida; spring and fall in North Florida.

MY FAVORITES

There are hundreds of pansy varieties, but the following have all been tested and proven superior for Florida.

'Accord/Banner Purple' (purple); 'Baby Bingo Beaconsfield' (purple with white blotch); 'Baby Bingo Blue Blotch' (solid blue); 'Baby Bingo Lavender Blue' (purple with light center); 'Bingo Red/Yellow' (yellow with dark blotch); 'Midnight' (purple with dark center); 'Pandora's Box' (a mix of gold, burnt orange, yellow, and rose), 'Penny Yellow' (yellow), 'Scala White' (white); and 'Scala Yellow' (yellow).

GARDEN COMPANIONS

Grow pansies massed in beds, in winter borders of mixed annuals, and in containers. Combine them with other cold-hardy annuals, such as dianthus, petunias, snapdragons, and statice (Limonium).

When Pansies prefer cool temperatures, so plant in midfall after the heat of summer has passed. Sow seeds in flats 8 to 10 weeks before the outside planting date, or start with nursery transplants, which is much easier.

Where Choose a location in sun or partial shade. Where warm weather arrives early, a partly shady spot may prolong vigorous flowering. Pansies need well-drained, amended soil.

How Space plants 6 inches apart in the garden, closer in containers. Incorporate a controlled-release fertilizer before planting. Lightly fertilize after planting with a water-soluble fertilizer.

TLC Water as needed to keep the soil evenly moist but not wet. Deadhead regularly to prolong flowering. Pansies are vigorous self-seeders and tend to show up in the least likely places, but they're always welcome. New transplants will be damaged by temperatures below freezing.

TOP RIGHT: 'Pandora's Box' flowers blend gold, orange, yellow, and rose. BOTTOM RIGHT: Baby Bingo series pansies overwinter well.

Pentas
Pentas lanceolata

It's hard to beat this tropical African native for continuous, eye-catching color. Pentas is an ideal annual plant for home gardeners and landscape professionals throughout Florida. It is a perennial where winters are not too severe, but a hard freeze in an unprotected area will kill even the strongest plant.

Pentas is a spreading, multistemmed plant that grows 2 to 3 feet high and wide, depending on the variety and whether the plant is shaded or in full sun. Its leaves are deep green, lance-shaped, and about 6 inches long. When weather is warm, 4-inch-wide clusters of red, pink, lavender, or white starlike flowers shoot up over the leaves. The blooms—especially the red and dark pink ones—attract a host of butterflies and hummingbirds. Bouquets of flowers last up to 2 weeks.

Filling a raised brick planter, pink and red pentas add color and attract many kinds of butterflies and hummingbirds.

PEAK SEASON

Year-round; spring to fall in central and North Florida

MY FAVORITES

'Butterfly Blush' has very light pink flowers on 12-inch-tall, very full, bushy plants. Its light pink color is not attractive to hummingbirds, but the butterflies enjoy it. Compared with other varieties, this one has a touch more panache.

'Butterfly Cherry Red' is, as the name implies, a bright cherry red, and produces so many blooms they almost cover the entire 12-inch-tall plant. Hummingbirds love it.

'Cranberry Punch' produces clusters of cranberry red flowers, each one with a ring of purple in its center, on 24-inch-tall stems.

'New Look Violet' is a vigorous 12-inch-tall plant that serves well in either the landscape or in containers or window boxes. The bright violet flowers don't attract butterflies, but their intense color is worth having in the garden.

GARDEN COMPANIONS

Use pentas in flower gardens as well as in containers and window boxes. Combine it with cool-season annuals, including delphinium, lobelia, foxglove, lupine, monkey flower, pansy, snapdragon, stock, and sweet William.

When In North Florida, plant in early spring and remove after killing frost. In warmer areas of the state, plant any time of year.

Where Pentas does best in at least 4 hours of direct sunlight a day and in fertile, well drained soil. Plants are not drought tolerant.

How Set plants from cell-packs or 4-inch pots into well-prepared, fertile garden soil. Plant at the same level that they were growing in the pots, being careful not to get soil in the crown (where roots and stems meet) of the plant. Firm the soil around the root ball and water well to eliminate air pockets.

TOP LEFT: *'Cranberry Punch'*
TOP RIGHT: *White pentas*
BOTTOM RIGHT: *Purple pentas*

TLC Fertilize with water-soluble fertilizer every 3 weeks; feed monthly in summer. Remove spent flowers to encourage more blooms. Prune heavily each year before spring growth begins to keep it compact and encourage flowering. Propagate from stem cuttings any time of year.

Snapdragon
Antirrhinum majus

S napdragons are among the best flowers for sunny borders and for cutting throughout Florida. They reach their greatest perfection in spring and early summer in North Florida, and in winter and spring in central and South Florida.

'Coronette Mix' snapdragons grow about 2 feet tall and produce flowers in a range of colors.

Individual snapdragon flowers have five lobes, which are divided into unequal upper and lower "jaws." A slight pinch at the sides of the flower will make the dragon open its jaws. Showing this trick to kids is a fun way to get them interested in the flower garden.

Some new varieties of snapdragons have different flower types: double; bell-shaped with round or open flowers; and azalea–shaped, which is a double bell flower. All are available in many colors. Plants range from 6 inches across for smallest types to 2 feet wide for the tallest. Both the traditional snapping and the bell-flowered types range in height from tall (2½ to 3 feet) to intermediate (12 to 20 inches) to dwarf (6 to 8 inches). A single plant can produce 10 to 12 blossom spikes in the course of a season. Snapdragons make excellent cut flowers.

PEAK SEASON

Winter and early spring in South Florida; early spring in North Florida.

MY FAVORITES

Several strains of snapdragons are available, but I get the best results from the Coronette and Liberty Classic series. The best among them are the following:

'Coronette Orchid' makes a very strong, sturdy, and densely branched garden plant that is better able than most varieties to withstand wind and rain.

'Liberty Classic' produces tall, full spikes of snapping flowers. All the colors are good, but my favorite is rose. That color, combined with its disease resistance, easily make it one of the best. All grow about 15 inches tall; the plants self-branch and become very dense.

GARDEN COMPANIONS

Tall and intermediate forms of snapdragons are splendid vertical accents in beds and borders with delphinium, iris, daylily (Hemerocallis), and foxglove. Other companion plants include winter annuals such as calendula, California poppy, delphinium, lobelia, foxglove, lupines, monkey flower, pansy, petunia, stock, and sweet William.

When Plant snapdragons in the garden when nighttime temperatures reach 50°F (10°C) in the fall. Pull the plants out when daytime temperatures reach 80°F (27°C) during the day. Sow seeds in flats from late summer to early spring for later transplanting. If snapdragons set out in early fall reach bud stage before night temperatures drop below 50°F (10°C), they will bloom through winter until weather gets hot the following spring.

Where Choose a location in full sun with richly amended, well-drained soil. Plant in cottage gardens and in beds, and to use as a cut flower. Dwarf kinds are quite effective as edgings and in rock gardens, raised beds, and containers.

How Start with nursery transplants, or grow your own transplants from seeds. Plant at the same level that the plant was growing in the pot, being careful not to get soil in the crown of the plant. Firm the soil around the root ball and water well to eliminate air pockets.

TLC Two or three weeks after planting your snapdragons, pinch varieties that aren't self branching back an inch or two to encourage side branches. Keep plants well watered, but avoid overhead watering (or do it only in the morning or on sunny days). Fertilize every 3 weeks with water-soluble fertilizer. Once temperatures go above 80°F (27°C), flowering stops.

LEFT: *'Liberty Classic Yellow'*
RIGHT: *'Liberty Classic Light Pink'*

Torenia, Wishbone Flower
Torenia fournieri

For many, many years, the original species form of torenia was the only option if you wanted to grow this plant here in Florida. But now there are new options for shade color, such as 'Summer Wave Blue', and over the last decade breeders have worked hard to create even more new varieties of torenia. Today, remarkably, there are varieties that grow in either sun as well as shade, and what a welcome addition they are.

Torenia is a tender annual, native to Vietnam and tropical Asia. The delicate, trumpet-shaped, gloxinia-like flowers are typically light blue or violet. They cover the mounding, 18-inch-tall plants by the hundreds from summer into fall. Varieties with pink, deep blue, burgundy, and blue-white bicolor blossoms are also available. Torenia's other common name comes from the arrangement of the stamens, which looks like a wishbone. Torenia makes a colorful plant in shaded rock gardens. Or use it in containers, as a companion to ferns or impatiens. And it's easy. Given fertile, well-drained soil and plenty of water, torenia is trouble free.

'Crystal White' zinnia backs a low edging of blue torenia, producing a colorful effect.

PEAK SEASON

Spring to fall

MY FAVORITES

Duchess hybrids prefer more shade, are more compact (6 to 8 inches tall and wide), and offer blooms in four color combinations: light blue with blue throat; blue with white throat; deep blue with blue throat; and pink with white throat. 'Duchess Deep Blue' grows only 6 inches tall and blooms 10 weeks after sowing the seeds indoors for transplanting into the garden. 'Duchess Burgundy' is similar, but flowers are red-purple with a white throat.

Summer Wave hybrids take more heat and more sun than most varieties, and their spreading habit makes them a good choice for hanging baskets. 'Summer Wave Amethyst' is my favorite, delivering outstanding color right through the hottest months of the year. It performs well in pots and window boxes.

GARDEN COMPANIONS

Plant with other warm-season annuals, including *Angelonia*, cuphea, begonia, cosmos, floss flower *(Ageratum)*, flowering tobacco *(Nicotiana)*, heliotrope, impatiens, blanket flower *(Gaillardia)*, Madagascar periwinkle *(Catharanthus)*, moss rose, nasturtium, petunia, strawflower *(Helichrysum)*, alyssum, verbena, and zinnia.

When Plant torenia seeds indoors 8 to 10 weeks before your anticipated garden planting date. Plant them outdoors after the danger of frost is past.

Where Set plants in part shade or full sun, depending on the variety, in fertile, well-drained soil. Use as edging plants or in pots and window boxes.

TOP LEFT: *'Summer Wave Amethyst'*
TOP RIGHT: *'Summer Wave Blue'*
BOTTOM RIGHT: *'Dutchess Burgundy'*

How Sow seeds in pots and transplant to garden after frost danger is past, or buy nursery plants. Set plants directly into well-prepared, fertile garden soil. Plant at the same level that the plant was growing in the pot, being careful not to get soil in the crown (where roots and stem meet) of the plant. Firm the soil around the root ball and water well to eliminate air pockets.

TLC Torenia is not drought tolerant. Keep roots cool with a mulch, and be alert for slugs, controlling them with bait if necessary. Fertilize every 3 weeks with water-soluble fertilizer. If plants stop flowering, trim them back and fertilize.

Verbena

Verbena

Clusters of 'Tapien Purple' flowers rise above dark red flowers of million bells (Calibrachoa).

As though it had been designed especially for Florida, verbena revels in summer heat while covering itself in colorful flowers. And it thrives with just moderate watering. Whether grown in the ground or in containers, these amenable plants can be counted on to provide low mounds of bright color from late spring into fall, until stopped by chilly weather or, in North Florida, knocked out by hard freezes.

Small, dark green leaves make a solid backdrop to the dense, dome-shaped clusters of small individual blossoms. The colors are clear and pure—white, pink, red, purple, and blue are the options, with the colored ones often featuring contrasting white centers. The many named strains vary not only in color but also in plant size; heights run from about 6 to 12 inches, with spreads equal to or somewhat greater than the heights. The new varieties have been bred for early flowering, resistance to disease (especially powdery mildew), and the ability to withstand Florida's intense summer heat. Gardeners in central and South Florida can treat verbena as a short-lived perennial, just giving plants a good "haircut pruning" in late winter before new growth starts.

Verbenas are trouble-free ground covers for Florida's summer gardens. The ½-inch flowers are held above the foliage in 3-inch-wide clusters. Verbena blooms from late spring until first frost.

PEAK SEASON
Spring into fall

MY FAVORITES
'Homestead Purple' has dark purple flowers on 10-inch-tall stems. It's hard to beat for disease resistance and heat tolerance.

'Novalis White' is dense and vigorous, very flowerful, and more tolerant of hot weather than other varieties.

'Tapien Purple', with its waves of purple flowers, makes an ideal flowering ground cover or hanging-basket plant.

'Tukana White' is dense, disease resistant, and very vigorous, sporting a thick mat of 2½- to 3-inch blooms from late spring until frost.

RELATED SPECIES
Verbena bonariensis, with its 3-foot-tall flower stems topped with purple flowers, blooms all summer on plants that have reseeded themselves from the previous year.

GARDEN COMPANIONS
Plant with other warm-season annuals, including cuphea, cockscomb, (*Celosia*), cosmos, floss flower (*Ageratum*), flowering tobacco (*Nicotiana*), impatiens, blanket flower (*Gaillardia*), lantana, moss rose, nasturtium, petunia, torenia, and zinnia.

When Plant verbena seeds indoors 8 to 10 weeks before your anticipated outdoor planting date. Transplant from cell-packs or 4-inch pots in spring as early as possible after all danger of frost is past.

Where Plant in a sunny, warm location that has good air circulation and well-drained soil. Low-growing verbenas make good ground covers and edging plants; they're also great in hanging baskets and containers or tumbling over rock walls. Use the taller types in borders.

How Transplant from cell-packs or 4-inch pots into well-prepared, fertile garden soil. Plant at the same level that the plant was growing in the pot, being careful not to get soil in the crown of the plant. Firm the soil around the root ball and water well to eliminate air pockets.

TLC Give plants moderate watering, and periodically remove spent flower clusters to keep plants tidy. Water during periods of extreme drought and heat to prevent spider mites. Fertilize every 3 weeks with water-soluble fertilizer.

TOP: *'Homestead Purple' is particularly effective combined with pastel-colored flowers.* RIGHT: *'Novalis White' is notably compact, creating a very uniform look.*

Bulbs

Ask any gardener about flowering bulbs and chances are, he or she will picture either tulips or daffodils. These most popular bulbs, or perhaps drifts of fragrant hyacinths or naturalized displays of crocus, are what usually come to mind. Unless, of course, you are a Florida native. For us, amaryllis, caladiums, and Peruvian daffodils will top the list.

This is the dichotomy of gardening in Florida. If you were born and raised here, you know about sandy soil, summer heat, and the litany of pests and diseases that befall plants in the Sunshine State. But if you've recently moved here, you might assume that plants like amaryllis, often sold in holiday gift boxes, are indoor plants. One of the most exciting days in your new gardening life will be when you realize you're "not in Kansas anymore," and that bulbs you've only read about before will thrive happily in your Florida garden.

In that one moment, you realize the potential of growing exotic bulbs in this climate.

Think of it: elephant's ear (page 48), amaryllis (page 38), and blood lily (page 42) will flourish here. Sure, some bulbs need a bit of shade to withstand the blazing sun, and not all can take the sandy soil and therefore need the help of compost. But given the right conditions, you can plant and forget glorious flowering bulbs with mysterious names like *Alocasia* and *Xanthosoma*.

Sometimes it gets a bit confusing determining whether a bulb is, in fact, a bulb and not a corm or a tuber or a tuberous root. But these differences are why plants such as daylily (page 46) and lily-of-the-Nile (page 52) are usually

OPPOSITE PAGE: *Elephant's ear (Colocasia 'Black Magic') combined with castor bean (Ricinus), purple Verbena bonariensis, and 'Pretoria' canna.*
TOP RIGHT: *White and blue lily-of-the-Nile provide midsummer color.*
BOTTOM RIGHT: *One of the showiest Florida bulbs is amaryllis.*

sold in containers, just like many landscape plants, even though they have tuberous roots like many bulbs. In fact, sometimes even the experts can't tell the difference between different bulb types, and in the end, it really doesn't make much difference.

The good news is that there are many bulbs to add the bright colors and dimension of visual interest to your garden that no other plants can provide. Include bulbs in a shrub bed or a flower border. They add depth to any planting and are virtually maintenance free. Provided the following bulbs are watered at the appropriate times, most of them can flourish in the same spot for many years.

Amaryllis
Hippeastrum

Florida's climate makes it possible to grow a wide variety of tropical and subtropical bulbs, and perhaps the showiest of all is the amaryllis. Atop a single tall, hollow stalk appear 6 to 12 large flowers in a variety of colors that punctuate the landscape with their exotic shape. The flowers are trumpet shaped and, depending on the selection, can be single or double. The bulbs are quite large, to 5 inches in diameter, and very easy to grow.

With big, uninhibited blooms, amaryllis make an unforgettable garden show. Winter-blooming houseplants in many other places, they are perennial in gardens here.

The leaves of the amaryllis are long and broad like a strap. After the flower has bloomed, cut off the flower stalk but allow the foliage to remain. It is this leathery foliage that processes nutrients that are then stored in the bulb for next year's flowers. If you remove the leaves, the following year's flowers will be fewer and smaller. Wait until the foliage turns yellow before removing it.

When Plant anytime between September and January.

Where Choose a location with full sun to partial shade and well-drained soil. If the soil is heavy, consider planting in raised beds made up of compost and native soil.

How Spacing for these big bulbs is personal preference and depends on the design of your garden. Normal spacing, however, is considered to be 14 inches apart. Plant the bulbs with just their necks aboveground and water well to establish strong roots. Apply mulch no deeper than 2 inches.

TLC Buy the largest and best-quality bulbs you can: a larger bulb will produce more stems and flowers. Pick off any grasshoppers that find their way to the leaves. Keep soil moist for maximum flower production. Red-blotch disease is sometimes a problem during periods of high humidity. Watering too frequently also encourages it. Symptoms are red blotches on the leaves, flowers, and stems, and on the bulb itself. Treat minor infestations by drenching the planting area with the fungicide thiophanate methyl, or dip bulbs in 105°F (41°C) water for 30 minutes, followed by a dipping in the same fungicide.

RIGHT: *'Apple Blossom' blends pink and white.*
BELOW: *'Picotee' petals are edged in bright red.*

PEAK SEASON
Late spring through summer

MY FAVORITES
'Apple Blossom' (glistening white with pale pink feathering) and 'Picotee' (bright white with a vivid red edge) are the most common.

'Lemon and Lime' has luminous white and pale yellow blossoms with green throats.

'Red Peacock' is a tall double red with narrow, white midveins.

If your garden needs a shorter amaryllis, try 'Baby Star', with its deep red flower with a white starburst center and a luminous green eye.

For a special amaryllis for the Florida garden, choose 'La Paz' cybister amaryllis *(Hippeastrum cybister).* The slender, pointed upper petals are dark coral, while the lower petals are greenish white edged in dark coral. The star-shaped flower has darker midveins and a faint green throat.

GARDEN COMPANIONS
Amaryllis are most effective in groups of eight or more in flower beds surrounding or below trees, near the entrance walk, along perennial borders, and as foundation plantings. Use them with 'Green Island' ficus, small ornamental grasses such as *Muhlenbergia* and *Stipa,* and perennial salvia.

Blackberry Lily, Leopard Flower

Belamcanda chinensis

Many of the more common kinds of iris, such as the luxuriant bearded iris, can't take Florida's heat and humidity. Fortunately, we have an amazingly diverse group of iris relatives that are suitable for many areas of our gardens. Among these, blackberry lily (also called leopard flower) is by far the most heat tolerant. If your garden has broiling hot sun and sandy soil, this member of the iris family is for you.

Clumps of blackberry lily grow to about 36 inches tall with broad, medium green, sword-shaped leaves that are arranged in an overlapping, fanlike fashion. Beginning in early summer, 48-inch-tall flower spikes appear. They produce bright golden flowers with five long, narrow petals that are spotted with deep orange. Blooming continues through fall. After some of the flowers finish blooming, a seed capsule appears adjacent to those still blooming. After ripening for 7 to 10 days, the capsule opens, displaying a tight group of 8 to 10 round, black berries for which the plant earned its name.

Speckled flowers of blackberry lily are 2 to 3 inches across on stems up to 4 feet high. Individual flowers last only a day, but new blossoms continue opening for weeks.

LEFT: *Seed capsules open to reveal shiny black seeds that resemble small blackberries.*
RIGHT: *Dazzler series plants are stockier than the species, and flowers are larger.*

PEAK SEASON

Late spring through fall

MY FAVORITES

Blackberry lily has only one known cultivar, 'Hello Yellow', which is free of spots. It's a favorite of many swallow-tail butterflies.

RELATED PLANTS

Blackberry lily and vesper iris (*Pardanthopsis*) have been hybridized to create a similar plant called *Pardancanda*. The flower shape is similar to blackberry lily, but the plant is only 12 to 18 inches tall and the flowers come in a broader range of colors. Named pardancandas include the following: The Dazzler series, with colors ranging from yellow to orange, red to pink, and lavender to purple; and 'Petite Pastels', which are delicate blends of yellow, peach, and pink flowers atop diminutive plants only 12 inches tall. Other varieties include 'Jungle Colors Improved' (shades of purple) and 'Sunset Tones' (pinks, yellows, and oranges).

GARDEN COMPANIONS

Use blackberry lily toward the back of a perennial border or wherever you need a coarse-textured, medium green upright plant. Plant with 'Victoria Blue' mealycup sage, black-eyed Susan (*Rudbeckia hirta*), and 'Blue Danube' Stokes' aster.

When You can plant container-grown nursery plants anytime, but fall is best, as it allows the plant to become well established before the following summer.

Where Plant in just about any well-drained soil with full sun. If there is a spot in your garden where other plants have failed, blackberry lily may be a good substitute.

How Soil amendments are beneficial but not essential. Don't plant in soggy areas, and keep the crown (where roots and top growth merge) of the plant above the soil level. Give this plant plenty of room. Blackberry lilies will grow to 48 inches tall and 36 inches wide in just a few years. They grow readily from seed sown in seed flats and covered with ¼ inch of fine soil.

TLC Blackberry lily is very easy to grow. Remove yellowing stems after seed production to encourage new growth from the base. To prevent the stems from falling over during the summer, place a peony ring over the clump and allow the fans of foliage to grow up through the support. Blackberry lily has no known pests or diseases.

Blood Lily
Scadoxus multiflorus katherinae

Huge ball-shaped clusters of flowers emerge atop foot-tall stalks of blood lily. Plant it in a container, or where you can see it up close.

Regardless of where you live, spring in Florida is spectacular. Flowering trees, shrubs, and bulbs of every color and description make our state one of the most colorful in the country. As with all things, however, spring comes to an end. From a gardener's perspective, there is typically a lull in color until the summer annuals and perennials kick in. But an interesting flowering bulb from South Africa called blood lily fills the gap by blooming in late spring. The 12-inch-tall stalk erupts out of the soil without leaves, bearing a blossom cluster with hundeds of individual red flowers.

Hummingbirds are attracted to the red, 8-inch-diameter flowers, but they can't quite figure out how to get to the nectar. After blooming over a period that lasts about 14 days, wide, flat foliage emerges from the soil and remains there until fall. This amaryllis relative gets its name from the flat, hockey puck–sized bulb that has flecks of red on the scales.

When Plant the bulb in the fall.

Where South of Gainesville, you can plant blood lily right in the garden and use it as a typical landscape plant. Farther north, plant it in pots. Store the pots inside during the winter and you won't have to dig up the bulbs. Freezing temperatures will kill the plants. In South Africa, blood lily grows in grassland and woodlands, in humus among boulders, and on termite mounds.

PEAK SEASON
Late spring; foliage is attractive summer through fall.

RELATED SPECIES
Giant stove brush, *Scadoxus puniceus*, bears 4-inch-wide clusters of scarlet to red flowers. The plant grows about 20 inches high.

GARDEN COMPANIONS
Blood lily performs well in a variety of garden settings. When planted in a perennial border, the large flower balls are a welcome addition for their unusual form and beautiful red color. Blood lily can also be planted among shrubs in a foundation planting, where the form and color of the blossoms will surprise the neighbors, and, later in the season, the broad green foliage will be attractive.

Giant stove brush is combined with maidenhair fern and iris in a narrow planting bed.

How Blood lily grows best in a soil that is rich

Flowers of aptly named giant stove brush are similar to blood lily, but tighter and aligned in an upward direction.

in humus and has good drainage. Bury the entire bulb so that the top is just below the soil surface. When the flower begins to bloom, start watering and feeding with a complete fertilizer and continue doing so throughout the summer. In August or September, fertilize with a high-phosphorus "bloom booster" product. Around November, the plant will start to go dormant again. During dormancy, reduce the watering, let the soil dry out a little, and don't fertilize.

TLC Fight the urge to remove the green foliage—it's there to produce food for next year's bloom.

Butterfly Ginger

Hedychium

The fragrant white flowers produced by this bed of butterfly ginger spread their delicate scent throughout the summer garden.

Gingers are used often in the Florida landscape because of their tropical appearance and pleasing fragrance that is similar to honeysuckle. The most common kinds are often called butterfly ginger because the upside-down flowers resemble butterflies.

Butterfly gingers can be grown in all areas of the state and will live through an ordinary winter with a little protection. Plant them near swimming pools, at the beach, in shade gardens, or in deep borders. They'll grow in containers, but their size will be restrained by the pot. In a container however, they can be moved out of the way at those times when they are less attractive.

Flower colors range from pure white to bright orange to soft yellow. The blossoms come on dense spikes, 6 to 12 inches long. They make good cut flowers. These gingers have bold tropical foliage, sometimes to 7 feet tall, and are a staple for any Florida garden.

When Plant gingers in May, once soil is thoroughly warmed but while it is still early in the season.

Where Choose a site with full sun to partial shade and plenty of moisture. Gingers are very tolerant of wet or heavy soils and some grow in water. They need at least 4 hours of sun to stand up tall and bloom well; too much shade causes them to grow horizontally to the ground.

How Butterfly ginger is a bit shy to bloom, so grow it where it can get maximum heat (against a wall, for example) and give it plenty of water. In North Florida, cover the crowns with leaf mulch in winter to protect them from cold. To increase butterfly ginger, divide the roots in spring.

TLC In late November, cut plants back and water only every other week. The butterfly ginger is a vigorous grower and needs to be divided every 4 or 5 years. Sometimes the butterfly ginger is attacked by stem borers. To prevent them from damaging the entire plant, destroy the affected stems early. Remove the old stems after flowers are spent to promote new growth.

LEFT: *Flowers of hidden ginger* (Curcuma petiolata).
BELOW: *'White Butterfly' butterfly ginger.*

PEAK SEASON
Late summer and fall

MY FAVORITES
'Dr. Moy' has clusters of fragrant, orange sherbet–colored flowers with dark orange centers, and the dark green leaves are streaked white.

'Elizabeth' grows 3 to 7 feet high and produces long clusters of deeply perfumed raspberry pink flowers that look like butterflies.

'Filigree' is delicate with thin light yellow flowers.

'White Butterfly' has pure white flowers atop 48-inch stems.

'Yellow Snow' is white with a bright yellow spot right in the middle.

RELATED PLANTS
Hidden ginger (*Curcuma petiolata*) grows 2 to 3 feet tall and produces 6-inch-long purple bracts in midsummer. Common ginger (*Zingiber officinale*) is the ginger used in cooking.

GARDEN COMPANIONS
In North Florida, plant butterfly gingers in the back of the perennial border as a backdrop for bleeding heart (*Dicentra*), columbine (*Aquilegia*), ferns, and foxglove. In southern areas, use butterfly gingers with elephant's ear (*Colocasia*), powder puff (*Calliandra*), bamboo, and banana (*Musa*).

Daylily
Hemerocallis

Enjoying a well-deserved reputation as easy to grow, daylilies are popular throughout Florida. They are available in a rainbow of colors and a variety of shapes and sizes.

Daylilies will survive in many types of landscapes with very little care. They are drought resistant and almost disease and insect free. Best of all, they are adaptable to various soil and light conditions and bloom from late spring until fall.

Once you start looking closely at daylilies, you'll begin noticing the ways in which they vary. Flowers may have a smooth, crepey, or ribbed texture, and the petal thickness, or *substance*, varies considerably. Blossom size, ranging from miniature to large, is an obvious distinction, as is the number of flower buds produced (anywhere from 10 to 100!). Thanks to new technologies in hybridizing, the days when the daylily color choice was limited to plain orange are long gone. Colors of the new varieties range from light purple to vivid red and nearly white.

LEFT: *Key members of the perennial border, daylilies provide season-long color.*
BELOW: *'Wedding Band' is one of the daylily hybrids that are well adapted to Florida.*

LEFT: 'Night Embers'
CENTER: 'Midnight Magic'
RIGHT: 'Butterscotch Ruffles'

PEAK SEASON

Late spring through later summer

MY FAVORITES

'Butterscotch Ruffles' grows to 24 inches tall; the ruffle-edged flowers are peach with gold overtones.

'Crystal Cupid' is a clear, dark yellow daylily that grows to 14 inches tall; it blooms early and reblooms well.

'Midnight Magic' grows to 28 inches tall, has fragrant 5½-inch-wide, velvety black-red flowers with a yellow-green throat.

'Night Embers' grows to 30 inches tall; the blossoms have 5-inch rich purple red petals with gold edges and a green throat.

'Paper Butterfly' grows 28 inches tall. The fragrant flower is a creamy peach and blue-violet blend with a blue-violet eye zone and a green throat.

'Wedding Band' has cream-colored 5½-inch-wide flowers. The petals have a delicate ruffled edge colored deep yellow, hence the name. It grows 26 inches tall.

GARDEN COMPANIONS

Combine with cuphea, phlox, iris, and scabiosa. The upright foliage contrasts well with annuals such as snapdragons, marigolds, and petunias.

When Plant nursery-grown plants in either early spring or very late fall. Daylilies planted in July, August, or September, when temperatures and humidity are extremely high, are more likely to rot.

Where Most daylilies do best in full sun. They will tolerate part-shade conditions, but require a minimum of 6 hours of direct sun per day. Light yellow cultivars, many shades of pink, and the delicate pastels need full sun to bring out their colorings. Many red and purple cultivars benefit from partial shade during the hottest part of the day because these heat-absorbing dark colors do not withstand the sun as well.

How Any fertile, well-drained garden soil is appropriate. Space plants no less than 18 to 24 inches apart and plant them about as deep as they grew originally. Do not set the crown more than 1 inch below the surface of the soil.

TLC Spider mites, thrips, aphids, and slugs are common pests, but usually do only minor damage. In poor soils or in light or sandy soils, fertilize with a complete fertilizer such as 5-10-10 or 5-10-5 in the spring or early summer. Follow with a low-nitrogen fertilizer such as 3-12-12 or 4-8-12 in late summer or early fall. In more fertile soils, fertilize once, in fall. Sufficient moisture increases the number and size of daylily blooms, so consistent watering is most important in spring when the plants are making flower stems and buds, and again in the summer during bloom.

Elephant's Ear

Alocasia, Colocasia, and *Xanthosoma*

Elephant's ear makes a dramatic container plant. Here it is combined with rex begonias.

Elephant's ear bulbs produce large leaves that add a tropical look to any garden. There are three different groups of plants referred to as elephant's ear. All are wetland herbaceous perennials (page 58).

Alocasia grows from rhizomes and is native to Malaysia and Asia. These plants are grown primarily for their heart- or spade-shaped leaves, which can range in color from variegated to hues of bronze, green, purple, and red. The smallest species grows only a foot or so tall, but others grow to 10 feet.

Colocasia grows from a corm, has heart-shaped leaves, and reaches 8 feet in height. Its starchy tubers are the source of poi, a traditional Hawaiian food. There are wetland and upland (dry-soil) types; the latter is known as "dasheen" or "taro."

Xanthosoma has large green leaves about 2 feet wide by 2½ feet long and the overall plant may attain a height of 5 feet or more. In Florida, it is known as "malanga"; it is the source of the edible cocoyam.

Elephant's ears are great for filling in large areas or in containers. If you want the tropical look but don't have the time to maintain a variety of different plants, they are a top choice.

When Plant the corms and rhizomes anytime water is plentiful.

Where Plants need full to partial sun and rich, wet soil. Depending on the variety, give them plenty of room. If young plants are crowded, they will compete for sunlight. Never plant *Colocasia* near lakes or streams. Small pieces will escape cultivation and establish themselves, to the detriment of other plants and animals.

How Plant tubers 2 inches deep in the ground or in containers after the danger of frost has passed and the soil is warm. The "eye" of the bulb tends to look like a spade toward the top end; plant it pointing up.

TLC Elephant's ears are very easy to grow given adequate space, water, and fertilizer. Fertilize the plants consistently through the growing season. Remove yellow leaves (a sure sign the plant is not getting enough water).

TOP RIGHT: Xanthosoma *'Chartreuse Giant'*
BOTTOM RIGHT: Colocasia *with purple sugar cane*
BELOW: C. esculenta *'Illustris' with* Miscanthus *'Morning Light'*

PEAK SEASON

Year-round in zones 26 and south; spring and summer farther north.

MY FAVORITES

Alocasia 'Dewey's Reversa' is a dwarf variety that is darkest along the midrib and veins of the leaves. *A. micholitziana* 'Frydek' is a striking, 3-foot-tall variety with velvety deep green leaves and snow white veins.

Colocasia affinis 'Jennigsii' has a velvety charcoal leaf face with central charcoal veining and a silver blotch in the center. It spreads via short, creeping stems that form new plants every few inches. *C. esculenta* 'Illustris', imperial taro, has green leaves with purple between veins. *C. e.* 'Black Magic' has velvety, purple-black leaves. *C. e.* 'Nancyana' has 2-foot-wide leaves that emerge light green then turn light yellow along the center. It also sends out side shoots that will root into the soil where moisture is adequate.

Xanthosoma lindenii 'Magnificum', an improved form, has deep green, arrow-shaped leaves with broad, creamy-colored veins. It grows 24 inches tall.

GARDEN COMPANIONS

Tiger grass (*Thysanolena*), butterfly ginger (*Hedychium*), and tropical lilac (*Dichorisandra*) all combine well.

Fancy-leafed Caladium
Caladium bicolor

Caladiums are tropical foliage plants grown for their spectacular, decorative multi-colored, leaves. They are used as pot, border, and bedding plants throughout Florida to provide summer color in shady locations.

Fancy-leafed caladiums grow between 12 and 30 inches tall, depending on the cultivar and the growing conditions. Densely planted, or planted in the shade, they will grow taller. Leaves have colored midribs and contrasting backgrounds and borders in combinations of red, pink, green, and white. The varied leaf colors and patterns of these easy and fast-growing plants create many uses for caladiums in the landscape.

Three new types of caladiums have been developed in recent years: strap leafed, lance leafed, and dwarf. The bulbs are smaller in size but have more eyes to produce dense, low-growing plants. Strap forms produce more leaves, making them ideal for a ground cover or front-row planting.

Typically, strap-leafed caladiums stay under 12 inches in height. Lance forms have pointed leaves with ruffled edges. They, too, stay under 12 inches. Dwarf forms are nearly as tall as fancy-leafed kinds, but their leaves are smaller.

Leaves of sun-tolerant 'June Bride' caladium are mostly green their first year, but nearly pure white in subsequent years.

'Pink Beauty' caladium combines attractively with English ivy, impatiens, and ferns.

PEAK SEASON

Late spring to late fall

MY FAVORITES

'Florida Beauty' has large, light green leaves with rose-colored polka dots.

'Florida Elise' leaves have light pink blotches, a green central vein, and a wide green margin along the edges.

'Florida Fantasy' has white leaves with green veins and a bright red midrib.

'Florida Sweetheart' is a rose pink variety with frilly green leaf margins.

'June Bride' is nearly pure white, especially its second year and if not given too much fertilizer.

'Pink Beauty' shows a mottled pattern of pink and green.

'Pink Gem' is a bright pink strap-leafed variety that is perfect for hanging baskets.

'Red Flash' is dark red with fuchsia spots and has the added benefit of good disease tolerance.

'White Christmas' is white with green leaf margins.

GARDEN COMPANIONS

Use fancy-leafed caladiums in deep to partial shade wherever you need a spot of color. Plant with other shade-loving plants such as bugleweed *(Ajuga),* English ivy *(Hedera),* ferns, begonia *(Begonia grandis),* and mossy ground covers such as *Selaginella.*

When All caladiums require warm, moist soil. Planting in cool soil results in slow growth or tuber rot. A good rule of thumb in determining when to set out caladiums is to plant them when you plant okra seed in the vegetable garden. A soil temperature of 70°F (21°C) is preferred.

Where Leaves need protection from direct sun. Some newer varieties will tolerate some full sun for a couple of hours daily, but all prefer dappled or moderate shade.

How For best results, start with new tubers each year. To get a jump on spring, start tubers indoors in pots, then transplant them to the garden. Plant the knobby side of the tuber up, leaving the top level with the soil surface. Space tubers about 1 foot apart.

TLC Keep plants well watered, and fertilize lightly through the growing season. Fertilize regularly with a soluble fertilizer to promote strong foliage growth. Burning of the edges of older leaves and scorching of leaves usually are the result of fertilizer touching the leaves, watering during the hottest part of the day, or too little water. In South Florida, tubers can remain in the ground all year. If you are growing caladiums in a pot, just bring the entire pot indoors, allow it to dry out, and then store in moderately cool conditions. Most caladium varieties produce only a few colorful leaves if the large central bud is allowed to grow; remove it by snapping it off when it first appears.

Lily-of-the-Nile
Agapanthus

While our northern gardening counterparts carefully and meticulously care for their

Dwarf 'Peter Pan' lily-of-the-Nile edges a narrow pathway.

exotic flowering bulbs, we Floridians can plant the same bulbs just like any other land-scape plant, then walk away. Lily-of-the-Nile, a native of South Africa, is one of those.

With its broad, straplike foliage and delicate, small, tubular flowers, lily-of-the-Nile is a star of the summer garden. In past years, it was known for its azure blue blossoms atop stems about 36 inches tall. But over the last decade or so, hybridizers throughout the world have been working with this plant, and the results are breathtaking. Now, pure white forms are available, as well as dark blue and even purple.

Lily-of-the-Nile grows best in warm, sunny conditions in a moderately fertile soil, but plants are very tolerant of a wide range of conditions, as long as the soil is well drained. This also makes an excellent container plant if fertilized with a slow-release fertilizer each spring.

When Plant container-grown plants anytime or plant individual rhizomes in the spring.

Where A site with full morning sun and rich, well-drained soil is ideal.

How Dig a planting hole equal to the depth of the plant's root ball and twice its width. Remove the plant from its container and set it into the hole, making sure the top of the root ball is even with the surrounding soil, and then backfill. Cover the tops of the roots with 1 inch of soil. Space plants 8 inches apart and provide adequate water to establish roots.

ABOVE: *Dark blue flower clusters of 'Elaine' bloom atop 4-foot stems.*
BELOW: *A close look at an individual flower of 'Blue Giant' lily-of-the-Nile.*

TLC Morning sun is preferred, but if rich soil and adequate water are maintained lily-of-the-Nile can withstand full sun. The flowers can be cut for use indoors; they will last up to 7 days in a vase. The dried seed heads also look attractive in arrangements. There are no pests or diseases of note.

PEAK SEASON
Early to midsummer

MY FAVORITES
'Alba' is the tallest white-blooming form, sometimes reaching 48 inches in height.

'Blue Giant' grows 3 feet tall and produces large heads of dark blue flowers on dark green stems.

'Elaine' is a very vigorous evergreen variety that grows 3 feet tall and produces dark violet-blue, 8-inch-wide, open flower heads on 50-inch-tall stems.

'Flore Pleno' is a large, sturdy plant, with heavy, 3-foot stalks topped by very large, full clusters of deep lavender blue double flowers.

'Peter Pan' has light blue flowers on short, 1- to 1½-foot flower stalks. Leaves grow only a foot high at most.

GARDEN COMPANIONS
Lily-of-the-Nile is a great plant for the perennial border because it looks good with just about anything. Place taller kinds in the backs of beds or borders, and shorter ones toward or at the front. Combine it with other morning sun–loving perennials, including bee balm *(Monarda)*, bush daisy *(Euryops)*, butterfly weed *(Asclepias)*, and daylily *(Hemerocallis)*.

Louisiana Iris

Iris

Florida has such a diverse climate for growing plants that it can be difficult at times to locate the one specific variety of a flowering perennial that's best for your area. But with iris, there's no problem narrowing it down to the best.

Of all the iris that grow well in Florida, the Louisiana iris is the finest. Four distinct species of *Iris* native to the low-lying areas of southern Louisiana and the nearby states have been hybridized back and forth to create what's called Louisiana iris.

Louisiana iris comes in a wide range of colors, including blue, purple, yellow, pink, white, and shades of brownish red. The flowers appear in spring on 2- to 3-foot stems held above the striking foliage. A single thriving plant can form a clump 3 feet wide by 3 feet tall in 2 years. These clumps of green foliage add great architectural interest to the garden and will persist year-round where winters are mild. They are excellent companion plants for water gardens, growing both in the water itself and on its edges.

Louisiana iris blooming in its preferred habitat on the edge of a pond.

LEFT: *Flowers of giant blue Louisiana iris,* Iris giganticaerulea, *are nearly 6 inches across, and are borne atop 4- to 6-foot tall stems.*
RIGHT: *Flaring, dark purple flowers of 'Jeri' are borne on 3-foot-tall plants.*

PEAK SEASON

Late spring through fall, depending on the selection

MY FAVORITES

'Delta Dove' is a bright white with light blue lines down the center of each petal.

'Eolian' is a classic light blue with a hint of ruffle.

'Gerry Marstellar' is light purple fading to a cream-colored edge.

'Grace Duhon' has nearly black flowers with veins of a dark red-violet color around large brilliant yellow gold "falls" (the upright fuzz on each petal).

'Jeri', one of the darkest purples, is a garden classic.

GARDEN COMPANIONS

Louisiana iris works best when planted in masses for a bold upright linear architectural statement. Plant with other plants that like wet feet, including summer sweet (Clethra alnifolia), elephant's ear (Colocasia), flame azalea (Rhododendron), sweetspire (Itea), ironweed (Vernonia), New England aster (Aster novae-angliae), and Florida leucothoe (Agarista).

When Plant container-grown iris anytime.

Where Plant wherever iris can receive full sun and some late-afternoon shade. At least a half day of sun is needed in order for iris to bloom, and it must be watered during dry periods. Also desirable are sites that are protected from high winds, as well as locations that are away from large trees or other plants with extensive root systems.

How Louisiana iris requires acid soil with a pH of 5.5 to 6.5; add sulfur to acidify the soil if necessary. It performs best in very moist soil liberally supplemented with peat moss, leaf mold, or compost. Plant in the fall, 15 to 18 inches apart, and about 1 inch deep.

TLC Provided it receives adequate moisture and proper soil acidity is maintained, Louisiana iris has no special care requirements or pest problems.

Peruvian Daffodil
Hymenocallis narcissiflora

When you walk along the beaches of Florida, you can't help but notice the beautiful plants

Powerfully fragrant, Peruvian daffodil flowers are 6 inches across.

that bloom along the edge of the sand dunes. There is partridge pea with its beautiful lavender blossoms, and often nearby is the incredible sea grape with its edible fruit. But standing out among all the beach plants is the majestic Peruvian daffodil. A relative of the Florida native spider lily *(Hymenocallis latifolia)*, its bright white flowers resemble daffodils, but the central cup is surrounded by six slender, spidery segments. The flowers are produced on leafless, hollow stems. Although these bulbs grow best in rich, well-drained soil, they have been known to thrive in the poorly drained marl soils of South Florida, and even in boggy conditions.

A large number of native species of *Hymenocallis* are found across the southern United States. The flowers are usually similar: white or yellow and arranged in clusters.

PEAK SEASON

Summer

MY FAVORITES

'Advance' features a white, fringed cup with a green throat and attractive thin petals. Flowers bloom for 2 weeks, beginning in June. This variety is long lasting as a cut flower, a potted plant, or a landscape plant.

'Bellum' has attractive cream-colored flowers with a deep yellow-gold center.

'Carribea' blooms late compared to the species, and the white cup in the center is half as large, and the flower segments are lax. The blossoms last well up to one week as cut flowers.

'Sulfur Queen' has large yellow flowers with green-striped throats. This variety is very fragrant and makes an excellent cut flower. It begins blooming in June and is dormant by late summer.

'Tropical Giant' (or 'Hayward') is a fine landscape plant with luxuriant green leaves, often to 4 feet in height. It blooms in July.

GARDEN COMPANIONS

Combine them with summer perennials and annuals such as black-eyed Susan *(Rudbeckia),* blanket flower *(Gaillardia),* hummingbird mint *(Agastache),* and *Catharanthus.*

When Plant container-grown plants anytime and individual bulbs in the spring. The bloom time during the summer months depends on the selection.

Where Plant in full sun or partial shade in ordinary sandy, loamy soil; plants will also tolerate dry or wet soils. Peruvian daffodil can withstand salt spray and drought, but not cold. It is a great plant for South Florida and coastal areas.

Flowers of 'Sulfur Queen' are primrose yellow with prominent green stripes in their throats.

How Set bulbs with tips 1 inch below the soil surface. In northern, colder regions of Florida, dig and store dormant bulbs after leaves have yellowed, but do not cut off fleshy roots. Store roots upside down on open trays in a cool location.

TLC In general, these bulbs should be planted in a permanent location because they quickly form large clumps. Furthermore, they appear to resent transplanting and blooming may be interrupted for a year if the plants are moved.

Perennials

To a gardener, the word "perennial" sounds so reassuring: here today *and* here tomorrow. Indeed, the relative permanence of perennials, their guarantee of reappearance, is their signature virtue. In the wide world of plants, perennials occupy a key niche between durable shrubs and ephemeral annuals.

Once planted, perennials, like shrubs, remain in your garden year after year; in contrast, annuals must be planted anew each year. But unlike shrubs, the stems of perennials usually aren't woody. Some perennials, in fact, don't have stems at all.

TYPES OF PERENNIALS

Under this umbrella of long-lived but nonwoody plants (technically called *herbaceous perennials*), you'll find three distinct patterns of seasonal growth. One sort—exemplified by butterfly weed (page 66)—dies back to the ground each fall and sends up a totally new set of stems and leaves the following spring. Another type of perennial makes a significant growth retreat at the end of the growing season but never disappears totally, remaining visible through the winter as a low tuft of foliage. Mexican bush sage (page 76) follows this seasonal rhythm. But in mild-winter parts of Florida, the prevailing type of perennial hardly changes in appearance (aside from producing flowers) over a 12-month period. Most of the perennials discussed in this chapter are of this type.

In addition to these three seasonal growth habits, perennials offer distinct variations in what you might call plant construction. Ornamental grasses (page 74), for example, put up leaves directly from the soil; the plants have no stems aside from those that bear flowers.

Blanket flower (page 62) and Mexican bush sage do produce stems from ground level, but the stems simply elongate until they terminate in flowers. Bushy perennials like lion's tail (page 72), however, offer a more shrublike appearance, with stems that branch and rebranch to form a more intricate, interlaced plant.

WORKING WITH PERENNIALS

Among perennials, you'll find just about every plant style imaginable. Growth habits run the gamut, from bolt upright to flat-out spreading to fountainlike to all manner of "bushy." Leaves range from huge to minute, simple to complexly divided and subdivided, and green in all tints and shades as well as gray, bronze, purple, nearly yellow, and virtually blue. Add flowers to

ABOVE: *Oriental fountain grass produces pinkish flower plumes and has gray-green leaves. Red 'Raspberry Royal' salvia is an accent.*
OPPOSITE PAGE: *Showy blooms of Brazilian plume flower light up shaded gardens and attract hummingbirds.*

this mixed equation and the variations are seemingly endless.

With such diversity at your disposal, think of the plant pictures you could compose with perennials and other plant types—or just with perennials alone. When you choose and arrange your perennials, take advantage of their differences to create contrasts that highlight the individual plants. Keep in mind the possibilities of mixing not only different plant sizes but also different shapes, foliage sizes and textures, and, finally, flower shapes and colors. Whether you opt for subtlety or flamboyance, a garden of, or with, perennials need never be boring.

Black-eyed Susan
Rudbeckia

Trilobed coneflower (Rudbeckia triloba) grows 4 feet high and wide, covering itself through midsummer with hundreds of 3-inch-wide flowers.

If ever there was a plant that grows in just about any part of the state with little or no care, it is the black-eyed Susan. Ubiquitous in nearly every Florida county, this bright gold sunflower relative with a dark brown center cone has been beloved as long as Floridians have cared for flower gardens. With its tall 24- to 36-inch stems that often carry clusters of 2-inch-wide flowers, it is a favorite plant for butterfly gardens and naturalized plantings.

Plant black-eyed Susan in masses or with grasses and other prairie-type plants in a big, open landscape, where its dazzling color can be fully appreciated. Bees, butterflies, and American goldfinches all flock to it, so if you like to think of your garden as a habitat for wildlife, you'll love this plant. Its sturdy stems and long-lasting flower heads make this mid- to late-summer bloomer a good cut flower as well. In a small city garden, a little goes a long way, so keep black-eyed Susan in check.

When Plant container-grown plants in the fall to establish roots before the next blooming season. Flowers bloom midsummer through late fall.

Where Black-eyed Susan is a reliable summertime bloomer, providing bright splashes of color in a mixed perennial border or porch planter. Any full-sun location with ordinary soil will do.

How Amend the soil with organic matter before planting. Plant in groups of three, five, or more, spacing the plants 1 ½ to 2 feet apart, depending on the cultivar. Water thoroughly and keep the soil moist until plants are established.

TLC Apply a 1- to 2-inch layer of organic mulch to retain moisture, improve soil, and reduce weeds. Be sure to keep the mulch from covering stems where they emerge from the soil (the *crown*), as it may cause rot. Remove spent flowers to keep plants looking neat until the end of the season, when you might want to leave some seed heads on for the birds to enjoy. Staking may be necessary for taller types. Every 3 or 4 years, divide plants in spring to maintain vigor, splitting them through the crown and replanting the young sections with generous spacing between them.

PEAK SEASON

Midsummer through late fall

MY FAVORITES

Black-eyed Susan (*Rudbeckia hirta*) is a short-lived perennial that is easy to grow from seed. 'Irish Eyes' produces very large, bright yellow blossoms with bright green centers. 'Indian Summer' also produces large golden flowers but with dark centers.

Cut-leaf coneflower (*R. laciniata*) grows to 5 feet high. Its yellow petals are accented by a green center. It blooms August to September and is an excellent cut flower as well as a butterfly magnet. Give it room to sprawl.

Golden coneflower (*R. fulgida* 'Goldsturm') produces masses of 3-inch, golden, daisylike blooms and is ideal for late-summer color in the border.

R. occidentalis 'Green Wizard' has outstanding large, nearly black central cones bordered by bright green sepals that burst out like a star.

Trilobed coneflower (*R. triloba*) is by far the toughest. It prefers sandy or loamy moist soils, but it can withstand drought.

GARDEN COMPANIONS

Grow black-eyed Susan in the semi-wild garden with butterfly weed (Asclepias), aster, and Louisiana iris.

TOP: *The green center of 'Irish Eyes' black-eyed Susan is a striking feature of the 3-inch flowers.* BOTTOM: *Flowers of 'Indian Summer' black-eyed Susan grow 6 to 9 inches wide.*

Blanket Flower
Gaillardia grandiflora

One of the secrets to growing perennials in Florida is finding plants that have several good features. Plants that can withstand drought but will live in good garden soil, plants that provide color over a long growing season, and plants that attract butterflies are perfect for the Florida perennial garden. And for all that, look no further than blanket flower. It has brilliant, daisylike, yellow and rust-bicolored blooms, and is a tough 12- to 18-inch-tall perennial for the hottest garden location. Provided the spent blooms are clipped off often, blanket flower will be in constant bloom year-round in zones 26, 28, and 31 and will bloom spring through fall in zone 25.

Blanket flower is perfect for the hot, sunny border, as well as in flower beds mixed with other annuals, perennials, or shrubs. Some varieties are low growers and look great in containers, spilling over the pot's edge. And coastal dwellers, note that gaillardia is tolerant of salt spray.

'Burgundy' plants grow to 2½ feet, and the flowers are long-lasting.

PEAK SEASON

Spring through fall in the north; year-round elsewhere

MY FAVORITES

'Burgundy' is tough and easy to grow; it produces solid burgundy flowers.

'Dazzler' has long-lasting 2- to 4-inch daisylike flowers that have orange to cherry red petals tipped with a golden yellow ring.

'Fanfare' is a 24-inch-tall plant; the tubular blossoms are scarlet with bright yellow tips.

'Goblin' has 2½-inch flowers; the scarlet-rust petals have bright, gold-frilled tips.

'Red Plume' is a very dwarf, 1-foot-tall form with brick red double flowers that look like small zinnias.

'Sundance Bicolor' doesn't even look like a blanket flower. The bushy, free-flowering plants are covered in masses of very double, bicolored blooms of red and orange. 'Sundance Bicolor' is an All-America Selections Winner (annual award given for outstanding plant performance).

GARDEN COMPANIONS

Plant with other drought-tolerant Florida plants, such as black-eyed Susan *(Rudbeckia hirta)*, butterfly weed *(Asclepias)*, Copper Canyon daisy *(Tagetes lemonii)*, and tickseed *(Coreopsis)*.

TOP: *'Goblin' has 3-inch flowers on 1-foot-tall plants.*
ABOVE: *Trumpetlike flowers surround the central cone of 'Fanfare'.*
RIGHT: *Blanket flower produces 3-inch, multicolored daisies spring through fall.*

When Set out plants in either spring or fall. Plants are easy to grow from seed sown in fall; established plants will usually reseed themselves.

Where Blanket flower grows best in full sun and in rich soil that has been amended with compost. It is very tolerant of locations that are hot and dry.

How Plant the crown slightly higher than the surrounding soil to prevent rot. Keep well watered until the roots are established.

TLC Blanket flower doesn't need much care. In winter, keep soil on the dry side to prevent crown rot. Remove spent blossoms to prolong flowering.

Brazilian Plume Flower
Justicia carnea

Brazilian plume flower is a Florida classic for its colorful and showy flowers as well as its adaptability.

A favorite of hummingbirds, this shade-loving plant creates lots of interest in the shade garden. The 4-foot-tall perennial has lance-leafed, almost black, deeply veined leaves. They're accented by brilliant 8-inch-tall plumes of bright pink flowers. Grow plume flower as a shrubby perennial in central and southern Florida, and as a low-growing annual in northern Florida.

Normally a shade garden offers subtle color, but Brazilian plume flower changes that. It begins blooming in central Florida about midsummer and continues through the first frost. In South Florida, it blooms nearly all year. In North Florida, it is sold as an annual for the shade garden and discarded after a hard freeze; the top growth will freeze at 29°F (−2°C). Beyond Florida, Brazilian plume flower is a treasured exotic that is grown in greenhouses. Wherever it grows, it will quickly become the center of attention.

LEFT: *'Alba' is guaranteed to brighten shaded areas of the garden.*
RIGHT: *Orange plume flower grows well in either full sun or partial shade, and it is very drought tolerant.*

PEAK SEASON

Midsummer through late winter

MY FAVORITES

'Alba' grows taller than the species, to 50 inches, and has bright white flowers.

RELATED SPECIES

Justicia aurea has a similar plume but in bright yellow; *J. a.* 'Compacta' has the same flowers on plants that grow only 24 inches tall.

Mexican plume flower (*J. fulvicoma*) has orange-red, flaring, two-lipped flowers in late summer and fall. It reaches 24 inches in height and can grow in sun or shade.

Orange plume flower, or Mexican honeysuckle (*J. spicigera*), has orange flowers in late summer through fall. It can grow to 6 feet in warm areas and can tolerate drought.

GARDEN COMPANIONS

Brazilian plume flower is a large perennial for the back of the shade garden. Shrubs that enhance its form and color include fringe tree (*Chionanthus virginicus*), holly (*Ilex*), anise tree (*Illicium*), banana shrub (*Michelia*), gardenia, Chinese cleyera (*Ternstroemia*), hydrangea, Japanese fatsia (*Fatsia japonica*), lady palm (*Rhapis*), Oregon grape (*Mahonia*), and summersweet (*Clethra*). Perennials or annuals to plant around it include begonia, aspidistra, clivia, caladium, and a variety of ferns.

When Plant in either fall or early spring while temperatures are relatively cool.

Where Choose a location that will provide deep to partial shade. Plants will tolerate less than ideal soil, but will produce many more and larger flowers in fertile soil that is moist but well drained.

How Amend the soil with organic matter before planting. Set container-grown plants at the same depth that they grew in the nursery. Water thoroughly and keep the soil moist until plants are established.

TLC This is about as carefree a medium-sized shade plant as you can plant in the Florida garden. Lightly tip-prune young plants to promote branching and bushiness. Occasionally, and especially if stressed, Brazilian plume flower will get mealybugs. Spray with horticultural oil or neem oil to control. Brazilian plume flower will tolerate drought, but blooming will decrease.

Butterfly Weed

Asclepias tuberosa

Attracting wildlife, in particular butterflies and hummingbirds, into home gardens is quite popular in Florida. And because of our mild climate, butterflies are visible year-round if the right plants are there. Many plants supply nectar for adult butterflies, and others provide food for newly hatched caterpillars. A few plants, like butterfly weed, provide both. *Asclepias* (milkweed plant) is the primary food source of adult monarch butterflies, and its leaves are the sole food source for monarch caterpillars. Milkweeds are also visited by queen butterflies and a variety of hairstreak butterflies.

Partly because of their relationship with butterflies, milkweeds are a great way to introduce children to gardening. The plants are very easy to grow and because they support all the life stages of the monarch butterfly, they offer an easy way to introduce the process of metamorphosis. Aphids are always present on the new growing tips but they don't cause any damage. In fact, they are another way to help young people learn about insects in the garden.

Butterfly weed grows about 2 feet tall and produces star-shaped flowers arranged in round or flat clusters atop a tall stem. In cold weather, the stems and flowers will die

back to the ground but because of the large tuber-like roots, the plant grows back with the onset of warm weather. Flower colors range from yellow-orange to red. In the fall, each milkweed seed bears a tuft of long, silky hairs that readily carry the seed great distances.

Butterfly weed is colorful and hardy, and it attracts monarch butterflies, making it a particularly charming component of a perennial border.

PEAK SEASON
Summer

MY FAVORITES
'Gay Butterflies' strain has yellow, red, orange, pink, or bicolored flowers.

'Hello Yellow' has bright yellow blooms, a welcome complement to the familiar orange.

RELATED SPECIES
Scarlet milkweed, or blood flower *(Asclepias curassavica),* is a tropical milkweed that has naturalized in Florida. It grows to 36 inches tall and is by far the most common milkweed in Florida gardens. The scarlet clusters bloom spring through fall in zone 25 and year-round in zones 26, 28, and 31. Yellow-flowered 'Silky Gold' is an improved variety.

Swamp milkweed *(A. incarnata)* grows primarily in central and northern Florida counties and is known for its pink-purple flowers that bloom during summer.

GARDEN COMPANIONS
Plant butterfly milkweed with other annual and perennial plants that attract butterflies, such as tickseed *(Coreopsis),* cardinal flower *(Lobelia),* false indigo *(Baptisia),* and goldenrod *(Solidago).*

TOP: *Bright 'Hello Yellow' has familiar milk-weed fortitude but in solid yellow.*
BOTTOM: *'Silky Gold' is a variety of scarlet milkweed that thrives in Florida.*

When Plant container-grown plants anytime. To propagate, sow seeds anytime or divide plants in the spring.

Where Plant butterfly weed in the cutting garden, where it will attract a wide array of butterflies as well as hummingbirds, and in natural landscapes and mass plantings. Choose a site in full sun to part shade with sandy soil. Butterfly weed needs well-drained soil and moderate amounts of water; it cannot tolerate heavy soils.

How Space plants about 2 feet apart, and, if space allows, in groups of three in order to have a full look the first few years. Water thoroughly after planting, and keep soil moist for two months or until roots are established.

TLC Butterfly weed will not bloom until it has become well established in the garden. It is slow to resprout in the spring so be careful not to injure the delicate crown. After the monarch caterpillars have stripped the foliage, cut the bare stems to the ground and apply a bit of fertilizer to encourage new growth. Milkweed contains steroids called *cardenolides,* which are consumed by monarch caterpillars during feeding and then transferred to the bodies of the adult butterflies. These cardenolides make monarchs toxic and bitter tasting to birds and lizards.

Firespike
Odontonema strictum

Firespike is one of those new plants on the gardening scene that has taken the market by storm. It is a very versatile plant for perennial and shrub borders in South Florida and in perennial borders in central to North Florida.

Bright green oblong leaves of firespike are 4 to 6 inches long.

Firespike has upright branches with thick, succulent stems and dark green, shiny, pointed leaves. And then it is topped off with 9- to 12-inch spikes bearing small, tubular red flowers. The individual flowers are about an inch long. In warmer areas of the state where frost rarely occurs, firespike will reach 6 feet tall. In cooler areas, it dies to the ground with the first cold weather but comes back with gusto the following spring. The flowers are excellent cut and long-lasting indoors.

Firespike prefers hot, full sun and plenty of water. It does grow in part to deep shade, but it will develop a more meandering, vinelike habit instead of growing upright, and it will flower more sparsely.

PEAK SEASON

Late summer to fall. Also blooms through fall and winter in zones 28 and 31.

MY FAVORITES

'Fuchsia' has many interesting purple to pink flowers.

'Gray White' is notable for its leaves, which are richly marbled, veined, and splashed with elegant pastels.

GARDEN COMPANIONS

Plant with other carefree plants such as beautyberry (Callicarpa), butterfly bush (Buddleia), pyracantha, juniper, oleander, blackberry lily (Bellamcanda), black-eyed Susan (Rudbeckia hirta), African iris (Dietes), four o'clock (Mirabilis), butterfly ginger (Hedychium), Russian sage (Perovskia), and Stokesia.

When Plant container-grown plants anytime of year.

Where Plant in full sun, in fertile to moderately fertile well-drained soil that stays continuously moist. Firespike can tolerate long droughts but will stop flowering. Plants can also tolerate slightly alkaline soil, but not salt spray.

How Amend the soil with organic matter before planting. Set container-grown plants at the same depth that they grew in the nursery. Water thoroughly and continue to keep the soil moist. Firespike propagates easily from stem cuttings that have not become woody.

ABOVE: *The deep red flowers of firespike are echoed by the brick wall.*
LEFT: *Hummingbirds and butterflies are attracted to the tubular red flowers of firespike.*

TLC The plant requires little attention once it's established. You will enjoy the brilliant red tubular flowers, and so will the butterflies and hummingbirds. If provided with adequate water, firespike will be the highlight of the fall garden. (If not, the shiny, wavy leaves will still be a welcome addition to the landscape all by themselves.) Cut the plants back in the spring to encourage branching and the production of new shoots. Plants are mostly free of pests but may occasionally be attacked by mealybugs. Control them with horticultural or neem oil. Deer like to browse on the leaves; plants will recover initially but will succumb to repeated defoliation.

Goldenrod
Solidago

'Crown of Rays' goldenrod covers itself in fall with acacia–like sprays of bright yellow flowers.

The bright lemon yellow flowers of goldenrod herald the end of summer and the beginning of fall. While other plants are thinking about going to sleep for the winter, goldenrod is just beginning with glorious blooms. There are more than 200 different types of goldenrods growing around the world and 20 species that are native to Florida. That alone tells you that goldenrod is a good, tough plant for Florida gardens.

The bright yellow sprays of the *Solidago* species that sway in the slightest breeze along roadsides and in old gardens from July until November have only lately drawn the attention of American gardeners. Northern Europeans long ago recognized the ornamental properties of goldenrod; they use it liberally to brighten gardens in autumn.

Like many tall flowers, goldenrod typically grows upright on sturdy stems. The blossoms make long-lasting cut flowers. Dried flowers are particularly useful in herbal wreaths and autumn wall ornaments.

If you are concerned about allergies, note that ragweed, not goldenrod, is the culprit in the fall. Ragweed blooms at the same time as goldenrod and generates a huge amount of pollen in the air. Goldenrod produces a sticky pollen designed to adhere to insects, not be carried by the wind.

PEAK SEASON

Fall into early winter

MY FAVORITES

'Crown of Rays' (Solidago canadensis) is bright yellow, and it grows to 36 inches tall. The shape of its plume-like flower spikes is different from other goldenrods.

'Fireworks' (S. rugosa) is a 1993 introduction from Ken Moore of the North Carolina Botanical Garden in Chapel Hill. It grows 36 inches tall and has 18-inch-long, arching spires of bright yellow flower spikes that look like exploding fireworks.

'Golden Fleece' (S. sphacelata) is a cute little 18-inch-tall selection with bright yellow flowers. It is by far the most popular goldenrod in cultivation and is often seen in mass plantings along roadsides.

GARDEN COMPANIONS

Goldenrod is excellent interspersed with native asters, fountain grass (Pennisetum), ironweed (Vernonia), and other wildflower plants. Also consider matching it with 'Autumn Joy' sedum.

When Ideally, plant goldenrod in early spring so that the plants are well established prior to the fall blooming season. In practice, however, container-grown plants can be planted any time of year.

Where Choose a location that receives full sun, and ideally with soil that is only slightly to moderately fertile. Soil that is too fertile will promote rank, aggressive growth. This showy plant is a prime candidate for late-season color in perennial plantings and wildflower gardens.

How Set container-grown plants at the same depth that they grew in the nursery. Water thoroughly and keep the soil moist until plants are established.

TOP: *Flowers of 'Fireworks' explode in fall. covering the plant.*
BOTTOM: *Closeup of 'Fireworks' flowers.*

TLC To prevent reseeding, remove stems in fall after the flowers fade. Every 4 or 5 years, rejuvenate crowded clumps in spring by lifting the roots and dividing each clump into pieces with at least three shoots.

Lion's Tail
Leonotis

'Staircase' lion's tail is a tall, gangly plant with large leaves and flowers that is well suited to the back of the border.

Given the heat and humidity that accompanies gardening throughout Florida, it's nice to add to the garden a plant like lion's tail, which grows robustly and blooms vigorously with little help from gardeners.

Lion's tail is a mint-family member from South Africa. It grows 4 to 6 feet tall in clumps that become nearly that wide. Hairy stems carry pairs of toothed, 2- to 5-inch-long leaves opposite each other. Flowers are tubular and dark orange; they come in dense whorls that encircle the 4-foot-long stems so that it looks as if the stems are growing right through the middle of the clusters.

In frost-prone areas, lion's tail will die back to the ground, but it comes back with a vengeance in the spring. Flowers appear in spring and again in fall. In warmer areas, it continues to grow and produce flowers throughout the year.

LEFT: *A mature clump of lion's tail catches and reflects late-afternoon light.*
RIGHT: *Closeup of whorled clusters of lion's tail flower shows its mint-family affiliation.*

PEAK SEASON

Blooms year-round in warmer areas, and in early spring and again in the fall elsewhere. Annual lion's tail blooms late spring through early summer.

MY FAVORITES

Leonotis ocymifolia raineriana grows fast and is loved by butterflies and hummingbirds. Its 2-inch flowers are very deep orange, and they appear earlier in the season. This variety is somewhat hardier, too, to 5°F (−15°C).

'Staircase' (*L. leunurus*) looks similar to annual lion's tail, but it has larger flowers and leaves.

RELATED PLANT

Annual lion's tail (*L. nepetifolia*) can reach 8 feet tall and more than 5 feet wide. It is less formal in appearance than perennial kinds. It reseeds readily and attracts hummingbirds.

GARDEN COMPANIONS

Plant with other drought-tolerant plants such as bluebeard (*Caryopteris*), broom (*Cytisus*), pineapple guava (*Acca sellowiana*), bottlebrush (*Callistemon*), nandina, senna (*Cassia*), smoke tree (*Cotinus*), and yellow bells (*Tecoma stans*).

When Plant from seed in midwinter and plant out in the garden in spring. Or plant container-grown plants in spring or fall.

Where Plant in full sun to part shade, and in well-drained, moderately fertile soil. Plants are tall, so position them toward the back of the perennial border or butterfly garden. Where it's native in Africa, lion's tail is considered very drought resistant.

How Lion's tail benefits from enriched soil. Set container-grown plants at the same depth that they grew in the nursery. Water thoroughly and keep the soil moist until plants are established. It is easy to grow from seed or from cuttings taken during biannual pruning.

TLC Water freely spring through fall and fertilize every 6 to 8 weeks. Water sparingly in winter. After the first flush of flowers in early summer, remove tall stems to encourage new growth for flowers in the fall. In spring, cut back old stems to the ground to make room for new growth.

Ornamental Grasses

When we think of grasses, we typically visualize green lawns. But turfgrasses are a special group, grown for their carpetlike uniformity. In contrast, ornamental grasses are strikingly individual. The foliage comes in tufts, sheaves, and fountainlike sprays, in colors of green, gray, silvery blue, red, and variegated patterns. And though the flowers are tiny, they're displayed in showy, foliage-topping plumes.

The striking purple leaves and flowers of purple fountain grass are outstanding in borders or in container gardens.

Some ornamental grasses grow best and have better foliage quality during the cool temperatures of spring and fall. These cool-season grasses will start to grow early in the spring and may even remain semievergreen over the winter. Other grasses prefer the heat of summer and remain good-looking even when temperatures are high and moisture is limited. These warm-season grasses do not begin to show growth until the weather becomes stable and the soil warms up.

When Plant in the fall to allow the roots to establish themselves before the onset of spring.

Where Plant in full sun in ordinary soil, and where ample water is available.

How Dig a planting hole as deep as the plant's root ball and twice as wide. Remove the plant from its container; if roots are matted on the root ball's sides, loosen them with your fingers. Set the root ball in the hole so it sits slightly above the surrounding soil level, fill in around it with soil, firming with your fingers, and then water thoroughly. Finish with a 2- to 3-inch layer of mulch that will help maintain soil moisture and temperature.

TLC During the first year or two, water young plants regularly. Once they've become established in your garden, clumps will thrive on regular to moderate watering. In late winter or early spring—before new growth emerges—remove dead leaves and stems. The previous season's growth usually turns brown in the fall, so cut the plants back to about 4 to 6 inches in the spring. Warm-season grasses usually do not require as frequent division as cool-season types. Divide clumps in the fall using a sharp shovel or machete.

PEAK SEASON

Year-round

MY FAVORITES

Dwarf pampas grass (*Cortaderia selloana* 'Pumila') grows 5 feet tall, and withstands hot sun and high humidity. *C. s.* 'Silver Comet' is shorter, to 48 inches, and has striped foliage.

Fakahatchee grass (*Tripsacum*) grows a whopping 6 feet tall in a single season, with 8-foot-long flower clusters. The dwarf version grows 36 inches tall with flowers that reach 4 feet in length.

Fountain grass (*Pennisetum*) is available in many forms: *P. setaceum* 'Burgundy Giant' grows 6 feet high, with 2-inch-wide burgundy leaves; 'Rubrum', or purple fountain grass, has maroon leaves and flowers; 'Tall Tales' is a fine-leaved grass with ever-present 60-inch white foxtail-like flower clusters. White feathertop (*P. villosum*) grows about 2 feet tall and has white flowers.

Muhly grass (*Muhlenbergia capillaris*) has very fine, almost hairlike foliage and in the fall produces clouds of purple seed heads. Bamboo muhly (*M. dumosa*) is a taller form.

GARDEN COMPANIONS

Plant ornamental grasses in full sun with other perennials and with coarse-textured foliage plants.

TOP: *Bamboo muhly.*
ABOVE: *Dwarf pampas grass.*
BELOW: *White feathertop.*

Sage
Salvia

Sage and Florida's hot summer weather go together. Unlike the short, spiked red annual salvia of your grandmother's era, the perennial sages are a mainstay of the full-sun perennial border, offering a brilliance and diversity in texture, form, and color to today's gardens. Perennial sages live from year to year, offering a certain permanency to the landscape. They are virtually unequaled in providing year-round color and interest. Variations in colors, sizes, habits, and time of bloom are almost endless.

Not all sages perform well in Florida. Most sages can adjust to a variety of soils, but some have soil requirements that Florida gardeners are unable to supply. And despite sages' ability to withstand hot daytime temperatures, many require cool evenings to survive. Although many sages have been trialed by research stations and botanical gardens around the state, often the best way to see if a particular sage will grow for you is to plant a few and see what they do. Or take my advice and try the ones that I know best, which are listed at right.

Mexican bush sage blooms fall to spring in South Florida, spring to fall elsewhere.

PEAK SEASON

Most bloom during the summer, but some bloom in early spring and late fall.

MY FAVORITES

Black-and-blue sage (*Salvia guaranitica* 'Black and Blue') is an elegant sage with deep blue flowers emerging from nearly black buds.

Forsythia sage (*S. madrensis*) is one of the few yellow forms. Plant it in large drifts in full sun.

Indigo spires sage (*S.* 'Indigo Spires') grows 30 inches tall. Remove spent blooms to prolong flowering.

Mealycup sage (*S. farinacea*) is a common annual sage for Florida gardens and can become a perennial in southern Florida. 'Victoria Blue' is an attractive lavender form.

Mexican bush sage (*S. leucantha*) grows 4 feet high and 5 feet wide, is drought tolerant, and has fuzzy white or purple flowers. 'Santa Barbara' is a neater, more compact form.

Scarlet sage (*S. splendens*) is best for attracting hummingbirds to your garden. 'Van Houttei' is a reliable cultivar.

GARDEN COMPANIONS

Sages are the perfect perennial for accompanying many sun-loving annuals and perennials, as well as small shrubs and trees in the garden.

ABOVE LEFT: *'Victoria Blue'*
ABOVE RIGHT: *'Van Houttei'*
LEFT: *Forsythia sage*

When Buy and plant when weather is mild in spring or fall.

Where Most sage plants enjoy full sun and enriched, moist, well-drained soil. But in the hottest locations, choose a spot where plants will be shaded during the late afternoon.

How Dig a planting hole as deep as the root ball and twice as wide. Remove the plant from its cell-pack or pot, gently loosen the sides of the root ball, and cut or pull off any matted roots at the bottom. Set the root ball into the hole so that its surface is even with the surrounding soil. Fill in around the root ball with soil, then water gently.

TLC Water regularly and fertilize about a month after planting; either apply controlled-release fertilizer pellets or begin a program of liquid fertilizing at 4- to 6-week intervals. Remove spent flower spikes to promote repeat flowers. Control mealybugs with either horticultural or neem oil.

Stokes' Aster
Stokesia laevis

Stokes' aster is best known as a reliable landscape ornamental or a specialty cut flower, but it is even more versatile than you might imagine. As a cut flower, it is very long lasting, and its early-season bloom provides nectar for spring butterflies. The foliage is evergreen, and the frilly flowers come in a variety of colors. Stokes' aster is easy to cultivate and is perfect where you need a low-growing plant in the front of the border. The plant, native to the southeastern United States, is hardy and thrives throughout Florida in a variety of soil types, in full sun to part shade, and in well-drained or moderately damp soils.

Native to the Southeast, Stokes' aster is one of the most reliable perennials for Florida.

Wherever it grows, Stokes' aster forms a rosette of lance-shaped leaves at the base of the plant. Height is about 18 inches, and in Florida, flowers appear in late spring and continue through summer and fall until frost.

Most Stokes' aster cultivars produce flowers that are blue or purple, but there are several new selections now available, my favorites of which are listed at right.

LEFT: *'Peach Melba'*
ABOVE: *'Mary Gregory'*
BELOW LEFT: *'Blue Danube'*

PEAK SEASON

Late spring through first frost

MY FAVORITES

There are many varieties of Stokes' aster available, mostly differing in flower color. Some of the best for Florida include:

'Blue Danube' (medium blue); 'Blue Moon' (deep blue); 'Bluestone' (dwarf, medium blue); 'Klaus Jelitto' (18 inches tall and wide, powder blue); 'Mary Gregory' (1 foot tall, creamy yellow); 'Omega Skyrocket' (2 feet tall, white to pale blue); 'Peach Melba' (creamy white with a peach center); 'Purple Parasols' (deep violet); 'Rosea' (rosy pink); 'Silver Moon' (silvery white); 'Wyoming' (dark blue).

GARDEN COMPANIONS

Plant Stokes' aster in drifts adjacent to large marigolds like 'Antigua' or 'Marvel' or with lantanas such as 'Lemon Drop' or 'Silver Mound'. A planting of 'Purple Parasols' Stokes' aster and 'Stella de Oro' daylily is very effective.

When   You'll find most Stokes' asters sold in cell-packs, 4-inch pots, and 1-gallon containers. Buy and plant when weather is mild in spring or fall.

Where   Choose a site with full to partial sun. In the hottest locations, choose a spot where plants will be lightly shaded during the late afternoon. If necessary, the soil should be amended for good drainage. Stokes' asters dislike heavy, wet soils and are particularly sensitive to poor drainage during the winter.

How   Dig a planting hole as deep as the root ball and twice as wide. Remove the plant from its cell-pack or pot, gently loosen the sides of the root ball, and cut or pull off any matted roots at the bottom. Set the root ball into the hole so that its surface is even with the surrounding soil. Fill in around the root ball with soil, firming with your fingers, then water gently.

TLC   To prolong flowering, remove the faded blossoms, and to encourage repeat flowering, cut the entire flower stalk off at the base of the plant after it finishes flowering. Every couple of years, divide the clumps in the late fall to prevent overcrowding and diminished flowering. Feed with a light application of fertilizer when growth emerges in the spring and again in midsummer.

Roses

Roses are *the* American flower and, as such, are ingrained in our collective imagination. The image of roses in full bloom, tumbling over arches and trellises, reminds us of the fragrances, the beauty, and the promise of spring blooms.

Roses are also thought of as being difficult to grow, a reputation earned largely because of breeding and our own desire for perfection from this most generous of flowering plants. Wild roses grow throughout the temperate regions of the Northern Hemisphere without any help from us, blooming freely in spring and setting fruit abundantly through the fall.

The growth habits, leaves, flowers, and hips of wild roses remind us of the many strong and beautiful ancestries of our garden roses.

Old garden roses, primarily European, were notable for their soft, open flowers and the handsome plants that fit well into gardens. Asian roses, both wild kinds and the ones cultivated for centuries in gardens, offered a larger range of colors on repeat-flowering plants. In the 19th century, rose breeders began crossing these Asian and European roses, along with species roses, creating new types of roses for later generations of home gardeners. These crosses have resulted in our hybrid tea roses, floribundas, and large-flowered climbers, all of which are valued for their ability to bloom repeatedly through the season and for their amazing array of colors.

The downside is that many of our modern roses inherited disease susceptibility along with their improved fragrance and colors. In addition, some of the grace and romance of the old garden roses was sacrificed. With that in mind, there has been an increasingly suc-

RIGHT: *Flowers of 'Brass Band' crowd together on the plant like a bouquet.* OPPOSITE PAGE: *'Double Delight' offers rich rose scent and red and cream bicolored flowers on long stems.*

cessful movement in the last several years to introduce improved versions of older roses into our gardens. Plant hybridizers have focused on introducing new types of roses that are disease resistant and easy to care for, have better growth habits, flower nearly continuously, and have colorful, fragrant blossoms. We want our roses perfect, and with some help, they do come close.

There are many roses that are beautiful and easy to grow. You can grow climbers (page 84) to disguise a small mailbox or ramble up into a large tree; hybrid teas (page 92) for their showy, exhibition-type blossoms to make stunning bouquets; vigorous grandifloras (page 90) that are lush with rose fragrance; and old garden roses (page 96). Try also miniatures (page 94) that spill over the edges of window boxes and patio containers.

If you want a long-lived rose, make sure to buy and plant only roses grafted onto the

Rosa fortuniana rootstock. It is immune to the microscopic roundworms known as *nematodes* that are abundant in our soil. Don't be tempted by less expensive roses of the same variety that are available. They are grafted onto either 'Dr. Huey' or *R. multiflora* rootstock. Perfectly fine throughout most of the country, roses on those rootstocks will fail here, usually within two years. They are only suitable to plant as annuals or short-lived perennials.

Keep in mind that categories of roses are human inventions imposed on nature's infinite variety. For instance, 'Blush Noisette' is an old rose, but also a climber. In this chapter, I've used categories that I think are useful to Florida gardeners. The key to enjoying the queen of flowers is to know what you like and where you want the plants to grow, and then to choose varieties that perform well in your region of Florida. Growing roses should be easy and fun!

Bermuda Mystery Rose

TOP: 'Smith's Parish' forms an open, 6-foot-tall bush. It has been traced back to a central parish on Bermuda.
BOTTOM: 'Vincent Godsif' makes a compact bush that is in bloom every month of the year.

If you are looking for a rose that requires very little, if any, care, then consider one of the so-called "Bermuda mystery roses." The history of these Bermuda roses is sketchy, but we do know that no roses are indigenous to the island and that all roses arrived there in the 18th century on clipper ships, along with their cargoes of spices, tea, and silks.

These are called mystery roses because they have no known name or pedigree. Some may be natural mutations, called *sports,* or seedlings of roses first planted three centuries ago. Others may have been imported and their proper names forgotten. In most cases, the roses have been given the name of the owner of the garden or the location where they were found growing.

Regardless of their origin, the great virtue of these robust roses is that, having excelled in Bermuda for generations, they are obviously well adapted to Florida's similar climate. This means they tolerate the summer heat that dooms so many roses, and they resist most of the common rose ailments. They accomplish this (with some exceptions) by becoming essentially dormant in summer!

In short, if you're looking for hardy and well-adapted roses, consider the Bermuda mystery roses.

PEAK SEASON

Late October through May

MY FAVORITES

'Smith's Parish' flowers are either white, striped, or completely red, and 2 to 3 inches wide. Fragrance is mild. The plant grows 6 feet tall and has abundant light green foliage.

'Soncy' has small, light yellow, lightly scented flowers that fade to ivory. Outstanding bloom spring and fall. It grows to 5 feet tall.

'St. David's' makes a compact, 4-foot-tall bush. Red flowers are about 3 inches wide, and slightly scented.

'Vincent Godsif' is the toughest—and smallest—Bermuda mystery rose. Unlike most others, it blooms nearly year-round in Florida. The hot pink flowers are 2 inches wide and semi-double, with a very light to non-existent scent. Its upright, 4-foot-tall growth habit makes this rose useful as a specimen or low hedge. It's tolerant of poor soil and is virtually trouble free.

GARDEN COMPANIONS

Combine Bermuda mystery roses with plants that have contrasting textures and forms, such as hollyhocks, porter weed (*Stachytarpheta*), and with tall salvias, cape plumbago, upright ornamental grasses, and crape myrtle (*Lagerstroemia*).

When Plant in the early fall while the soil is still warm enough to encourage root development. When spring arrives and the foliage begins to require water, the roots will be well prepared.

Where Like most roses, Bermuda mystery roses require at least 6 hours of full sunlight every day. Choose a location where the roots can stretch out, and where the branches can reach full size; with good care, some plants will grow 6 to 8 feet tall. Good air circulation will help minimize disease and pest problems. Use Bermuda mystery roses in mass plantings or as specimens.

How Choose roses that are grafted on *Rosa fortuniana* rootstock. Before planting, soak the roots of bare-root plants in a bucket of water for a few hours and amend the soil with organic matter. If well-drained soil is not available, build islands of elevated garden soil and mulch well.

TLC Keep plants well watered. Fertilize 5 times a year. Prune in late winter, just before growth begins, to remove dead and crossing branches and to control size; prune through the growing season to remove faded flowers. Bermuda mystery roses are trouble free and are very well adapted to Florida's hot and humid climate.

TOP: *'Soncy' is a delicately scented flower that blooms profusely in both spring and fall.*
BOTTOM: *'St. David's' is named for the northern Bermuda island.*

Climbing Roses

Given Florida's summer heat, gardeners throughout the state need a shady refuge during the heat of the day. What could be more appealing than to withdraw to an arbor covered with the delicately perfumed blossoms of a climbing rose?

Climbing roses perform splendidly throughout the peninsula, and, given their penchant for aggressive growth, they are the perfect choice for covering outdoor structures. When you choose a climbing rose, it's important to know the plant's growth habit. Some climbers are suited for picket fences or a fan trellis on the front of the house; others will cover an 8-foot arbor with ease. For example, 'America' grows to only 10 feet and is the perfect solution for a small space. Others, such as Lady Banks's rose, which can grow to 25 feet, have been known to cause damage to structures not strong enough to support them. Choose a climber that will grow to the height you have available, and then provide adequate support. These are large plants and can be a part of your garden for many years.

Planted on both sides of a gate, 'America' readily climbs to form a continuous arch of flowers.

TOP: *Its rich color and fragrance make 'Don Juan' an especially desirable climber.*
BOTTOM: *'Golden Showers' is a classic and still the best yellow climbing rose.*

PEAK SEASON

Year-round throughout most of the state; spring to fall in the north.

MY FAVORITES

'America' has medium-sized flowers that are a light yellowish pink and very, very fragrant. It grows about 10 feet tall. All-America Rose Selections (AARS) winner in 1976.

'Don Juan' is my favorite. Its fragrance and velvety, crimson flowers are outstanding. Their damask-rose scent can perfume an entire garden. This variety grows to 10 feet, so it is suitable for training up a post.

'Fourth of July' is also a terrific rose, which is why, in 1999, it was the first climbing rose in two decades to win an AARS award. Flowers are red and white striped, come in large sprays, and have a green apple fragrance.

'Golden Showers' flowers are a deep gold yellow that gradually fades to cream. Stems are nearly thornless and leaves are glossy green.

GARDEN COMPANIONS

Plant densely foliaged plants around the base of climbers to hide their large, bare stems. Try smaller polyantha roses, tall annuals, blackberry lily *(Belamcanda),* ornamental grasses, junipers, boxwood, small forms of butterfly bush *(Buddleia),* foxglove, and small yellow dewdrop *(Duranta).*

When Plant in the early fall while the soil is still warm enough to encourage root development. When spring arrives and the foliage begins to demand water, the roots will be well prepared.

Where Choose a location with enough space for the roots to stretch out and for the branches to reach full size. Plants need at least 6 hours of full sun daily. Good air circulation will help minimize disease and pest problems. Plant with other roses in the foreground, or train up a post, over an arbor, or on chains loosely draped between posts at the back of a perennial border.

How Choose plants that are grafted onto *Rosa fortuniana* rootstock. Before planting, soak the roots of bare-root plants in a bucket of water for a few hours and amend soil with organic matter. Space fan-trained climbers about three-fourths of their mature height apart; space upright growers about one-fourth of their height.

TLC When weather is dry, water new roses approximately twice a week and established roses once a week. Water deeply, preferably in the early morning. In spring, place a 1-inch-thick layer of mulch around the plants. Fertilize 4 or 5 times per season. Climbers respond well to the application of organic fertilizer between regular fertilizer applications. Apply sprinklings of cottonseed meal, alfalfa pellets, or diluted fish emulsion for maximum bloom size and lots of bright green foliage.

English Roses

Flowers of 'Abraham Darby' look and smell very much like the European roses of centuries ago, but they bloom throughout the season.

These shrub roses represent a shift in gardeners' opinions of what defines a great rose. For nearly a century, hybrid tea (page 92), grandiflora (page 90), and floribunda (page 88) types set the standards of rose beauty and performance. But through breeding over many years, the best elements of both the old roses (those introduced before 1867) and the modern types were combined. The results have been stunning. These so-called English, or David Austin, roses first became available here in the United States in 1969, and Florida rose gardens have never quite been the same. English roses have the shapes and fragrances of old roses, but they repeat-flower like a modern rose.

Perhaps the finest attribute of the English roses is their heady scent. They offer all the variety of rose fragrance, from damask (page 96) and hybrid tea to even citrus. English roses also come in a variety of colors and hues, such as yellow and coral, which, up until now, were not common in shrub roses.

When Plant in the early fall while the soil is still warm enough to encourage root development. When spring arrives and the foliage begins to demand water, the roots will be well prepared.

Where Choose a location with enough space for the roots to stretch out and for the branches to reach full size. Plants need at least 6 hours of full sun daily. Good air circulation will help minimize disease and pest problems. Use English roses as specimens or towards the back of a large perennial border.

How Choose plants that are grafted onto *Rosa fortuniana* rootstock. Before planting, soak roots of bare-root plants in a bucket of water for a few hours and amend soil with organic matter. Space plants about three-fourths of their mature height apart. Keep the root zone moist but not soggy. These roses produce large quantities of flowers and foliage, so fertilize 4 or 5 times per season. Apply sprinklings of cottonseed meal, alfalfa pellets, or diluted fish emulsion in addition to regular rose fertilizer for maximum bloom size and bright green foliage.

TLC When weather is dry, water new roses approximately twice a week and established roses once a week. Water deeply, preferably in the early morning. In spring, place a 1-inch-thick layer of mulch around the plants. In North Florida where winter cold can be severe, cover the center of each bush in late fall with mulch to protect it. In late winter, remove the mulch and fertilize. Little pruning is needed. Remove some of the oldest canes, along with weak and crossing branches.

PEAK SEASON

In warmer regions of the state, English roses can bloom year-round. In cooler areas, they go dormant in winter but rebloom in the spring.

MY FAVORITES

'Abraham Darby' has a warm pink-peach-apricot flower color and a very strong, fruity scent. Its robust growth habit is wide and arching.

'Heritage' flowers are a delicate shell pink, and although they aren't as long lasting as some other cultivars, they are as beautiful as any. The plant grows to 5 feet at most. This rose is best in cooler regions of North Florida.

'L. D. Braithwaite' produces crimson red, cup-shaped flowers that are lightly scented on a shrub of medium height.

'Pat Austin' flowers are a bright copper on the inside of the petals, and pale copper yellow on the outside. The flowers have a light tea scent and are large and deeply cupped. The shrub grows very vigorously to 5 feet tall.

GARDEN COMPANIONS

Plant a grouping of English roses as specimens in the garden or even as an informal hedge. Many have substantial thorns, making it difficult to maintain other plants placed near or around them.

TOP: *'Pat Austin'*
BOTTOM: *'L. D. Braithwaite'*

Floribunda Roses

The defining characteristic of floribunda roses is their ability to produce large quantities of hybrid tea–

'Europeana' is noted for very dark green and red leaves and rich, red flowers.

quality flowers that are slightly smaller than the hybrid teas and held in clusters above the leaves. Originally the result of crosses between hybrid teas (page 92) and polyanthas (page 98), floribundas retain much of the hardiness and repeat bloom of the polyanthas, but have much larger blooms. Cultivars vary—many produce strong, sizable bushes, while others are smaller varieties that work well in limited spaces. In Florida, floribunda roses typically reach 3 to 4 feet tall when grown on *Rosa fortuniana* rootstock.

The line between hybrid tea and floribunda roses has become blurred over time. With their tall, perfectly formed buds, hybrid teas are still known for the "one flower, one stem" rule, whereas floribundas may have large tealike flowers but in clusters. As with hybrid teas, there are challenges for some floribundas in Florida. But given adequate sunshine and water, floribunda roses are very resilient and can survive with little care.

PEAK SEASON

Year-round in southern and coastal regions; spring and fall elsewhere.

MY FAVORITES

'Amber Queen' has large, ruffled, amber gold flowers that come in small clusters that contrast the dark green, veined, shiny leaves.

'Brass Band' has delicate yellow buds that open into cantaloupe orange flowers, scented like a damask rose. Leaves are dark and glossy green.

'Europeana' has brilliant crimson red double blossoms held in clusters of up to 30. This is a reliable rose that's been proven over many years.

'Iceberg' covers itself in pure white double flowers throughout the summer. It grows about 3 feet tall.

'Sunsprite' has deep golden yellow flowers that are surprisingly resistant to fading, and sweetly scented. The leaves are dark green and shiny. Plants grow 3 or 4 feet high.

GARDEN COMPANIONS

Plant with other roses or in an ever-blooming border with perennials and small shrubs such as acacia, azaleas, abelia, sweetspire (Itea), summer-sweet (Clethra), angel's trumpet (Brugmansia), bluebeard (Caryopteris), butterfly bush (Buddleia), flowering maple (Abutilon), and cat's whiskers (Orthosiphon).

When Plant in the early fall while the soil is still warm enough to encourage root development. When spring arrives and the foliage begins to demand water, the roots will be well prepared.

Where Choose a location with enough space for the roots to stretch out and for the branches to reach full size. Plants need at least 6 hours of full sun daily. Good air circulation will help minimize disease and pest problems.

How Choose roses grown on *Rosa fortuniana* rootstock. Before planting, soak roots of bare-root plants in a bucket of water for a few hours and amend soil with organic matter. Space plants about three-fourths of their mature height apart.

TLC When weather is dry, water new roses at least twice a week and established roses once a week. Keep the root zone moist but not soggy. Water established roses deeply, preferably in the early morning. In spring, place a 1-inch-thick layer of mulch over the soil around plants. Remove spent blooms to encourage repeat flowering. Floribunda roses respond well to the application of organics between regular rose fertilizer applications. Apply sprinklings of cottonseed meal, alfalfa pellets, and diluted fish emulsion for maximum bloom size and lots of bright green foliage. In late winter, prune back to approximately half the normal height of the rose, cutting just above outward-facing buds. Remove weak and inward-facing canes, as well as any damaged by pests.

TOP: 'Iceberg'
CENTER: 'Amber Queen'
BOTTOM: 'Sunsprite'

Grandiflora Roses

In the United States, grandiflora roses are recognized as a class similar to but distinct from both floribundas (page 88) and hybrid teas (page 92). Some grandifloras have hybrid tea–like individual blossoms on long stems, and others have clustered flowers in floribunda style. In most cases, the flowers are as large as those of hybrid teas. More important, grandifloras are "flower factories" that equal hybrid teas in blossom production.

Just as with hybrid teas and floribundas, choosing the right grandiflora plant, putting it in the right place, and providing it with all the basics needed for survival helps ensure that you will get many years of pleasure from your rose. Once again, what's most important isn't the differences between the classes of roses, but rather which varieties of each type perform best in Florida's heat and humidity.

LEFT: *'Cherry Parfait' combines sumptuous colors with a light and sweet scent.*
RIGHT: *The grandiflora class of roses was created to accommodate this uniquely vigorous and hardy rose, 'Queen Elizabeth'.*

PEAK SEASON

Year-round in mild-winter regions; spring and fall in North Florida.

MY FAVORITES

'Candelabra' has large coral-and-orange flowers and dark green, glossy, and disease-resistant leaves. It grows about 4 feet tall.

'Cherry Parfait' has white to pale pink petals with red edges that contrast nicely with its dark green leaves. Of all the grandiflora types, 'Cherry Parfait' will receive the most compliments in your garden.

'Melody Parfumée' has deep plum buds that open to blooms of rich lavender with the fragrance of an old-fashioned rose. Leaves are lush green and disease resistant. Plants grow to 5 or 6 feet tall.

'Queen Elizabeth' has an outstanding pink flower and is a vigorous plant. No listing of superior grandifloras would be complete without it.

GARDEN COMPANIONS

Plant with other roses or in a border of mixed perennials and small shrubs including acacia, azaleas, abelia, sweetspire (Itea), summersweet (Clethra), angel's trumpet (Brugmansia), bluebeard (Caryopteris), butterfly bush (Buddleia), flowering maple (Abutilon), and cat's whiskers (Orthosiphon).

When Plant in the early fall while the soil is still warm enough to encourage root development. When spring arrives and the foliage begins to demand water, the roots will be well prepared.

Where Choose a location with enough space for the roots to stretch out and for the branches to reach full size. Plants need at least 6 hours of full sun daily. Good air circulation will help minimize disease and pest problems. Grandiflora roses are ideal for mass plantings, barriers, or hedges, where they will provide a colorful display all season.

'Melody Parfumée' has a rich, spicy scent.

How Choose plants that are grafted onto *Rosa fortuniana* rootstock. Before planting, soak roots of bare-root plants in a bucket of water for a few hours and amend soil with organic matter. Space plants about three-fourths of their mature height apart.

TLC When weather is dry, water new roses approximately twice a week and established roses once a week. Water established roses deeply, preferably in the early morning. In spring, place a 1-inch-thick layer of mulch around the plants. Fertilize at least 4 times per season, using cottonseed meal, alfalfa pellets, or diluted fish emulsion for maximum bloom size and lots of bright green foliage. Remove faded flowers to encourage repeat bloom. In late winter, prune back to approximately half the normal height of the rose, cutting just above outward-facing buds. Remove weak and inward-facing canes, as well as any damaged by winter or pests.

Hybrid Tea Roses

Of all the classes of roses, hybrid tea roses are by far the most popular in home gardens as well as in exhibitions. They are the favorite of rose gardeners who love to cut long-stemmed, large flowers. The blossoms have many petals and are usually fairly tall and upright, and most have great fragrance. These roses work well in both formal gardens or informal plantings. A cross between two types of old garden roses (page 96), hybrid perpetual roses and tea roses, hybrid teas are represented by more than 7,000 cultivars. On *Rosa fortuniana* rootstock, hybrid tea roses can last more than 20 years in the garden.

Hybrid teas flower best on new growth, and they must get a heavy pruning in late February to encourage strong new stems that will support the large blossoms. Depending on temperature and water availability, hybrid tea roses will rebloom every 8 to 9 weeks.

TOP: *'Double Delight'*
CENTER: *'Midas Touch'*
BOTTOM: *'Brandy'*

LEFT: *'Ingrid Bergman'*
RIGHT: *'Tiffany'*

PEAK SEASON

In warmer regions of the state, hybrid teas can bloom year-round. In cooler areas, they go dormant but rebloom in the spring.

MY FAVORITES

'Brandy' flowers are an apricot color. They come singly on long stems and have a pleasant but mild tea fragrance.

'Double Delight' flowers shift colors in a most beautiful way: scarlet buds open to a whitewashed pink and then mature to a buttery yellow and strawberry red. Perhaps because the fragrance is every bit the equal of the colors, this rose has been a Florida favorite for more than 20 years. Plants grow 4 to 5 feet tall.

'Ingrid Bergman' is a classic: dark velvety red, strongly scented, large flowers come singly on long stems. Plants grow 2 to 3 feet tall.

'Midas Touch' flowers are a deep and rich golden yellow, and fragrant.

'Tiffany' is one of the top-rated hybrid teas. The blossoms are pink with a hint of yellow at the base of every petal, and they have a clear, fresh fragrance.

GARDEN COMPANIONS

Plant with other roses or in a border of mixed perennials and small shrubs, including lavender and germander.

When Plant in the early fall while the soil is still warm enough to encourage root development.

Where Choose a location with enough space for the roots to stretch out and for the branches to reach full size. Plants need at least 6 hours of full sun daily. Good air circulation will help minimize disease and pest problems.

How Choose plants that are grafted onto *Rosa fortuniana* rootstock. Before planting, soak roots of bare-root plants in a bucket of water for a few hours and amend the soil with organic matter. Space plants about three-fourths of their mature height apart.

TLC When weather is dry, water new roses approximately twice a week and established roses once a week. Keep the root zone moist but not soggy. Water established roses deeply, preferably in the early morning. In spring, place a 1-inch-thick layer of mulch around the plants. Remove faded flowers to encourage repeat bloom. Fertilize hybrid tea roses 4 or 5 times per season. In addition to regular rose fertilizer, use cottonseed meal, alfalfa pellets, or diluted fish emulsion for maximum bloom size and bright green foliage. In late winter, cut back to approximately half the normal height of the rose, always cutting just above an outward-facing bud. Remove weak and inward-facing canes, as well as any damaged by winter or pests.

Miniature Roses

It was way back in 1810 that a miniature rose was discovered by British botanists on a small island in

The penetrating fragance of the small 'Sweet Nothing' flowers is a surprise.

the Indian Ocean. The first miniatures were introduced to America in 1840 but remained virtually nameless and led an obscure life, given the Civil War and the expansion to the west. In 1917, however, a tiny rose was discovered growing on a kitchen windowsill in Switzerland by a Swiss botanist, who named it for his close friend Colonel Roulet. Thus *Rosa roulettii* was introduced into our modern rose world, and the stage was set for the role of its many descendants.

Miniature roses are typically small shrubs (trees and climbers are available) with small flowers and small foliage. As with other rose groupings, the category of miniatures is a little blurry. The defining characteristic, however, is that even though the shrub itself may be 3 feet tall, the flowers are still smaller than those of roses in any other group.

When Plant in the early fall while the soil is still warm enough to encourage root development. When spring arrives and the foliage begins to demand water, the roots will be well prepared.

Where Choose a location with enough space for the roots to stretch out and for the branches to reach full size. Plants need at least 6 hours of full sun daily. Good air circulation will help minimize disease and pest problems. Use miniature roses in the garden, on windowsills, or in containers.

How Before planting, soak roots of bare-root plants in a bucket of water and amend soil with organic matter. Plant container plants at the same level they grew in the pot. Space plants about three-fourths of their mature height apart.

TLC Roots of miniature roses are shallow, so water and fertilizer are needed more frequently than for larger roses. Use the same rose fertilizers recommended for other roses (commercial rose fertilizer, cottenseed meal, alfalfa pellets, fish emulsion) but at lower concentrations and more frequently. This is especially true if the plants are growing in containers. Though hardy, miniatures still need some winter protection in the northern half of the state; cover plants with mulch in late fall. In late winter, prune back to approximately half the normal height of the rose, cutting just above outward-facing buds. Remove weak and inward-facing canes, as well as any damaged by winter or pests.

'Black Jade' is a perfectly formed rose that is miniature in size.

PEAK SEASON

Year-round in the south, spring through fall in the north.

MY FAVORITES

'Bees' Knees' has beautiful medium yellow blossoms with pink edging on long stems. It has beautiful foliage as well. Even in heat, it blooms constantly.

'Black Jade' flowers are classic in every way but size. Buds open to dark red flowers that come singly on long stems. Leaves are dark glossy green. The plant grows about 2 feet tall.

'Sweet Nothing' has beautiful pink flowers that have incredible fragrance. The plant grows 3 feet tall.

'Tiffany Lynn' flowers are light to medium pink at the edges, blending to white in the center, and they are slightly fragrant. For a miniature, it has a large (1¼ inches wide) blossom. The foliage is dark green. The bushy plant grows to 3 feet in height.

'Winsome' has perfectly formed lilac lavender flowers that win as easily in flower shows as in gardens. Plants are disease resistant and grow about 1½ feet tall.

GARDEN COMPANIONS

Use miniature roses in mixed borders or containers or window boxes with verbena, marigolds, torenia, dianthus, nasturtiums, gomphrena, zinnia, and nicotiana.

Old Garden Roses

If you want a rosebush that is easy to grow, virtually pest free, deeply fragrant, and reminiscent of grandmother's roses, you want an old garden rose. The old garden roses are primarily those that were grown in Europe before the hybrid teas (page 92) came along. Typically, these roses have graceful flower shapes, very fragrant blossoms, and a nostalgic charm that provides a perfect counterpoint to modern roses.

Some old garden roses bloom only once a year, usually in spring, but others are repeat bloomers. The bushes are handsome, and many offer showy hips in fall.

Old garden roses have a rose shape that is reminiscent of old hand-colored rose etchings, with seemingly hundreds of delicate, tissue-thin petals. But the shrubs, on the other hand, are often large with lots of thorns and large, thick stems. Several of these roses earn a place in the garden just for their heady fragrance. The blooming of the old garden roses signals not just the beginning of summer, but the onset of a particular sort of olfactory pleasure as well, one that can evoke memories and feelings outside of our normal range of perceptions. Perhaps that is why rose attar, the distilled oil of rose fragrance, was once nearly priceless.

Among the old garden roses are subgroups such as damask, bourbon, centifolia, hybrid perpetual, China, tea, and noisette. But these groupings aren't as important as finding the cultivar that fits your specific requirements and your garden.

The pink flower buds of 'Céline Forestier' open to fragrant, pale yellow blooms. Leaves are an attractive bright green.

PEAK SEASON

In warmer regions of the state, some old garden roses can bloom year-round. Others go dormant in summer but rebloom in the spring.

MY FAVORITES

'Blush Noisette' (subgroup: noisette) flowers are white blushed with pink, cup shaped, and nicely scented. The plant grows 4 to 8 feet tall.

'Céline Forestier' (subgroup: noisette) flowers are fragrant and pale yellow and come in clusters of 3 or 4. Leaves are a dark glossy green, and the plant grows to about 6 feet high.

'Old Blush' (subgroup: China), with its light pink flowers, has been a Florida favorite for many years. It blooms just about every month of the year in some regions, even through our hot and steamy summers. Plants grow about 5 feet tall.

'Sombreuil' (subgroup: tea) has creamy white flowers that often show a significant pink tint. The plant is large and essentially a climber.

GARDEN COMPANIONS

Use old garden roses in a variety of garden locations, including rose gardens, perennial borders, and specimen plantings, as well as to create informal hedges.

When Plant in the early fall while the soil is still warm enough to encourage root development. When spring arrives and the foliage begins to demand water, the roots will be well prepared.

Where Choose a location with enough space for both the roots and the branches to reach full size, and where plants will receive at least 6 hours of full sun daily. Good air circulation will help minimize disease and pest problems. Plant these roses toward the back of a mixed bed that also includes perennials and annuals.

TOP LEFT: *'Blush Noisette'*
TOP RIGHT: *'Sombreuil'*
BOTTOM RIGHT: *'Old Blush'*

How Choose roses grafted onto *Rosa fortuniana* rootstock. Before planting, soak roots of bare-root plants in a bucket of water for a few hours and amend soil with organic matter. Space plants about three-fourths of their mature height apart.

TLC When weather is dry, water new roses approximately twice a week and established roses once a week. Water established roses deeply, preferably in the early morning. Fertilize 4 or 5 times per season, using cottonseed meal, alfalfa pellets, or diluted fish emulsion for maximum bloom size and lots of bright green foliage. In spring, place a 1-inch-thick layer of mulch around the plants. Prune to remove older canes and weak growth. Prune repeat-flowering kinds in late winter, spring-blooming kinds after bloom.

Polyantha Roses

Normally a knee-high bush, the climbing form of 'Margo Koster' gracefully grows up and over an entry arbor, trailing its numerous 2-inch flowers all the way.

If you want to plant an easy-to-grow, profusely blooming, highly colorful rose that will never, ever win a blue ribbon at a rose show, then polyantha roses are for you.

Individual polyantha flowers are small, even insignificant, and they are usually not fragrant. But these charming little plants cover themselves with clusters of these tiny but delightful blossoms, and the overall effect from the masses of blooms can be amazing. In warmer areas of the state, the small plants are covered with blossoms for long periods beginning in March, continuing through peak season in late spring and early summer, and well into fall.

The small, bushy plants grow no more than 3 feet tall, so are ideally suited for borders and garden beds. Many polyanthas are also good in containers—even indoors—and provide a casual, colorful look not offered by many other garden plants.

Polyanthas are easy to grow, relatively disease resistant, and hardy. Most are small, so if they are in mixed borders, they need to be in front of other plants. Some larger forms that can make large shrubs are also available. Give a polyantha a spot in your garden with good soil, nutrition, light, and water, and it can be an incredibly rewarding plant. Polyantha roses are one of the parents of the original floribundas (page 88) and have many characteristics in common with them.

PEAK SEASON

In warmer regions of the state, poly-anthas bloom early spring through late fall.

MY FAVORITES

'China Doll' develops large sprays of pink, 1- to 2-inch-wide, slightly fragrant flowers. Plants grow to a compact 1 to 2 feet high and wide, and stems are nearly thornless.

'Fairy Queen' produces clusters of dainty double blooms in a deep shade of dark pink to red. An improvement over 'The Fairy' (which is a spider mite magnet in Florida), it is hardy, disease resistant, and easy to grow.

'Margo Koster', with its unique soft orange blooms, is by far the most popular polyantha rose at garden centers. Its popularity is well de-served—it is tough and it flowers profusely.

'Mother's Day' has dusty rose-colored blossom on 30-inch-tall plants.

GARDEN COMPANIONS

An effective use of polyantha roses is in large containers mixed with verbena, marigolds, torenia, dianthus, nasturtiums, gomphrena, zinnia, and flowering tobacco (Nicotiana).

When Plant in early fall while the soil is still warm enough to encourage root development. When spring arrives and the foliage begins to demand water, the roots will be well prepared.

Where Choose a location that in-cludes enough space for the roots and the branches to spread out and reach full size. Plants need at least 6 hours of full sun daily. Good air circulation will help minimize disease and pest problems. Use in containers, mixed borders, and patio plantings. Many polyanthas stretch out over the ground, making them an attractive choice for bordering a walkway.

'China Doll', a fragrant, nearly thornless rose.

How Choose plants grafted onto *Rosa fortuniana* root-stock. Before planting, soak bare-root plants in a bucket of water for a few hours and amend soil with organic matter. Space plants about three-fourths of their mature height apart.

TLC When weather is dry, water new roses approximately twice a week and established roses once a week. Water established roses deeply, ideally in the early morning. Fertilize 4 or 5 times a season, using cottonseed meal, alfalfa pellets, or diluted fish emulsion. In spring, place a 1-inch-thick layer of mulch around plants. In late winter, reduce the size of the plant by approximately half, cutting just above outward-facing buds. Remove weak and inward-facing canes, as well as any damaged by winter or pests.

Shrub Roses

Compared with the hybrid teas (page 92), which are cultivated for their near-perfect flowers, modern shrub roses are bred to be all-around garden plants. Rose breeders have responded to gardeners' requests for hardy, good-looking, low-maintenance roses, and for the last several years, many of the more exciting breeding breakthroughs have occurred in this large and diverse group of roses, which has many uses in gardens.

Among the most popular shrub roses are those that look and smell like old-fashioned roses, but are much more disease resistant and flower repeatedly through the season. The trademarked David Austin English roses (page 86) are a leading example of these.

The ultimate toughness test for any flowering shrub is a median strip, and roses such as 'Knock Out' pass this test, blooming all season long.

These newer shrubs are ideal for Florida gardeners who desire an attractive, easy-care rose.

'Simplicity' rose flowers virtually year-round and serves well as a colorful barrier hedge.

PEAK SEASON

In warmer regions of the state, shrub roses can bloom year-round. In cooler areas, they go dormant but rebloom in the spring.

MY FAVORITES

'Carefree Wonder' covers itself all season with lightly scented, bright pink flowers that have cream petal backs. The plant grows 4 to 6 feet high and has bright green and very disease resistant leaves.

'Knock Out' has cherry red single flowers in clusters that come non-stop all season long. Very resistant to black spot disease, this rose has taken the Florida rose market by storm and sells more than all other shrub roses combined. Leaves are glossy and dark green. Plants grow 30 to 36 inches high and wide. Gardeners tell me that pruning will reduce bloom.

'Simplicity' grows tall and dense and is very flowerful, so it is a natural for use as a hedge. Pink flowers come in clusters all season. The plant is disease free and easy to grow.

GARDEN COMPANIONS

Combine shrub roses in a border of mixed perennials and small shrubs such as acacia, sweetspire (Itea), summerweet (Clethra), angel's trumpet (Brugmansia), bluebeard (Caryopteris), butterfly bush (Buddleia), flowering maple (Abutilon), and cat's whiskers (Orthosiphon).

When Plant in the early fall while the soil is still warm enough to encourage root development. When spring arrives and the foliage begins to demand water, the roots will be well prepared.

Where Choose a location with enough space for the roots to stretch out and for the branches to reach full size. Plants need at least 6 hours of full sun daily. Good air circulation will help minimize disease and pest problems. Use shrub roses as specimens or in mass plantings, or group them to create impenetrable hedges.

How Choose plants grown on *Rosa fortuniana* rootstock. Before planting, soak bare-root plants in a bucket of water for a few hours and amend soil with organic matter. Space plants about three-fourths of their mature height apart.

TLC Shrub roses are very resilient and can survive much neglect, provided they receive adequate sunshine and plenty of water and fertilizer. They produce massive quantities of flowers and foliage, so fertilize them at least 4, even 5, times per season and be sure to keep the root zone moist but not soggy. They respond well to the application of organics between regular rose fertilizer applications. Apply sprinklings of cottonseed meal, alfalfa pellets, or diluted fish emulsion for maximum bloom size and bright green foliage.

TOP: *'Carefree Wonder'*
BOTTOM: *'Knock Out'*

Shrubs

Everyone knows what shrubs are. They're those bushy, woody-stemmed blobs you stick into the garden wherever you require something leafy that is roughly 3 to 10 feet high, doesn't need fertilizing or pruning, or can be repeatedly chopped into unnatural shapes, and makes do with whatever water the rest of the garden gets.

Well, some shrubs—even some good ones—fill that bill, but shrubs offer so much more than just durable and low-maintenance utility. Perhaps their status as a necessary evil began in times past when homes were built on foundations that rose several feet above ground level. Shrubs—especially dense, bulky ones—were pressed into service as "foundation plants" to provide a transition from house to garden by masking the often unattractive exposed foundation.

But in today's gardens, shrubs are an integral part of the diverse tapestry better known as "the landscape." Shrubs can still serve as foundation plants (where high foundations exist), but more often their role is to form the framework of a landscape: the permanent plantings that influence views, guide visitors, and create a graceful transition from tree canopy to ground level. Shrubs can also be used to punctuate the landscape as featured attractions; some especially showy flowering shrubs—azaleas (page 104) and camellias (page 108), for example—can become a garden's theme plant, playing a dominant role to which all else is secondary.

CHOOSING SHRUBS

You may ultimately be disappointed with the shrubs you choose if you let yourself be guided solely by flashy color or sentimental attachment. Instead, keep in mind the following guidelines:

ADAPTABILITY Gardeners expect most shrubs to be easy-growing, virtually trouble-free plants that will always look presentable. But success depends on choosing a shrub that is suited to your climate zone, your soil, and your garden's environment.

PLANT SIZE If you have space for a 4- by 4-foot plant but install one that's determined to reach 12 feet in all directions, you will be unhappy and frustrated, and your options will be frequent restrictive pruning (marring the plant's

inherent beauty) or removal. The better plan is to match a shrub's ultimate size with the space available. The most attractive shrubs (except those intended for formally sheared hedges) are ones that can reach their natural size and form without severe restraint.

GROWTH RATE Check the information on how fast your shrub selections will grow. This doesn't mean to always look for the rapid growers; rather, you should be aware of growth rates so your expectations will be realistic. Many choice shrubs are slow to moderate growers—but they are well worth the years it takes them to reach mature size.

Azalea
Rhododendron

Large flowers of early- to midseason-blooming 'Southern Charm' are spectacular in a mass planting. Individual plants grow 4 to 6 feet tall.

Azaleas are a staple on the plant-selection menu of gardeners throughout Florida. Available in a variety of colors, forms, and bloom times, azaleas are grown as majestic spring specimens or as regal back-drops to other southern plants. Ranging in colors from purest white to bright pink and lavender to the deepest crimson red, azaleas play an important role in creating what we know as the landscape.

Most azaleas bloom at various times in the spring, although the new Encore series blooms in late summer and early fall. A few, like 'Red Ruffle', bloom sporadically through-out the year and are quite popular for that reason. Azaleas can reach 8 feet in height if left unattended; a few dwarf varieties barely reach 2 feet tall. Azaleas are most often grown in the shady areas of the garden; how-ever, the Southern Indica types ('Red Formosa', 'Mrs. G. G. Gerbing', and 'George L. Taber', to name a few) thrive in Florida's full sun and heat, provided they get plenty of water and have adequate soil drainage.

PEAK SEASON

Spring primarily, though a few bloom throughout the year and the Encore series blooms late summer into fall.

MY FAVORITES

Evergreen azaleas

The Southern Indica types perform best in most areas of Florida, provided they have well-drained and acidic soil. Grow them in containers if your soil is alkaline. The best include: 'George L. Taber' (pink lavender); 'Lavender Formosa' (lavender); 'Mrs. G. G. Gerbing' (white); 'Pink Formosa' (pink); 'President Clay' (brick red); 'Pride of Mobile' (watermelon); 'Red Formosa' (wine red); and 'Southern Charm' (rich pink).

Deciduous azaleas

These perform admirably in the northern areas of the state where cool winters and plentiful water are the norm. A reliable choice is the flame azalea (Rhododendron calendulaceum), which bears large clusters of 2-inch flowers in spring. Plants usually grow 4 to 9 feet tall.

GARDEN COMPANIONS

Plant azaleas with dogwood (Cornus), redbud (Cercis), mondo grass, live oak, camellias, silverbell (Halesia), Oregon grape (Mahonia), magnolia, chaste tree (Vitex), crape myrtle (Lagerstroemia), and river birch.

When Plant azaleas from mid- to late fall through winter; you can even plant them while they're blooming, but try to do it before new growth starts.

Southeastern woodlands are alive in springtime with the brilliant flowers of flame azalea.

Where Choose a garden spot that gets either filtered sunlight all day or some sun in the morning followed by light shade from noon on. Where summer is typically foggy and cool, you can grow azaleas in parts of the garden that are more open and exposed to the sun.

How Azaleas must have soil that drains rapidly yet retains moisture, so be sure to amend your soil liberally with organic matter prior to planting. In addition, they need soil that is acidic, or at least neutral; organic matter initially helps to acidify conditions, but in regions where alkaline soil prevails, fertilizers are the long-term solution. To plant, dig a hole roughly three-quarters as deep as the plant's root ball and twice as wide. Remove the plant from its container and place it in the hole: The crown (the juncture of stems and root ball) should be above soil grade—1 to 2 inches in well-drained soil, 2 to 3 inches where soil drainage is only moderately good. Where soil is poorly drained, grow these shrubs in raised beds containing a specially formulated planting soil.

TLC Give azaleas plenty of water, and monitor the pH to keep it between 5 and 6.5. For best growth and flowering, apply an acid fertilizer twice a year: before bloom as buds begin to swell, and again just after flowers have finished. Azaleas roots are very shallow; don't cultivate the soil around them, as it could cause long-term damage. Add a layer of good organic mulch such as pine straw, pine bark, or recycled wood products (but not cypress).

Beautyberry
Callicarpa

Beautyberry is a graceful deciduous shrub with long, arching branches that are appreciated mostly for their pleasing displays of small, round, long-lasting lavender to purple fruits in late summer and fall.

Tight clusters of berries hug cascading stems of purple beautyberry.

Beautyberry typically grows to about 8 feet high. In spring it produces clusters of lavender flowers along the branches. The flowers ultimately turn into round clusters of incredible bright purple berries that last well into winter. The berries grow so that it looks as though the branch has been driven right through the center of each cluster. There are 1 to 15 clusters per branch.

These are tough and good-looking shrubs that fit well into native and woodland gardens or shrub borders. A number of beautyberry cultivars have been introduced in the last several years, offering the Florida gardener a wide range of shrub types and berry colors. Beautyberry grows best in full sun and ordinary soil.

When Plant in late fall or early winter to establish the root system before the onset of summer heat.

Where Plant in ordinary, slightly acid soil in full sun to part shade.

PEAK SEASON
Late fall once branches are laden with berries

MY FAVORITES
American beautyberry (*Callicarpa americana*), a native of the southern United States, grows 8 feet high and wide and has large, 6-inch-long leaves. Peppercorn-sized berries are deep purple. *C. a. 'Lactea'* is just as prolific but has white berries.

Profusion bodinier beautyberry (*C. bodinieri giraldi* 'Profusion') is an upright shrub with cascading branches. Small mauve flowers in spring are followed by heavy clusters of rich violet-purple fruit.

Purple beautyberry (*C. dichotoma*) grows 4 to 5 feet tall. 'Early Amethyst' has a rounded habit, smaller leaves, and berries that mature early. Issai Japanese beautyberry (*C. dichotoma* 'Issai') has striking lilac violet berries.

White Japanese beautyberry (*C. japonica* 'Leucocarpa') has white berries in the fall that cover its arching branches. This rounded deciduous shrub is typically 4 to 6 feet high.

GARDEN COMPANIONS
Pair with trees such as dogwood (*Cornus*) or redbud (*Cercis*), native ornamental grasses, azalea, Cape plumbago, or lion's tail and sun-tolerant ferns.

How Dig a planting hole twice the width of the container and slightly shallower, then dig deeper around the hole's perimeter to leave a firm central core. Remove the root ball from the container and set it on the firm center, making sure the root ball's surface is just a bit higher than the surrounding soil. Roughen the sides of the root ball. Then return the soil to the hole and water well. Or, remove the ripened seeds after they have turned dark brown and sow in a seed flat; allow up to 3 months for germination. Three-foot-tall plants can be grown in one season from seed sown the previous fall.

TLC Other than the American holly, beautyberry produces more berries than any other native shrub in Florida gardens.

The ripening comes at the perfect time for the northern birds flying south during their fall migration. Plants bloom and fruit on new growth, so remove the previous season's branches in spring.

LEFT: *White-fruited Japanese beautyberry,* C. japonica *'Leucocarpa'.*
BELOW: *Native American beautyberry has large leaves that turn purple in fall.*

Camellia
Camellia

Along with southern magnolia and palms, camellias symbolize gardening in Florida. They have the ability to thrive in a variety of conditions and soils and, with a little attention, will reward you with breathtakingly large blossoms of deepest carmine red to bright white, as well as pinks and variegated forms.

There are two main types of camellia: the common camellia, *Camellia japonica,* and the sasanqua camellia, *C. sasanqua.* Both are symmetrical, broad-leafed, evergreen plants that would grace any garden even if they never bloomed. The common camellia is larger. Its

glossy oval leaves are about 4 inches long and make a dense cover on plants that can be upright, rounded, or spreading, depending on the variety. Heights generally run from 6 to 12 feet and are eventually matched by an equal spread. Ultimately, some varieties can reach 20 feet or higher, but the plants' slow to moderate growth rates make this a long, slow climb. The sasanqua camellia is more sprawling and broad. After many years, it may grow 20 feet wide and 12 feet tall. Both leaves and flowers are smaller than the common camellia, but the flowers are more numerous.

Camellia sinensis, an evergreen shrub that grows 6 feet tall, is the source of oolong, black, and green teas.

'Lady Clare' features carmine rose semidouble flowers with prominent, bundled stamens. Blooming time is mid- to late season. Plants are more cold hardy than most.

PEAK SEASON

Camellia sasanqua blooms October to December; and *C. japonica* blooms January to March.

MY FAVORITES

Camellia japonica

Red: 'Governor Mouton' (often splashed with white); and 'Mathotiana Supreme' (deep red with hint of blue on the petal edges).

Pink: 'C. M. Wilson' (light pink); 'Debutante' (clear pink); 'Lady Clare' (carmine pink); 'Pink Perfection' (light pink); and 'Sawada's Dream' (white to pale pink).

White: 'Alba Plena' (pure white); 'Imura'; 'Leucantha'; and 'Purity'.

Red variegated: 'Dixie Knight Supreme' (deep red with white); and 'Rebel Yell' (burgundy with white).

Camellia sasanqua

'Fuji-no-mine' (single white with light pink edges); 'Leslie Ann' (white with pink margins); 'Mine-no-yuki' (pure white); 'Setsugekka' (pure white tipped in rose red); 'Stephanie Golden' (pink); 'William Lanier Hunt' (medium red); and 'Yuletide' (single red with yellow stamens).

GARDEN COMPANIONS

Camellias combine well with many other shade plants. Consider azaleas, banana shrub (*Michelia*), fringe tree (*Chionanthus*), and gardenia.

Flowers of the classic and early-blooming 'Pink Perfection' are relatively small and fully double.

When Container-grown camellias are available year-round, but mid-October through February is the best time to plant. You want to get the shrubs in the ground during the cooler months and before new growth begins in early spring.

Where Plant *Camellia japonica* in dappled shade. *Camellia sasanqua* prefers full sun, although it will thrive in dappled shade. Soil pH is important and needs to be maintained in the 6.0 to 6.5 range. Give camellias a well-drained loam soil amended with organic matter.

How Dig a planting hole twice the width of the camellia's container and about 2 inches shallower than the plant's root ball. Then dig deeper around the hole's perimeter (leaving a firm central plateau) and roughen the hole's sides to encourage the roots to grow into your garden soil. Set the root ball on the plateau—making certain the top of the root ball is 1 to 2 inches higher than the surrounding soil—then fill in the hole with soil amended with organic matter, firming the soil with your fingers as you add it. Finally, water the plant well.

TLC Camellias are synonymous with gardens of the Deep South and grow very well in Florida. Just make certain they get plenty of fertilizer and water, and they will reward you with abundant blooms from October through March.

*Grow in containers filled with an acidic potting soil mix.

Cape Plumbago
Plumbago auriculata

Growing some plants in Florida can be a challenge: full, hot sun, poor soil, inadequate water, and not enough growing time. Wouldn't it be great to discover a plant that grows during the hottest time of the year, with little or no supplemental water, and that doesn't require much of a gardener's time? It's no fantasy. Such a hardworking garden plant actually exists.

Cape plumbago, with its brilliant blue, phloxlike flowers, evergreen foliage, arching habit, and penchant for hot, dry weather, is too often overlooked by gardeners. Despite its ability to grow in the worst of adverse conditions, there is no plant society dedicated to growing it and no one sings its praises on the Saturday morning gardening talk shows. All the same, it is a hardworking and handsome plant in all areas of Florida.

If you need something to cover a large space in the land–scape without much care, plumbago is the best choice.

Large clusters of dark blue flowers cover 'Royal Cape' nearly year-round.

Phloxlike clusters of sky-blue flowers cover Cape plumbago most of the year.

PEAK SEASON

All year in southern areas of 26 and 31. Spring to fall in zone 25 and in northern areas of zone 26.

MY FAVORITES

'Royal Cape' has been around for a number of years and is a superior variety. Its flowers are a brighter blue, even through the most intense summer sun.

RELATED SPECIES

Red plumbago *(Plumbago indica)* has deep red flowers in the spring and again in late summer or early fall, but not in the same quantity as Cape plumbago. In hottest regions, it prefers a bit of shade.

GARDEN COMPANIONS

Cape plumbago looks great with a wide variety of heat- and sun-tolerant flowering plants. Consider planting with annuals such as pentas, marigolds, and torenia; perennials such as blanket flower *(Gaillardia)*, gaura, or salvia; and shrubs such as crape myrtle *(Lagerstroemia)*, nandina, and cleyera. An evergreen tree such as evergreen magnolia or holly *(Ilex)* will provide an attractive dark green backdrop.

When Fall is ideal but any time of year is fine.

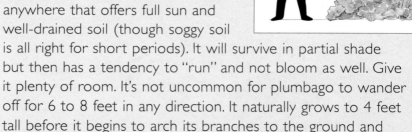

Where Plant Cape plumbago anywhere that offers full sun and well-drained soil (though soggy soil is all right for short periods). It will survive in partial shade but then has a tendency to "run" and not bloom as well. Give it plenty of room. It's not uncommon for plumbago to wander off for 6 to 8 feet in any direction. It naturally grows to 4 feet tall before it begins to arch its branches to the ground and ramble about.

How Dig a planting hole twice the width of the container and about 2 inches shallower than the root ball. Plant so that the top of the root ball is 1 to 2 inches higher than the surrounding soil, then fill in the hole with soil amended with organic matter, firming the soil with your fingers as you add it. Water the plant well.

TLC Cape plumbago is a landscape plant you won't have to worry about. Prune lightly in late winter for shape. The flowers bloom on new wood, so don't worry about giving it a trim in spring. It will withstand heavy pruning, but is at its best when allowed to grow to its full potential.

Crape Myrtle
Lagerstroemia indica

Ask anyone who has gardened for any length of time in Florida to choose a favorite summer-blooming tree and odds are, the answer will be crape myrtle. It comes in a variety of colors, sizes, and shapes, with some types becoming 40-foot-high trees, and others reaching only a few feet!

A potentially tall crape myrtle, 'Natchez' is very disease resistant.

Crape myrtle may also be the most misunderstood plant. Even though breeding programs have produced many named varieties of specific sizes and shapes, gardeners still plant them where they don't fit. This leads to the cutting of crape myrtles in the late winter or early spring, an annual tradition known as "crape murder."

The key is to find a named cultivar with the size and color desired. Don't plant one that will ultimately reach 30 feet tall in a space suited for a 12-foot specimen. It may take a little research to find the right color and the right height but it can be done, and the time spent will garner you large rewards in the years to come.

PEAK SEASON

Late spring through fall

MY FAVORITES

Don't buy an unnamed plant: It might grow to 40 feet or to 10 feet.

8 to 10 feet: 'Acoma' (clear bright white flowers); and 'Pink Velour' (coral pink flowers with wine-colored foliage that fades to dark green).

12 to 15 feet: 'Dynamite' (purple new growth and intense red flowers); 'Sioux' (clear pink flowers); and 'Tonto' (beet red flowers).

20 feet: 'Apalachee' (light lavender flowers and a vase-shaped habit).

40 feet: 'Biloxi' (pale pink blossoms); 'Muskogee' (lavender pink flowers that repeat-bloom in fall); and 'Natchez' (white flowers and beautiful cinnamon and gray mottled bark).

GARDEN COMPANIONS

Many plants go well with crape myrtles. Good companions include annuals such as pentas and verbena, and shrubs such as Cape plumbago.

When Plant in late fall or early winter to establish the root system before the onset of summer heat.

Where Choose a site with well-drained soil in full sun. Crape myrtle can withstand partial shade, but bloom will be diminished. Plant the right-sized plant in the right location. If the site calls for an 8-foot plant at maturity, spend a little time and find the correct variety for that location.

How Dig a planting hole twice the width of the container and slightly shallower, then dig deeper around the hole's perimeter to create a firm central plateau. Remove the root ball from the container and set it on the plateau, making sure the root ball's surface is just a bit higher than the surrounding soil. Then return the soil to the hole and water well. Stake the shrub so it won't whip about in the wind.

TLC Crape myrtles are very easy to grow, provided they receive adequate moisture and get a dose of a complete fertilizer three or four times a year. Remove spent flowers for a repeat bloom throughout the summer; it's possible to have three bloom cycles in one summer. Crape myrtles do get powdery mildew if night temperatures hover around 65°F (18°C), and some varieties are more susceptible than others. Once the cooler nights pass, the mildew won't be a problem again until late fall. Wash any aphids off new growth in spring with a strong stream of water.

TOP: 'Sioux' develops a narrow, vaselike shape.
BOTTOM: 'Natchez' blooms earlier than most others.
LEFT: 'Apalachee' flowers are lightly scented.

Fringe Tree
Chionanthus virginicus

In spring, it's hard to imagine that anything could be more beautiful in Florida gardens than this large white-flowering shrub (or small tree), a native plant of the southeastern United States. It's often called "grancy gray beard" or "old man's beard" for its showy fringelike white blooms that cascade downward like the white beard of an old man. Of all the native white spring-flowering shrubs, fringe tree may have the most plentiful flowers. The fragrant blossoms cover the tree from May to June (about the same time as the dogwoods and azaleas are in bloom), and this shrub is renowned for its delightful sweet scent. Fringe trees are typically the last plant to leaf out in the spring; the leaves are large and arranged opposite each other on the stems.

Fringe tree is one of the most beautiful flowering shrubs. Slow growing, it is adaptable to a variety of light and soil conditions. Fringe tree has no common insect or disease problems and is easy to transplant.

The only reason fringe trees are not more common is that they are difficult to propagate—but, new methods of growing plants are making them more available. Still, if your local nursery does not have them, check with a nursery that specializes in native plants.

PEAK SEASON

Spring

RELATED SPECIES

Chinese fringe tree *(C. retusus)* is native to China and Japan. It makes an ideal shade or specimen tree and thrives in fertile, well-drained, moist soil.

Pygmy fringe tree *(Chionanthus pygmaeus)* is an endangered species restricted to the scrub communities of central Florida. Look for it at nurseries that specialize in native plants.

GARDEN COMPANIONS

Place with other spring-blooming plants including azaleas and dogwood *(Cornus).* In shady locations, plant fringe trees with camellias, gardenias, Florida pinwheel *(Tabernaemontana),* cleyera, and lady palm *(Rhapis).* In sun, plant fringe tree as a specimen or with sasanqua camellias, viburnum, sago palm, or Chinese witch hazel *(Loropetalum).*

OPPOSITE PAGE: *A native plant, fringe tree is a spectacular shrub or small tree during its spring bloom time.*

When Planting in fall is recommended.

Where Choose a site with full sun or partial shade and ordinary well-drained soil. Fringe trees are difficult to grow in South Florida because of the alkaline soil.

How Prepare a planting hole that is slightly shallower than the fringe tree's root ball and twice as wide; then dig a bit deeper around the perimeter of the hole, leaving a firm central plateau. Set the plant onto the firm center, making sure the top of the root ball is slightly higher than the surrounding soil. Fill in with soil around the root ball, firming with your fingers, then water thoroughly.

TLC Little pruning is required, but you can prune to shape the plant to your preferences and available space. To develop it as a shrub, prune the tips of the branches after the flowers fade. To develop it as a tree, remove the lower branches from the central trunk. Fringe tree is not bothered by pests or disease.

TOP: *Greenish white and lightly scented flowers of fringe tree come in ample, impressive, and lacy clusters.*
BOTTOM: *Compared to fringe tree, flowers of Chinese fringe tree are smaller, pure white, and more numerous. They also appear about 3 weeks earlier.*

115

Gardenia
Gardenia jasminoides

Among the wonderful characteristics of Florida gardens are the exotic fragrances that seem to materialize from nowhere as you stroll through them. As a member of the club of "not to be missed garden fragrances," gardenia may be the queen of late-spring flower perfumes. Its heady, elegant scent emanates from glorious velvety soft, white flowers, and the glossy evergreen leaves are a welcome addition to any garden. Provided they receive adequate water and nutrients, gardenias will live to be grand old plants, sometimes reaching 10 feet in height and width.

Gardenias are native to eastern Asia (China, Taiwan, and Japan) and prefer an acidic, well-drained, highly organic and moist soil. In cooler areas of Florida, gardenias grow with vigor in full sun; the farther south you plant them, the more shade they need.

Few other plants are as identified with the charm of the South as the gardenia. On summer nights, its scent is one of the most powerful and most memorable.

ABOVE: *The velvet-like petals are marred quickly by the touch of a fingertip.*
BELOW LEFT: *A dwarf, single-flowered, exceedingly fragrant gardenia.*

PEAK SEASON

Most gardenias bloom in late spring or early summer. A few cultivars bloom during the summer months.

MY FAVORITES

'August Beauty' is a large plant (to 6 feet) with large, 4-inch flowers that appear sporadically throughout the summer.

'Coral Gables' grows to 4 feet and produces large, 4-inch flowers.

'Fortuneiana' has double, carnation-like flowers up to 4 inches in diameter.

'Golden Magic' grows 3 feet tall and has unusual, almost double, pure white flowers that deepen to a golden yellow color.

'Radicans' grows 1 foot tall and 3 feet wide and produces 1-inch-wide flowers; 'Radicans Variegata' is the same but with variegated leaves.

GARDEN COMPANIONS

Gardenias are happiest when planted in the shade of live oak trees, camellias, azaleas, and hydrangeas.

When Container-grown gardenias are available year-round, but mid-October is the best time to plant. Plant them during the cooler months and before new growth begins in early spring.

Where The best location for all gardenias is in partial shade: in the dappled light beneath tall trees, on the north side of a house, or beneath an overhead structure (such as lath) that will filter sunlight. Give them well-drained soil amended with organic matter. Gardenias prefer an acidic soil (5.0 to 6.5 pH) and have a difficult time staying healthy in the alkaline soils of South Florida.

How Dig a planting hole twice the width of the gardenia's container and about 2 inches shallower than the root ball. Then dig deeper around the hole's perimeter (leaving a firm central plateau) and roughen the hole's sides to encourage roots to grow into your garden soil. Set the root ball on the plateau so the top is 1 to 2 inches higher than the surrounding soil, then fill in with soil amended with organic matter, firming it with your fingers as you go.

TLC Gardenias need moist soil. In addition to helping the plant grow, adequate water will prevent flower-bud drop. The most common complaint is yellow leaves. The cause is poor nutrition, nematode (roundworm) damage, poor soil drainage, insufficient light, or cold soil. Treat plants with yellow leaves in spring with an all-purpose fertilizer (15-5-15) and a dose of iron chelates. Gardenias suffering from either inadequate drainage or poor nutrition attract insect pests; aphids and spider mites are the most common. To reduce their numbers, apply horticultural oil or neem oil to the bottom sides of the leaves during the cooler times of the year (to prevent leaf scorching).

Princess Flower
Tibouchina

The huge, 9-inch-long leaves of large-leaf princess flower are covered on both sides with silky hairs.

One of the most glamorous Florida shrubs is princess flower, *Tibouchina urvilleana*. A native of Brazil, it has the lush growth and colors you might associate with a tropical jungle. The shrub grows at least 8 feet tall and wide and has 2- to 4-inch-long, deeply veined leaves that are fuzzy on the top side. The leaves are dramatic, but it's the flowers that stop passersby in their tracks. About 5 inches across, they are an intense, striking violet purple. Whether singly or in clusters, they have conspicuously long, twisted stamens that inspired the name "spider flower" in the plant's native Brazil. Bloom is intermittent throughout the year, or, in central Florida, intermittent spring through summer.

Princess flower is a treasured landscape plant and, as such, is typically given a prominent location. Unfortunately, it is cold sensitive, so is grown primarily in central to southern Florida.

When The best planting period is the cooler part of the year—from mid- or late fall to midwinter. The roots can take advantage of the cooler, moister conditions to begin growing into the soil of your garden.

Where Princess flower grows best in full sun and rich, well-drained, slightly acid soil. Use it as an informal, unclipped hedge or screen, as a specimen in a prominent location, or in a container. It can be trained as an espalier against a wall that gets at least 6 hours of full sun during the day.

How Dig a planting hole twice as wide as the plant's container and slightly shallower than the root ball. Then dig deeper around the perimeter of the hole to create a firm plateau in the center, roughing up the sides in the process. Remove the plant from its container, set the root ball on the plateau, then fill in with soil. After firming the soil with your fingers, water the plant well.

TLC Princess flower has a tendency toward legginess that is easy to counteract—lightly pinch it back after the spring bloom and following each subsequent bloom cycle. This will also increase the number of flowers. The plant will rebound quickly after heavy pruning. This shrub is very easy to grow and has no serious pests.

PEAK SEASON

Year-round in South Florida; spring to fall in central Florida.

MY FAVORITES

'Athens Blue' princess flower (*Tibouchina urvilleana*) is a hybrid that produces familiar violet-blue flowers on a much more compact 3- to 5-foot-tall plant.

'Jules' is very similar to 'Athens Blue', and grows about 3 feet high. It is the most cold sensitive of all the cultivars but is the perfect size for a container or for use as a border plant.

Large-leaf princess flower (*Tibouchina grandiflora*) grows 4 to 6 feet tall. Its inch-wide flowers rise above leaves in foot-long spikes.

GARDEN COMPANIONS

Combine princess flower with exotic plants. Consider powder puff (*Calliandra*), bottlebrush (*Callistemon*), angel's trumpet (*Brugmansia*), banana (*Musa*), butterfly ginger (*Hedychium*), bromeliads, palms, ornamental grasses, floss silk trees, Chinese hat plant, and elephant's ear.

RIGHT: *Brilliant royal blue flowers of princess flower* (Tibouchina urvilleana) *are 3 to 5 inches wide.*

Sweetspire, Virginia Willow

Itea virginica

Tiny, scented sweetspire flowers are packed into long, bottlebrush-like clusters.

Beautiful, warm weather is one of the primary reasons people from all over the world move to Florida. After the long, hot summer, however, gardeners long for cooler days, and with those fall days, perhaps a little foliage color. The folks in North Florida are rewarded with rich red, gold, and even purple in fall; most trees and shrubs in South and Central Florida, however, don't provide the same colorful show—unless gardeners there plant sweetspire.

When plants like sweetspire are used in the landscape, gardeners in southern areas can finally have a hint of the fall color enjoyed by their northern neighbors. Its leaves turn the rich red to purple hue that gardeners seek. In addition to the fall color, sweetspire produces bright white, very fragrant flower spikes in early summer.

Sweetspire is perfect for a formal or informal hedge and can be used in mass plantings. Once established, it is a resilient plant, able to take dry or wet soil conditions. In fact, it will do quite nicely in dry soils, though you will have to water it frequently the first year. It is one of our most attractive native shrubs.

When The ideal time to plant is late fall just after most of the leaves have fallen off, but you can successfully plant container-grown plants any time of year.

Where Sweetspire ordinarily grows in wet areas along streams and ponds; it prefers moist, fertile soil but will tolerate dry soils once established. It is also pH adaptable. Although it grows best with a little shade, it can take a few hours of full sun every day.

How Prepare a planting hole that is slightly shallower than the root ball and twice as wide; then dig a bit deeper around the perimeter of the hole, leaving a firm central plateau. Set the plant on the plateau, making sure the top of the root ball is slightly higher than the surrounding soil. Fill in with soil around the root ball, firming with your fingers, then water thoroughly.

TLC In wet areas, sweetspire can create dense thickets, so give it plenty of room. And because it's native, there are no concerns about planting it adjacent to streams and lakes. Sweetspire is very easy to grow and is rarely bothered by either pests or diseases.

LEFT: *Bumblebees and other pollinators are strongly attracted to sweetspire flowers.*
BELOW: *Compared to the species, 'Henry's Garnet' has a deeper red fall color and longer flower clusters.*

PEAK SEASON

Early summer for flowers; fall for leaf color

MY FAVORITES

'Henry's Garnet' flower spikes are twice as long as those of the species, and they arch and cascade above the foliage beautifully. Leaves take on a reddish tinge in early fall and deepen to a dark crimson red and scarlet as the weather turns colder.

'Little Henry' is 2 to 3 feet tall, so it is perfect for mass plantings or a perennial border.

'Merlot' grows to about 3 feet high, with a dense, compact habit and red fall color.

'Saturnalia' glows shocking pink, yellow, red, orange, and burgundy in the fall.

'Scarlet Beauty' is a new large (4 to 5 feet), upright selection that has proved itself to be hardy in the heat of Florida.

GARDEN COMPANIONS

Give sweetspire plenty of room. Combine with azaleas, caladium, camellias, dogwood (*Cornus*), gardenia, Oregon grape (*Mahonia*), holly (*Ilex*), hydrangea, Florida leucothoe (*Agarista*), osmanthus, toad lily (*Tricyrtus*), pawpaw, redbud (*Cercis*), silverbell (*Halesia*), and snowbell (*Styrax*).

Tropical Hibiscus
Hibiscus rosa-sinensis

TOP: *'Seminole Pink' has dark leaves and bright pink flowers.*
BOTTOM: *A salmon-pink variety of tropical hibiscus.*

If ever there was a signature plant of Florida, it is the hibiscus. Its exotic and alluring flowers display every color of the rainbow and exhibit a variety of shapes and forms.

Hibiscus like it hot and humid. Give them lots of water and fertilizer and they will reward you with flowers that are beyond description. They are tropical plants and perform best in tropical conditions.

In Florida, three types of hibiscus are grown. The first and most abundant group comprises the modern hybrids of tropical hibiscus. The second—and flashiest—are the grafted hibiscus hybrids. They always generate lots of interest, but they are more sensitive to cold, pests, and diseases. The third group—selections of rose mallow with flowers of various colors—is the toughest.

Hybridizers have been working on three specific characteristics of the hibiscus flower: size (larger or smaller), color (the elusive blue hibiscus), and blossom quality. The breeding has led to an array of unusual colors ranging from silver to lavender and even gray. By now, there must be thousands and thousands of named varieties of hibiscus.

When Plant in late fall or early winter to establish the root system before the onset of summer heat.

Where Choose a site with well-drained soil, and, for most types, in full sun. Many of the grafted hybrids are so delicate, however, their blooms will burn in the hot sun; they prefer a little shade during the day. Plant rose mallows either in wet soil or where moisture is readily available.

How Dig a planting hole twice the width of the container and slightly shallower, then dig deeper around the hole's perimeter to create a firm central plateau. Remove the root ball from the container, roughen its sides and set it on the firm plateau, making sure the root ball's surface is just a bit higher than the surrounding soil. Then return the soil to the hole and water well. Stake the shrub so it won't whip about in the wind.

TLC Water generously, and fertilize hibiscus hybrids monthly from April through September. For good branch structure of young plants and to rejuvenate mature plants, prune plants in early spring. Pinch off branch tips through summer to increase flowering.

LEFT: *Bicolored blossoms, such as 'Jason', are available with grafted hibiscus.*
RIGHT: *'John Paul Jones' flowers are 7 inches in diameter.*

PEAK SEASON

All year in South Florida; spring to late fall in central Florida; summer in North Florida.

MY FAVORITES

Modern hybrids

'El Capitola' (red with white edge); 'John Paul Jones' (orange-red); and 'Seminole Pink' (solid pink flower with red-tipped flower parts).

Grafted hybrids

'Byron Metts' (pure white); 'Hawaiian Sunset' (yellow and red); 'High Voltage' (white flower with a dark red center); 'Jason' (yellow with a burgundy and violet center); 'Macintosh' (orange-red); 'Seminole Pride' (garnet with a brilliant gold band); 'Shelley Lynn' (red, purple, and orange with yellow rings); and 'Snapper' (spotted white).

RELATED SPECIES

Rose mallows *(Hibiscus moscheutos)* grow to 4 feet tall and have blossoms up to 12 inches across. Selections include: 'Disco Belle Mix' (white to dark red); 'Lady Baltimore' (pink with red centers); and 'Luna Blush' (white blushed with pink).

GARDEN COMPANIONS

Hibiscus serve well as specimens in the landscape with other summer-flowering shrubs. The smaller forms work well in the perennial border.

Whether they are trumpet trees lighting up the sky near Miami beaches or dogwoods coloring Tallahassee neighborhoods with blossoms or foliage, trees help define the general character of a landscape. They serve so many purposes—both aesthetic and practical—that few homeowners would consider doing without them.

Trees offer cooling shade, provide shelter, and establish perspective. They can also frame special vistas and block out unattractive ones. Dominant features of the landscape, trees can make dramatic statements or enhance the yard or garden with sculptural effects.

Although trees are often the most expensive individual plants to buy, they are a worthwhile long-term investment. They can be relied on to give a feeling of permanence to any landscape, so, not surprisingly, they are particularly valued in new housing developments.

Often overlooked is the role trees play in conserving energy in your home. For example,

a tree-shaded house will require less air conditioning in summer than an exposed one. And when deciduous trees are planted on the south side of a house, the winter sunshine can help to reduce heating and lighting costs.

Your choice of trees will be determined largely by their intended purpose in your landscape. To block the sun, for example, select only trees that develop widely spreading branches. If you need a screen, look for trees that produce branches on their lower trunks, or combine shrubs or walls with trees that have bare lower trunks. For a focal point, choose a tree that displays eye-catching flowers or colorful fruits, or

OPPOSITE PAGE: *A large, cup-shaped flower of evergreen magnolia is cradled by the tree's leathery leaves.*
RIGHT: *Semievergreen pink trumpet tree is glorious in spring, when blooms emerge and cover bare branches.*

one with attractive foliage, interesting bark, or a striking winter silhouette.

Trees usually live for decades, even centuries. Each year, new growth springs from a framework of last year's branches to form a gradually enlarging structure. Tree silhouettes vary greatly from one species to another and a tree's ultimate shape is usually not obvious in young nursery specimens, so be sure you are familiar with a tree's mature shape before you plant it.

Although the range of tree shapes is enormous, all trees are classified as either deciduous or evergreen, though a few are inbetween. Most deciduous trees produce new leaves in spring and retain them throughout the summer. In the fall, leaf color may change from green to warm autumnal tones, and the trees then drop their foliage for the winter, revealing bare limbs. Broad-leafed evergreens, such as evergreen magnolia (page 128), have leaves year-round, but drop the oldest ones just the same. Needle-leafed trees, including pines (page 136), are usually evergreen, but not always. Bald cypress (page 126) is deciduous.

STAKING AND TRAINING

Try to avoid trees that are too weak to stand upright on their own. If you have such a tree, cut it back a little at a time until it can support itself. This way, a stronger trunk will develop. If cutting back is not practical, you can stake the tree, though usually staking prolongs the time that support is required. The method depends on the tree's size. For trees with trunks up to 2 inches thick, place two stakes on either side of the tree, and secure the tree to them at about chest height. Use three stakes to support trunks 2 to 4 inches thick.

Bald Cypress
Taxodium distichum

If there is a tree that typifies Florida's swamplands and waterways, it has to be the bald cypress, with its imposing pyramidal shape draped in gray Spanish moss. Although it has traditionally been seen and grown in swampy areas throughout the Deep South, its many ornamental virtues and adaptability have recently been discovered by landscape architects and designers and as a result, you'll now find bald cypress in home gardens and even in urban environments as a street tree.

One of the biggest misconceptions about bald cypress is that it requires wet or boggy soil. In fact, it will thrive in either wet or dry soils. Bald cypress is so adaptable, there are almost no sites in which this tree can't grow (the one exception is soil with a high pH).

Bald cypress has attractive reddish brown, fibrous bark, and with age shows a characteristic buttressed trunk near its base. If it is in waterlogged soil, it develops knobby growths called *knees*. Bald cypress are long-lived and can become huge trees, easily reaching 50 or more feet within 30 years.

Branch tips of 'Pendens' bald cypress gracefully droop, lending a refinement to the tree. Note the "knees" rising from the waterlogged soil at the edge of the pond.

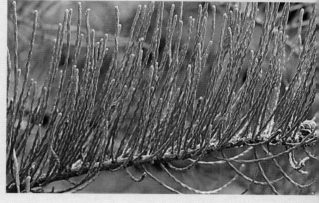

TOP: *Delicate new needle-like growth is yellow-green and soft.*
BOTTOM: *Awl-shaped leaves of 'Prairie Sentinel' pond cypress stand erect along pendant branchlets.*

PEAK SEASON

Bald cypress has soft conifer-like foliage from spring through fall and drops its "needles" in the fall, hence its common name.

MY FAVORITES

'Monarch of Illinois' is a newer variety and is most notable for its wide-spreading habit (to 90 feet tall with a spread of 70 feet). The width of this variety is unusual, given the typically pyramidal or columnar habit of the species.

'Pendens' is sometimes offered by specialty nurseries. This old variety differs mainly in its drooping branch tips. The overall shape is pyramidal, with horizontal primary limbs.

RELATED SPECIES

Pond or upland cypress, *Taxodium ascendens* 'Nutans', is a columnar, slow-growing tree with short branches; *T. a.* 'Prairie Sentinel' is also columnar in overall shape but has more horizontal branching. Both are somewhat more drought tolerant than bald cypress.

GARDEN COMPANIONS

Combine with bayberry *(Myrica)*, buttonbush *(Cephalanthus)*, Florida anise tree *(Illicium floridanum)*, summersweet *(Clethra)*, sweetspire *(Itea)*, and pentas.

When Plant container-grown plants anytime.

Where Plant in full sun to part shade and in soil that is slightly acidic. Bald cypress is a large tree. Use it as an accent plant or a specimen— it is outstanding on a stream bank or on the edge of a lake or pond. It also works well as a background plant to screen unwanted views. Never plant under utility wires or wherever vertical space is limited.

How Dig a planting hole twice as wide as the plant's container and slightly shallower than the root ball. Then dig deeper around the perimeter of the hole, creating a firm plateau in the center. Rough up the sides of the hole in the process so the roots will grow into the surrounding soil. Set the root ball on the plateau, then backfill with the excavated soil. After firming the soil with your fingers, water thoroughly. Keep soil moist until the roots are established.

TLC Prune to remove dead wood and unwanted branches. Bagworms may be a nuisance some years, but no treatment is needed. Otherwise, bald cypress is little bothered by pests or diseases.

Evergreen Magnolia
Magnolia grandiflora

Given the space it needs to develop, evergreen magnolia becomes a stately tree with a classic look.

No doubt about it, the evergreen magnolia has personality. I confess to a sense of reverence when I see it towering above diminutive-by-comparison camellias and azaleas growing beneath it. Its glossy dark leaves, contrasted with its creamy white, 10-inch-wide flowers, create a sense of grandeur and stateliness unmatched by few other trees.

Evergreen magnolia is a dense tree, featuring broadly oval, leathery, glossy leaves. Typically, the leaves are dark green on both the top and the bottom, but some varieties are rusty brown underneath. They can grow to 8 inches long. The sumptuous silken blossoms, which have been called the most elegant floral offerings found on any tree, exude a heady perfume. Flowering begins in spring and continues through summer into early fall. Be aware, however, that named seedlings often take 10 years after planting before they come into bloom.

In favored locations, this tree may eventually reach 80 feet in height, with a spread of 60 feet. It grows best in acidic soils in the central and northern areas of the state, where it also gets the few chilly nights it needs in winter.

The dense shade cast by the tree, as well as its shallow roots, make it nearly impossible to grow grass beneath it. And considering that the large leaves drop year-round, planting a leaf-swallowing ground cover, such as periwinkle (page 210), beneath it makes good sense.

When Fall is the best time to plant, although you can plant container-grown trees any time of year.

Where Plant magnolias in full sun or part shade and in soil that is slightly acid. Keep the root zone moist but not wet. Evergreen magnolias can withstand short periods of drought without long-term damage.

How Dig a planting hole twice the width of the container and slightly shallower than the root ball. Dig deeper around the hole's perimeter to create a firm central plateau. Set the root ball on the plateau, making sure the root ball's surface is just a bit higher than the surrounding soil. Then return the soil to the hole, water well, and mulch.

PEAK SEASON

Peak flowering is midsummer. Evergreen leaves look attractive year-round.

MY FAVORITES

'Bracken's Brown Beauty' is by far superior to all of the other varieties. Leaves have a rusty brown "felt" on their undersides. It tops out at 30 feet, so it is much more compact than the species.

'Claudia Wannamaker' is a new variety that is reported to bloom at a very young age. It also shows a rusty brown felt on leaf undersides.

'D. D. Blanchard' grows in a more open pyramidal shape than 'Bracken's Brown Beauty'. The leaves are particularly lustrous and their undersides are a very showy orange-brown. It grows 50 to 60 feet high and 30 feet wide.

'Little Gem' is a dwarf magnolia. A much more compact and narrow form, it grows about 20 feet high and has slightly smaller leaves than is typical.

'Majestic Beauty' has very dark green, almost black, leaves, and it flowers heavily. It grows 50 feet tall and about 20 feet wide.

GARDEN COMPANIONS

Leave an unplanted and mulched space beneath an evergreen magnolia, where fallen leaves and seedpods can decay over time. Or use a ground cover that can absorb the debris.

TLC Mulch the soil around the tree to conserve moisture and to cool the soil. Avoid digging or cultivating beneath a magnolia, as this could damage the fleshy surface roots. If growth is sparse or weak, fertilize. Prune only to remove lower branches on the trunk as the tree gains height.

LEFT: *Flower petals catch the fallen stamens of a 'Little Gem' magnolia blossom.*
BELOW: *In fall, beadlike red magnolia seeds are embedded in woody fruit.*

Flowering Dogwood
Cornus florida

Native to the eastern United States from New England to central Florida, flowering dogwood has been called the most beautiful native tree of North America. In some situations, it grows 40 feet tall and as wide, but closer to half that size is more typical. The tree branches low to the ground, sending out horizontal branches that turn up at the tips. The effect is a distinctive appearance through the growing season, and an equally interesting and good-looking winter silhouette.

The flowers that come in spring are the main attraction. The 2- to 4-inch-wide flowers, called *bracts*, cover the tree in midspring before the leaves have fully emerged. The typical color is white, but there are numerous named selections that have colors ranging between white and red. Dogwoods provide more than a show in spring, however. In fall, the leaves turn a glowing red before dropping, and clusters of small, oval, scarlet fruits remain for several weeks more, providing a treat for the birds.

The second half of dogwood's Latin name speaks to the tree's significance to our state. In fact, for many years the largest known dogwood in North America thrived in Tallahassee's famous clay loam. As important as flowering dogwood is here, it grows well only in the northern third of the state. South of Gainesville, 'Pendula' and the pink forms don't get enough cold to either grow well or produce bright pink colors.

Flower bracts of 'Weaver's White' are larger than the common species. They're followed by red fruits that birds greedily consume.

When Plant container-grown trees in fall just as weather is beginning to cool. Plant bare-root trees in winter as soon as they become available.

Where Select a location with some afternoon shade and well-drained, fertile soil. Dogwoods in Florida are strictly a midlevel tree best used under the canopies of taller trees.

How Dig a planting hole twice the width of the container and slightly shallower than the root ball, then dig deeper around the hole's perimeter to create a firm central plateau. Set the root ball on the plateau, making sure the root ball's surface is just a bit higher than the surrounding soil. Return the soil to the hole and water well. Stake the tree so it won't whip about in the wind.

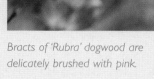

TLC Prune out dead, damaged, or diseased wood, and remove crossing branches that rub against each other, causing wounds. When pruning, take

Bracts of 'Rubra' dogwood are delicately brushed with pink.

care to not remove too many branches at one time or water sprouts (upright growing shoots that are out of character with the plant's form) will result. Water dogwoods well through the first two growing seasons, never allowing them to suffer from drought. After the leaves drop, fertilize with a controlled-release fertilizer or organic equivalent and water it in.

*Cooler areas of zone 26.

PEAK SEASON

Peak flowering is midspring, about the same time as the Indica azaleas.

MY FAVORITES

'Cherokee Chief' has deep red bracts that are paler at the base.

'Pendula' has white bracts and an attractive weeping shape.

'Rubra' has attractive winter flower buds, followed by pink flowers.

'Weaver's White' is by far the most widely adapted flowering dogwood for Florida. Its white flowers are very large, fall leaf color is red to maroon, and the fruits are bright red.

GARDEN COMPANIONS

Plant dogwoods under the high canopies of oak and pine trees. Or combine them with other spring-flowering trees and shrubs, including azaleas, camellias, Japanese magnolias, star magnolias, redbud (Cercis), snowbell (Styrax), and silverbell (Halesia).

White bracts of dogwood surround small yellow flowers.

Live Oak
Quercus virginiana

The wide-spreading live oak, with its heavy, nearly horizontal branches, is one of the most familiar trees in Florida.

With their large, stout trunks and long, sweeping branches that often rest on the ground, southern live oaks are one of the most beautiful trees of North Florida. Always draped in gray, swaying Spanish moss, live oaks are reminiscent of antebellum mansions, sweeping entrance drives, and front-porch mint juleps on sultry evenings.

These are magnificent and robust trees that live long, dignified lives; many reach 400 years in age. Live oak trees grow very slowly and, in so doing, develop strong wood. In hurricane-plagued Florida, it is the southern live oak that remains standing, despite sustained winds of 100 miles per hour, while many other trees are destroyed.

New propagation techniques have allowed growers to select cultivars of live oak that have predictable growth habits. Many new selections have been released in recent years, making it possible to have a live oak in a variety of shapes in your garden.

Spanish moss (Tillandsia usneoides) *hanging from live oak branches adds a touch of mystery to the landscape.*

PEAK SEASON

Live oak trees are semideciduous. They hold their leaves all winter long and only drop them three weeks before the new growth emerges in the spring.

MY FAVORITES

'Highrise' has lustrous, dark green leaves and an upright branching habit around a central trunk. More compact than the species, it will grow to 40 feet tall by 25 feet wide.

GARDEN COMPANIONS

When planting live oaks with other plants, give each one plenty of room to grow properly. Live oaks provide the necessary shade for plants such as camellias, azaleas, aucuba, mountain laurel, Florida anise tree *(Illicium)*, banana shrub *(Michelia)*, gardenia, hydrangea, fatsia, lady palm *(Rhapis)*, Oregon grape *(Mahonia)*, sweet olive *(Osmanthus)*, and pittosporum.

Live oak leaves have smooth edges and are dark green on top, whitish underneath.

When The most favorable time to plant is early fall, but container-grown trees can be planted anytime.

Where Plant in partial to full sun and in just about any soil. Trees will thrive and grow fastest in deep, rich soil that has plenty of available moisture, but they'll grow and survive in soils that are much less favorable. Give the young tree plenty of space; it will eventually need a width of 75 feet.

How Dig a planting hole twice the width of the container and about 2 inches shallower than the root ball; then dig deeper around the hole's perimeter, creating a firm central plateau. Roughen the hole's sides to encourage roots to grow into your garden soil. Set the root ball on the plateau, making sure it is 1 to 2 inches higher than the surrounding soil, then fill in the hole, firming the soil with your fingers as you go. Live oak roots can grow up to 10 feet per year, so give them plenty of room to spread.

TLC Prune young trees to develop a strong structure; little care is needed thereafter. Oak galls, caused by tiny wasps, are unsightly but harmless. Unlike most other plants, live oak is not usually browsed by deer.

133

Maple

Acer

A maple does just about everything a tree is supposed to do. The full, rounded canopy sits atop a straight trunk. When the tree is planted on the south side of a house, the dense shade provided by the large leaves can significantly cool off the home's interior. In the cooler areas of Florida, maples produce what is often the only fall color in an ordinarily drab landscape. In warmer areas of the state, maples produce shades of gold and burgundy in late winter (depending on the species), and almost all produce tiny bright red "flowers" followed shortly by their distinctive double winged seeds, called *samaras,* in the spring. Place a Florida sugar maple, with its brilliant yellow fall color, in the landscape, and everyone will want to know what type of tree it is.

As with evergreen magnolias, maples' shallow roots and heavy shade can make it tough to grow anything beneath them. Try planting them amid shade-tolerant ground covers like periwinkle, where the fallen leaves and small stems will be "swallowed up" by the ground cover, making maintenance much easier.

Leaves of 'Autumn Flame' red maple change early—and brilliantly—in fall.

TOP RIGHT: *Glossy green leaves of trident maple show three lobes.*
BOTTOM RIGHT: *Red maple at fall peak.*

PEAK SEASON

Fall in North Florida and late winter and early spring in central and South Florida, when the leaves change color.

MY FAVORITES

Florida sugar maple, also known as southern sugar maple *(Acer barbatum or A. saccharum floridum),* produces a roundish crown to 25 feet tall. Its golden color above blooming camellias and beneath an overstory of pines can be breathtaking. The leaves drop days before the new growth emerges in the spring.

Red maple *(A. rubrum)* is one of the most prominent native trees in fall. 'Florida Flame' is by far the most often planted because of its persistent fall red color. 'Autumn Blaze', 'Autumn Flame', 'October Glory' and 'Franksred' (trademarked Red Sunset) have all been satisfactory in zones 31 and 28, and in cooler areas of 26.

Trident maple *(A. buergerianum)* is a small, broad understory tree with low-growing branches. It needs staking and pruning to become a high-branched tree. Its bark of brown-gray scales is attractive in winter.

GARDEN COMPANIONS

Combine smaller maples with camellias, azaleas, cleyera, gardenia, and various ground covers and ferns in the dappled light of a woodland garden.

When Plant container-grown maple trees anytime. Transplant in late fall or before the buds break dormancy in the spring. Trident and Florida sugar maples are tolerant of drought, but red maples need water.

Where In zones 31 and 28, and in cooler areas of zone 26, most maples prefer full sun. In zone 25 and in warmer areas of 26, maples will welcome a bit of dappled shade in the afternoon. Red maples perform best where water is plentiful and will tolerate poor drainage. They will even grow in soils that are periodically waterlogged.

How Remove the tree from its container carefully, keeping the root ball intact. Plant at the same depth that it was growing in the container, in a hole deep and wide enough to accommodate the roots without crowding. Dig deeper around the perimeter of the hole, creating a central plateau to support the root ball. Rough up the sides of the root ball, then backfill. Gently firm soil around the roots and water thoroughly, making sure there are no air pockets. Apply 2 to 4 inches of organic mulch, such as shredded bark, leaf compost, or wood chips, and replenish as needed throughout the growing season.

TLC Avoid pruning in late winter or early spring as cuts are likely to bleed. But cut off dead, damaged, or diseased branches anytime. Protect trunks of young trees from mowers and trimmers by creating wide circles of mulch around them.

Pine

Pinus

Loblolly pine is common throughout central Florida and northward, especially in abandoned fields.

Pines come in just about every shape and size, from compact little cushions to towering, open giants. They are the best known and most widely grown conifers. There are about 35 species of pine tree in North America, about a third of which are found growing throughout Florida.

All pines carry their needles in clusters around the branches, and their attractive, patterned cones hang straight down. In spring, the branch tips are decorated with upright, light-colored bundles of new growth, aptly named *candles*.

Pine trees are wonderful evergreen additions to Florida gardens. They are unmatched as dark green backdrops to flowering shrub borders, and their needle-shaped evergreen leaves and simple but attractive cones provide visual relief from the many brightly colored, exotic plants that thrive here.

Pines attract a wide variety of resident and migratory birds and are the backbone of any natural planting whose primary purpose is to attract wildlife. The larger pine trees, including the longleaf and the loblolly pines, are nesting sources for many unusual birds like the pileated woodpecker.

The thick bark of mature loblolly pines separates into distinctive and irregular dark brown "scales."

PEAK SEASON
Year-round

MY FAVORITES

Loblolly pine *(Pinus taeda)* grows 90 to 110 feet tall, with trunks that reach 2 to 4 feet in diameter. It's quick to colonize in sandy soils that have been cleared of other plants.

Longleaf pine *(P. palustris)* grows 80 to 100 feet tall and 3 feet in diameter. It is characterized by long, bright green, tuftlike needles—the longest needles of any pine that grows in North America.

Sand pine *(P. clausa)* rarely becomes taller than 25 feet. Its name speaks to its fondness for sandy soils. Like many other pines, sand pine relies on the heat of a fire to open its cones and release the seeds.

Slash pine *(P. elliottii)* is a common tree in Florida, where it is used primarily by the state's pulpwood industry. It looks good in Florida gardens, especially in lowland areas and adjacent to streams. It can reach 100 feet in height, but in gardens it's usually less than 70 feet tall.

GARDEN COMPANIONS

In the garden, a ground cover of periwinkle can absorb cones and fallen needles. In time, the high branches of pine trees will produce dappled shade.

When Fall is the best time to plant, but container-grown trees can be planted any time of the year.

Where Pine trees can withstand a variety of soil conditions, depending on the species; some prefer wet soils and others prefer sandy soils.

How Start with smaller plants (1- to 5-gallon size). Pine trees develop a taproot, making larger specimens difficult to transplant successfully. Dig a planting hole twice the width of the container and about 2 inches shallower than the root ball, then dig deeper around the hole's perimeter to create a firm central plateau. Roughen the hole's sides to encourage roots to grow into your garden soil. Remove circling roots to lessen the chance of them girdling and killing the plant years later. Set the root ball on the plateau, making sure the top of the root ball is 1 to 2 inches higher than the surrounding soil, then fill in the hole, firming the soil with your fingers as you go. Water thoroughly and mulch.

TLC In late spring, many pines drop their needles, which can be swept up and used as mulch elsewhere in the yard.

Redbud
Cercis canadensis

In spring just as the azaleas and dogwoods are flowering, this native tree bursts into bloom, opening thousands of bright blossoms that cover every branch as well as the main trunk. The exquisite flowers are followed in summer by large, heart-shaped leaves and then flat, beanlike pods that often cling to the tree well into winter.

Although the tree is called "redbud," the buds of this North American native are pink-purple, not red. They're small, only about ½ inch long, but so profuse that at their peak, they are like a spotlight in the garden.

Redbuds grow rapidly to 20 feet in height and width. Often multi-trunked in the wild, they are usually found at the edge of woodlands. Though they prefer highly organic, moist soils, they will survive periodic droughts if growing in partial shade. Redbuds make fine lawn trees, look good in groupings, and have their place in shrub borders and even foundation plantings.

The white-flowered form of redbud, 'Alba', complements the familiar pink form and adds to the chorus of early spring bloom.

LEFT: *A mature redbud at peak bloom is a sight to behold.*
RIGHT: *The pea-blossom structure of redbud flowers is apparent in this close-up.*

PEAK SEASON

Early spring at peak bloom, but trees remain attractive through summer and fall.

MY FAVORITES

'Alba' is a pure white form of the native species.

'Flame' ('Plena') has double pink flowers that, unlike those on other cultivars, appear at the same time as the leaves.

'Forest Pansy' has bright pink flowers and deep red to purple leaves that gradually change to dark green as summer progresses.

'Silver Cloud' has pink flowers and leaves that are marbled with white. It's more heat sensitive than other cultivars, so it grows better north of Gainesville.

RELATED SPECIES

Cercis canadensis mexicana is more sun tolerant than *C. canadensis*. Its leaves are more rounded and have scalloped edges. The blossoms are bright pink.

GARDEN COMPANIONS

Plant redbud with other woodland-type plants, including camellias, azaleas, fringe tree *(Chionanthus),* gardenia, live oak, dogwood *(Cornus),* and holly *(Ilex).*

When The best planting time is fall, but you can plant container-grown plants anytime as long as you provide adequate water during the hotter months.

Where Redbud prefers organic soils that are moist but well drained, and it can adapt to many less-than-favorable acidic or alkaline soils. In North Florida, plant it in full sun; in central and South Florida, choose a site in partial shade.

How Dig a planting hole twice the width of the container and about 2 inches shallower than the plant's root ball. Then dig deeper around the hole's perimeter, creating a firm central plateau. Roughen the hole's sides to encourage the roots to grow into your garden soil. Set the root ball on the plateau, making certain the top of the root ball is 1 to 2 inches higher than the surrounding soil. Fill in the hole, firming the soil with your fingers as you add it. Water the plant well. Stake the tree trunk until the roots are well established.

TLC For the first 2 years, keep the soil evenly moist from spring until fall, and maintain a 2- to 4-inch layer of mulch. Prune in winter or just after blooms fade.

River Birch

Betula nigra

River birch is one of those trees that immediately attracts attention. Usually grown as a multi-trunked specimen, its tiny leaves quiver in the slightest breeze. The most striking feature, however, is its outstanding dark brown bark that peels away to reveal an attractive rust color. Even in the middle of winter after it has lost its leaves, the tree is a standout in the garden.

This tree grows quickly in a variety of Florida soils. It loves our hot and humid summers, has no notable pest problems, and is very tolerant of urban conditions such as tight planting spaces, drought, and pollution. The Society of Municipal Arborists voted it Tree of the Year in 2002.

If you have room for only one tree in your yard, consider the river birch.

Fresh, light green leaves of spring attractively contrast the bark's color and texture.

PEAK SEASON

Year-round good looks, though I prefer its winter appearance.

MY FAVORITES

Several trademarked varieties are available. Their cultivar names follow in parenthesis.

Dura-Heat ('BNMTF') grows 40 feet tall and is resistant to Florida's ever-present aphids.

Heritage ('Cully') has dark purple, almost black, new stems that eventually turn light brown. Its exfoliating bark is the nicest of all the cultivars, but it does seem less tolerant of Florida heat than Dura-Heat.

'Little King' is a dwarf cultivar growing only 10 feet tall and forming a low-branched tree with peeling white bark.

Tecumseh Compact ('Studetec') stays a compact 12 feet high and has horizontal branches that become pendulous.

GARDEN COMPANIONS

River birch provides an attractive contrast to plants such as magnolia, trumpet tree (*Tabebuia*), beautyberry (*Callicarpa*), holly (*Ilex*), sea grape (*Coccoloba uvifera*), sumac (*Rhus*), wax myrtle (*Myrica cerifera*), and witch hazel (*Hamamelis*).

LEFT: *The peeling bark of river birch provides winter interest.*
RIGHT: *A ground cover of lily turf fills in beneath a multi-trunked river birch specimen.*

When Fall is the best time to plant, but you can set out container-grown plants anytime as long as you provide adequate water during the hotter months.

Where Although river birches are normally found growing in moist, sometimes flooded, soils, they will tolerate drier soils.

How Dig a planting hole twice the width of the container and about 2 inches shallower than the plant's root ball. Then dig deeper around the hole's perimeter, leaving a firm central plateau. Roughen the hole's sides to encourage roots to grow into your garden soil. Set the root ball on the plateau, making certain the top of the root ball is 1 to 2 inches higher than the surrounding soil. Fill in the hole with soil, firming it with your fingers as you add it. Water the plant well.

TLC For the first 2 years after planting, keep the soil evenly moist from spring through fall, watering deeply to encourage vigorous root growth. Maintain 2 to 4 inches of mulch. In summer, prune to shape or to correct growth.

Texas Olive
Cordia boissieri

It may seem a bit odd to grow a plant called Texas olive in Florida, but don't let the name throw you. It's one of the best trees for central and South Florida gardens. Given the tree's origin, its ability to survive extended drought is no surprise.

Texas olive is native to the southwestern United States and Mexico. It grows 20 feet tall and 15 feet wide. Showtime comes in spring, when the tree covers itself with 3-inch-wide, trumpet-shaped, snow white flowers that have a bright yellow throat. While peak flowering is in the spring, flowers will come again in fall and even intermittently through summer and winter if enough water is available. In winter, birds relish the olive-like white fruits as they ripen.

In warmer areas of Florida, the velvety, silver green, 4-inch leaves are evergreen. In cold weather they'll all drop, but this has no long-term ill effects; shortly after the return of warmer weather, the tree will sprout new leaves. The cocoa brown bark is deeply fissured and has a corky appearance.

Texas olive is a colorful, clean, and very low-maintenance tree, and its small size means it's easy to fit into most gardens. Florida nursery growers have recognized its merit by awarding it Plant of the Year. If you're shopping for a small tree, give this one a try.

PEAK SEASON
Spring and fall

GARDEN COMPANIONS
In addition to all of its other desirable qualities, Texas olive also has the ability to withstand drought. It can be planted with other drought-tolerant plants, including blue mist (Caryopteris), broom (Cytisus), butterfly bush (Buddleia), plumbago, holly (Ilex), pittosporum, juniper, bottlebrush (Callistemon), Oregon grape (Mahonia), needle palm (Rhapidophyllum hystrix), oleander (Nerium oleander), some senna (Cassia), sumac (Rhus), and yellow bells (Tecoma).

When Fall is the best time to plant but anytime is okay. If planting in spring or summer, be sure to water regularly until the roots are established.

Where Choose a location that receives full sun or partial shade and has well-drained soil. Use Texas olive as a small specimen tree, next to the sidewalk, or in a large container.

How Prepare a planting hole that is twice as wide as the container and slightly shallower than the root ball. Then dig a bit deeper around the perimeter of the hole, creating a firm central plateau. Set the root ball on the plateau, making sure the top of the root ball is slightly higher than the surrounding soil. Fill in with soil around the root ball, firming with your fingers, then water thoroughly. Provide regular moisture to the root zone until roots are established in the new soil.

TLC Prune young trees to the shape and habit you desire: single or multi-trunked, high or low branching. Once established, little additional water is needed.

Warmer areas of zone 26.

OPPOSITE PAGE: *At peak bloom, Texas olive is covered with 3-inch-wide white flowers.* ABOVE RIGHT: *Papery flowers belie the tree's otherwise rugged nature.*

Trumpet Tree
Tabebuia

There are few, if any, flowering trees that can match the beauty of the trumpet tree in bloom! The blossoms are particularly showy because there are no leaves on the tree during flowering, and because the bright flowers contrast with the light gray bark.

Native to the Amazon rainforest and other tropical parts of the Americas, trumpet trees are colorful, easy-to-grow, small to intermediate-sized trees (to 40 feet tall). The 3-inch-long, trumpet-shaped flowers are pink, purple, or yellow, depending on the species. They appear in spring and are borne in rounded clusters that become larger and more profuse as the trees mature. Leaves are green and may have up to seven leaflets arranged like fingers on a hand.

Few ornamental trees or shrubs can compare to the spring flower display produced by the purple trumpet tree.

PEAK SEASON

Mid- to late spring

MY FAVORITES

Golden trumpet tree (*Tabebuia chrysotricha*) has deep yellow flowers on attractive, wide-spreading branches in early spring.

Pink trumpet tree (*T. heterophylla*) has a rounded habit and reaches up to 40 feet in height. The bright pink, 3-inch-long flowers are borne in clusters at the end of each branch.

Purple trumpet tree (*T. impetiginosa*), or ipe, has purple flowers.

Yellow trumpet tree (*T. umbellata*) grows 25 to 35 feet tall. It has light yellow flowers in spring.

GARDEN COMPANIONS

Combine trumpet trees with other sun-loving tropical plants, including Australian tree fern (*Cyathea cooperi*), banana (*Musa*), bottlebrush (*Callistemon*), ornamental fig trees (*Ficus*), orchid tree (*Bauhinia*), palms, traveler's tree (*Ravenala madagascariensis*), angel's trumpet (*Datura*), copper leaf (*Acalypha*), plumeria, hibiscus, princess flower (*Tibouchina*), cannas, *Calathea*, butterfly ginger (*Hedychium*), and elephant's ear (*Colocasia*).

When The best time to plant is fall, but you can plant container-grown trees any time of the year if you provide adequate water until roots are established.

Where Trumpet trees are well adapted to South Florida. Plant in full sun and in any well-drained soil. All are useful as color accents and as stand-alone flowering trees. Larger types are excellent as street trees. Smaller species make beautiful patio trees or even container plants.

How Prepare a planting hole that is twice as wide as the container and slightly shallower than the root ball. Then dig a bit deeper around the perimeter of the hole, leaving a firm central plateau. Set the root ball on the plateau, making sure the top of the root ball is slightly higher than the surrounding soil. Fill in the hole, firming the soil with your fingers, then water thoroughly. Stake the tree until the roots are well established.

TLC Keep soil evenly moist through the first summer after planting, or until the roots are well established. In subsequent years, reduce watering 6 to 8 weeks prior to flowering in spring, but then water well in early summer to get a good bud set for next year's bloom. Trumpet trees tend to be gangly when young, so don't neglect training them in their early years to achieve the shape and habit you want. They respond well to regular fertilizing.

*Warmer areas of zone 26.

The brilliant yellow of golden trumpet tree produces a stunning effect against a blue sky.

Palms

Few plants symbolize the mild climate of Florida the way that palms do. Only a few are native here, however; most originated instead from similar tropical and subtropical regions around the world. Many are surprisingly cold hardy and can withstand brief periods of freezing temperatures, making them good candidates for central and North Florida.

Although palms aren't suited to every landscape, they can really shine in the right setting. They can line an avenue, shade a deck, serve as dramatic accents, or form an evergreen backdrop. Some, such as saw palmetto, stay shrublike for many years, thriving under taller trees as well

as in entryway plantings, mixed borders, and courtyards.

Palms are especially effective near swimming pools, because they don't drop leaves and their roots don't cause paving to buckle. Fronds, whether fanlike or feathery, reflect beautifully in the water, as does the curved trunk of the Senegal date palm (page 159), which creates an atmosphere reminiscent of the tropics.

Carefully placed, palms produce dramatic effects. Night lighting, in particular, shows off their stateliness and spectacular leaves. You can backlight them, shine spotlights on them from below, or direct lights to silhouette them against a pale wall. Sunlight also casts evocative palm shadows onto walls.

So many different palms exist for the home garden, it's hard to keep up with them all. The modest array here represents tried-and-true choices for just about anywhere palms can be grown. I've picked my top 10, but in most cases I included alternative palms for you to consider.

Palms are one of the few plants that can be transplanted easily as large, mature specimens.

ABOVE: *Coconut palms frame the entrance to a historic Key West mansion. The compact palm to the right of the steps is a latan palm.*
RIGHT: *Coconut palms leaning over thatched roofs cast delightful shade patterns on the lawn.*
OPPOSITE PAGE: *The glossy green leaves of paurotis palm, an Everglades native, shimmer in morning light.*

Even tall plants can be dug up, placed in relatively small boxes, and replanted with almost certain success. Planting specimen palms usually requires heavy equipment and expert help, but it's one of the best ways of instantly converting an empty garden into a tropical paradise. Although expensive, planting a few choice mature palms around a new pool or patio or as a stunning focal point in the front yard may be a worthwhile investment.

Bismarck Palm
Bismarckia nobilis

Red and orange flower spikes of 'Big Harv' bromeliad (Aechmea) rise to contrast the silver-blue of bismarck palm.

The bismarck palm is one of the most spectacular palms. The large, bold, intense silvery blue leaves of the common variety create focal points that dominate their surroundings. The bismarck palm is native to Madagascar and the islands off the southeast coast of Africa, but it is entirely at home in South Florida.

Bismarck palm grows 30 to 40 feet tall in the landscape, and the plant is very drought tolerant once it is established. The leaves are large (each one is 5 to 10 feet wide) and the trunk is thick and heavy, so this palm needs some room in the landscape.

Given the drama of the large leaves, bismarck palm is very effective as a specimen plant or as an accent in front of plants with darker green leaves. Or, if space permits, a grouping of these palms makes a striking statement.

There are two forms of the bismarck palm. The most desirable one, also the most common, has silvery blue leaves; the other has green leaves. These different leaf colors are apparent even in young plants. Seedling leaves of the silver form have a maroon or purplish coloring; seedling leaves of the green form are green.

When Any time of the year is fine for planting, but spring or summer is optimal.

Where Plant in full sun and well-drained soil for the best growth and appearance. Remember, this palm has a large spread, so give it some room to grow. Also, until this palm forms a trunk, it is almost impossible to transplant, so make sure to plant it in its permanent location.

How Amend the soil with organic material such as compost or manure. Place the palm in the hole a few inches deeper than it was growing in the container. Water the palm well after planting and regularly for the first 4 to 6 weeks until it is established.

TLC The bismarck palm is a very low-maintenance palm once it is established. Remove lower leaves that have yellowed or died. Fertilize 3 to 4 times a year, using a good palm fertilizer with micronutrients. Bismarck palm is very drought tolerant but responds to regular watering.

In zone 26, in the Orlando area and south.

PEAK SEASON

Year-round good looks

SIMILAR PALM

Latan palm *(Latania)* looks very similar but is distinguished by its slightly more slender upper trunk and leaves that are smaller and more folded. Also, the trunk of the latan palm is much more swollen at the base. Slightly less cold hardy than bismarck palms, latan palms will grow in zone 25 and the warmest parts of 26.

GARDEN COMPANIONS

In the garden, place plants with dark green foliage behind the bismarck palm to show off its silver coloring. Some good choices include mirror-leaf viburnum *(Viburnum odoratissimum awabuki)*, Himalayan snailseed *(Cocculus laurifolius)*, broadleaf podocarpus *(Nageia nagi)*, fern podocarpus *(Afrocarpus gracilior)*, or Japanese podocarpus *(Podocarpus macrophyllus)*. Use plants with colorful foliage or flowers near or in front of this palm, such as bromeliad, croton *(Codiaeum variegatum)*, copperleaf *(Acalypha)*, purple queen *(Tradescantia pallida* 'Purple Heart'*)*, and giant redleaf crinum *(Crinum asiaticum procerum)*.

RIGHT: *A stunning specimen of bismarck palm at Fairchild Tropical Botanic Garden is underplanted with bromeliads* (Aechmea blanchetiana).

Cabbage Palm
Sabal palmetto

The cabbage palm, also called the sabal palm, is the most common palm in Florida. It is our state tree—despite the fact that, technically, palms are woody monocots, not trees. The cabbage palm is also one of our native palms, growing naturally throughout the southeastern United States, the Bahamas, and Cuba.

Cabbage palms are variable in their appearance. Some trees hold their leaf bases on the trunk for a long time, becoming quite tall while retaining them; others drop them promptly, revealing a fibrous, gray trunk at a young age. Cabbage palm grows slowly but gets quite tall, eventually reaching 30 to 60 feet.

The cabbage palm earned its name from its edible buds that, if cooked when young, taste a lot like cabbage. The early settlers, who were the first to apply the name, learned from the Native Americans how to prepare the buds. Unfortunately, harvesting the edible bud kills the palm.

Use this palm as an accent or specimen plant, or as a street tree. Some animals and birds eat the fruits, so cabbage palm can also be a source of food for wildlife.

The long and arching cabbage palm flower stalk will later be covered with black, 1/2-inch-wide, round fruits.

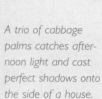

A trio of cabbage palms catches afternoon light and cast perfect shadows onto the side of a house.

PEAK SEASON

Year-round good looks

RELATED SPECIES

Carat palmetto, *Sabal mauritiiformis,* has a slender trunk and deeply divided leaves. It grows 40 to 50 feet tall. Zone 25 and the warmer areas of zone 26.

Dwarf palmetto, *S. minor,* is another native trunkless palm. It grows 3 to 5 feet tall. Zones 25, 26, 28, and 31.

Mexican palmetto, *S. mexicana,* looks similar to *S. palmetto* but is much more robust. It grows 30 to 40 feet tall. Zones 25, 26, 28, and 31.

Puerto Rican hat palmetto, *S. causiarum,* grows 30 to 50 feet tall and has a wide, massive trunk. Zones 25, 26, and the warmer areas of 28.

Scrub palmetto, *S. etonia,* is native to Florida. Trunkless, it grows only 3 to 4 feet tall. Zones 25, 26, 28, and 31.

Sonoran palmetto, *S. uresana,* grows 40 to 50 feet tall and has distinctive silvery green fronds. Zones 25, 26, and 28.

GARDEN COMPANIONS

The cabbage palm blends in well with either native or exotic vegetation. Some Florida natives that look good planted with the cabbage palm include *pink muhly grass (Muhlenbergia), sea oats (Uniola paniculate), and sea grape (Coccoloba).*

When Plant any time of the year, but spring or summer is best.

Where Choose a location in sun or shade and with any type of soil, wet or dry. Cabbage palm is also very salt tolerant and can be used in coastal locations.

How Cabbage palm is very easy to transplant once the trunk is developed; good-sized plants are often rescued from construction sites. Smaller plants are sometimes available in nursery containers. Prepare for them by digging a hole the size of the root ball; amend backfill one-third by volume with compost or manure. Plant the tree at the same height or slightly higher than at the original location, and remove all leaves to help the palm survive transplanting.

TLC Fertilize 3 to 4 times a year, using a palm fertilizer that contains micronutrients. This palm is very drought tolerant and does not require supplemental watering after it is established. Though you may see this palm in commercial landscapes with all but a few leaves removed, I recommend this practice only at planting time. Repeated heavy pruning will weaken the palm over time.

Clustering Sugar Palm
Arenga engleri

The clustering sugar palm is an underused palm here in Florida that is just now becoming available to gardeners at local nurseries. The leaves are dark green with silvery undersides. This is one of the few palms with fragrant flowers. The blossom clusters form in late spring and early summer, and the individual flowers have a peachy mango scent.

A pair of clustering sugar palms sprawl over a crinum lily (Crinum procerum).

This clustering palm grows 6 to 15 feet tall. It is native to the Ryukyu Islands of southern Japan and to Taiwan. Two forms are commonly available. The form from the Ryukyu Islands is smaller, reaching 6 to 8 feet tall, and it is slightly hardier to cold. The leaves are smaller and more grayish green in color. The form from Taiwan grows much larger—to 10 to 15 feet tall—and has leaves almost twice as long. It is slightly less cold hardy. Use the clustering sugar palm as a specimen plant or as a screen.

PEAK SEASON

Looks good all year, but especially in early summer when the fragrant flowers are in bloom and the bright purplish red fruits are forming.

RELATED SPECIES

Dwarf clustering sugar palm, *Arenga caudata,* only grows 4 to 6 feet tall. It likes a shady, moist spot and is a nice palm for a small location. It is native to southeastern Asia and will grow in zones 25 and 26.

SIMILAR PALMS

Clustering fishtail palm, *Caryota mitis,* is a very common palm in South Florida. It has a clustering growth habit with stems that grow 10 to 20 feet tall. The leaves and leaflets are shaped like a fish's tail. Zone 25 and the warmer areas of 26.

Wallichia densiflora is a clustering palm that grows 6 to 10 feet tall and likes shade. Native to the Himalayan valleys of northeastern India and Nepal, it grows in zones 25 and 26.

GARDEN COMPANIONS

Combine with camellias (*Camellia japonica* or *C. sasanqua*), pinwheel flower (*Tabernaemontana divaricata*), Formosa azalea (*Rhododendron* 'Formosa'), white butterfly ginger (*Hedychium coronarium*), lobster-claw (*Heliconia*), xanadu philodendron (*Philodendron xanadu*), or bromeliads.

When Any time of year; spring or summer is best.

Where This palm will look best where it receives some afternoon shade. If planted in full sun, keep it watered during dry spells.

How Before planting, amend soil with organic matter such as compost or manure. Set the palm at the same height that it was growing in the container. Water in well after planting.

TLC Fertilize 3 to 4 times a year, using a palm fertilizer that contains micronutrients. Clustering sugar palm is only slightly drought tolerant and looks best when provided with regular watering. Cut off old leaves as they yellow or turn brown and remove individual stems to open up the clump. Wear gloves when handling the inedible fruit; its peel and juice irritate skin.

*Warmest sections of zone 28.

TOP: *Nine-foot-long leaves of clustering sugar palm are silvery underneath.*
BOTTOM: *Chain mail–like inflorescence belongs to clustering fishtail palm.*

Coconut Palm
Cocos nucifera

The 20-foot-long, arching, featherlike fronds of this unusually straight-trunked coconut palm are silhouetted against a blue sky.

Just as the cabbage palm is the most common in Florida, the coconut palm is probably the most well known. It is, universally, the signature plant of the tropics. No tropical shoreline is complete without coconut palms lining the beach. This palm is so widely grown throughout the tropics that its exact native habitat is unknown, but it is thought to be originally from the South Pacific islands.

The coconut palm is economically important. Vast plantations of this palm are grown for its famous edible fruit, the coconut. The leaves are used for thatching and fiber, and the trunks for lumber.

The coconut palm is widely used in South Florida landscapes. It can grow to 30 to 60 feet high, and the trunk typically leans with a graceful curve. This palm can be used as a specimen, an accent, or even as a source of shade. Coconut palms also make great hammock "anchors."

The one caveat about coconut palm is lethal yellowing disease. No totally immune cultivar has been found, but many (listed at right) show good resistance to this disease.

PEAK SEASON

Year-round

MY FAVORITES

'Maypan', 'Green Malayan', 'Golden Malayan', and 'Red Malayan' are all fairly resistant to lethal yellowing disease. The Malayan types are some-times called dwarf types because they bear fruit when they are young and only have a few feet of trunk. They will eventually grow as tall as other coconut palms.

GARDEN COMPANIONS

Combine with traveler's tree *(Raven-ala)*, lobster-claw *(Heliconia)*, sea grape *(Coccoloba)*, clusia *(Clusia rosea)*, hibis-cus, croton *(Codiaeum variegatum)*, screw pine *(Pandanus utilis)*, and royal poinciana *(Delonix regia)*.

When Plant in either spring or summer.

Where Plant in either full sun or light shade, and in well-drained soil. Roots are very salt tolerant, so these palms grow along coastal dunes.

How Before planting, amend the hole with organic matter such as compost or manure. Plant the palm at the same level that it was growing in the container. Water in well after planting and mulch if desired.

TLC Fertilize the palm 3 to 4 times a year, using a palm fertilizer that contains micro-nutrients. Coconut palms are drought tolerant but will grow better with regular watering. Prune off old leaves as they yellow or turn brown. If the palm is near a heavily used area, consider removing ripening fruit—falling ones are a considerable hazard.

ABOVE: *Foot-long coconuts are yellow, green, or brown when mature.*
BELOW: *Curved or leaning trunks are the norm, especially near the coast.*

Warmest areas of zone 26.

Cuban Royal Palm
Roystonea regia

The Cuban royal palm is a common sight in South Florida, where it is often used to line streets and avenues. The massive grayish white trunk almost appears to be made of concrete. At the top of the trunk, just under the leaves, is a smooth, green section. Called the *crownshaft,* it is formed by the bases of the leaves. The slight bulge in the upper half of the trunk is another distinctive characteristic of this palm.

The Cuban royal palm grows relatively quickly, reaching 50 to 70 feet tall. It tolerates salt-laden air and strong winds. Its arched fronds stretch from 9 to 20 feet in length, with leaflets that stand out from the midrib at many angles. This palm is native to Cuba and coastal regions from southern Mexico to Honduras.

You can use this stately palm individually or in groupings, but it is in rows, with the massive trunks aligned like columns supporting some invisible superstructure, that it is most impressive.

PEAK SEASON
Year-round good looks

RELATED SPECIES
Florida royal palm, *Roystonea elata*, is very similar to the Cuban royal palm. (According to some plant experts, they are actually the same plant.) But the main differences that are apparent to me include the Florida royal palm's taller height (to 80 or 90 feet) and less pronounced bulging of the upper trunk. This palm, a native of South Florida, grows wild in the Everglades.

GARDEN COMPANIONS
Royal palms combine well with traveler's tree *(Ravenala)*, lobster-claw *(Heliconia)*, sea grape *(Coccoloba)*, bougainvillea, glory bush *(Tibouchina granulosa)*, hibiscus, croton *(Codiaeum variegatum)*, screw pine *(Pandanus utilis)*, and royal poinciana *(Delonix regia)*.

OPPOSITE PAGE: *The smooth gray trunk is marked with rings where leaves were attached, and it has a swollen base.*
TOP RIGHT: *Leaflets are attached at various angles, giving the whole leaf a feathery look.*
BOTTOM RIGHT: *Cuban royal palm's crown includes about 15 leaves atop a 6-foot crownshaft.*

When Spring and summer are the best planting times.

Where Royal palms prefer full sun or light shade, but are not particular about the soil type.

How Before planting, amend the hole with organic matter such as compost or manure. Plant the palm at the same level that it was growing in the container. Water in well after planting, and mulch.

TLC Fertilize 3 to 4 times a year, using a palm fertilizer that contains micronutrients. The Cuban royal palm is somewhat drought tolerant but will grow better with regular watering. Pruning is not necessary, as this palm naturally sheds its dead leaves.

Warmest areas of zone 26.

Date Palm
Phoenix dactylifera

One of humanity's oldest crops, date palm is also an attractive ornamental. Its upright, blue-green leaves grow up to 20 feet long.

Just as the coconut palm is the classic plant of tropical shorelines, the date palm is the symbol of the desert oasis. It has been cultivated in the Middle East for thousands of years for its edible fruit. Dates are still an important economic crop in many regions of the world, where this palm is grown on large plantations.

Date palms come in male and female versions; only the latter produce dates. They ripen in fall in large, hanging clusters.

Date palms grow 30 to 60 feet tall. Their slender, gray-green trunks are patterned with the bases of old leafstalks. The leaves are waxy and stiff and have sharply pointed leaflets. Some specimens have a single trunk, while clustering types form a sparse clump with one dominant trunk. The date palm is native from northern Africa to Arabia. Use it as a specimen, in formal settings, and as a street tree. Suitable varieties can also be planted for fruit.

PEAK SEASON

Year-round good looks

MY FAVORITES

'Medjool' and 'Zahedii' are the two fruiting varieties that will sometimes produce dates in Florida.

RELATED SPECIES

Canary Island date palm, *Phoenix canariensis,* grows 40 to 60 feet tall. It has a massive trunk topped with a wide crown of leaves. Zones 25, 26, and 28.

Cliff date palm, *P. rupicola,* is one of the most beautiful date palms. It has a slender trunk that grows 20 to 30 feet tall and soft, glossy leaves. Zone 25 and the warmer areas of zone 26.

Pygmy date palm, *P. roebelenii,* grows only 6 to 10 feet tall. It is available single stemmed or as a clustering type. Zone 25 and the warmer areas of zone 26.

Senegal date palm, *P. reclinata,* is from tropical Africa. It is an attractive clustering palm with slender trunks. Zone 25 and the warmer parts of 26.

GARDEN COMPANIONS

Combine with century plant *(Agave),* bougainvillea, spineless yucca *(Yucca elephantipes),* Jerusalem thorn *(Parkinsonia),* purple queen *(Tradescantia pallida* 'Purple Heart'), and aloe *(Aloe vera).*

When Plant any time of the year but spring or summer is optimal.

Where Date palms need full sun and a well-drained soil. Plant the larger kinds where they'll have the space they need at maturity.

How Before planting, amend the hole with organic matter such as compost or manure. Plant the palm at the same level that it was growing in the container, and water in well after backfilling the hole.

TLC Fertilize 3 to 4 times a year, using a palm fertilizer that contains micronutrients. Date palms are very drought tolerant but will grow better with regular watering. Cut off old leaves as they yellow or turn brown. If you desire a tree with a single trunk, remove the shoots that grow from the base.

TOP: *The favored candy of Moroccan royalty, 'Medjool' is one of the best date palms for Florida.*
BOTTOM: *Pygmy date palms are often planted in pairs, in borders near a patio or pool.*

Foxtail Palm

Wodyetia bifurcata

In recent years, the foxtail palm has become a very popular palm in tropical areas throughout the world. It was discovered relatively recently (the early 1980s), in remote northwestern Australia. Since then, seed has become available and many nurseries have begun growing it. This palm is now widely available in the southern half of Florida.

The modestly sized foxtail palm grows a respectable 20 to 30 feet high within just a few years, making it well suited to home gardens. But it's the arching, pale green fronds that draw the most attention. At 6 to 10 feet in length, the fronds are large for the palm's height, and they form a crown up to 20 feet wide. Most notably, leaflets radiate out from each frond at all angles, lending a bottlebrush or foxtail look to the crown. The slender trunk is ringed with scars where fronds have fallen off.

Similar to the Cuban royal palm, with its arching, feathery fronds and prominent trunk rings, the shorter foxtail palm is better suited to smaller home gardens.

PEAK SEASON

Year-round

SIMILAR PALMS

Christmas or Manila palm, *Veitchia merriillii,* bears bright red fruits around Christmastime. It has a narrow trunk, grows 10 to 20 feet tall, and has strongly arched fronds. Zone 25 and warm parts of 26.

King palm, *Archontophoenix alexandrae,* grows quickly to 30 to 40 feet. Zones 25 and 26. Piccabean palm, *A. cunninghamiana,* is similar but slightly hardier. Zones 25 and 26.

Montgomery palm, *Veitchia arecina,* grows 30 to 50 feet tall and has a slender trunk. Zone 25 and the warmer parts of 26.

Solitaire palm, *Ptychosperma elegans,* grows 10 to 20 feet tall and has a very slender trunk. Zones 25 and 26.

Triangle palm, *Dypsis decaryi,* native to Madagascar, grows 15 to 25 feet tall. Its erect leaves grow along the trunk in three vertical rows. Grow in full sun in zones 25 and 26.

GARDEN COMPANIONS

Plant with hibiscus, bird of paradise (*Sterlitzia*), purple fountain grass (*Pennisetum setaceum* 'Rubrum'), frangipani (*Plumeria rubra*), selloum (*Philodendron bipinnatifidum*), croton (*Codiaeum variegatum*), allamanda (*Allamanda catharticum*), or ixora.

When The best time to plant is spring or summer.

Where Foxtail palm grows best in full sun or part shade.

How Before planting, amend the hole with organic matter such as compost or manure. Plant the palm at the same level that it was growing in the container. Water the palm in well after planting, and mulch.

TLC Fertilize 3 to 4 times a year, using a palm fertilizer that contains micronutrients. This palm is somewhat drought tolerant but looks best with regular watering. Prune to remove dead or dying leaves only.

Warmest areas of zone 26.

TOP RIGHT: *Leaflets of piccabean palm are bright green and 3 feet long.*
BOTTOM RIGHT: *The refined appearance and habit of Christmas palm make it well suited for use on patios or as specimens.*

Queen Palm
Syagrus romanzoffiana

Parallel rows of queen palms frame a courtyard garden and shelter a reflecting pool. Fronds grow to 15 feet long, and leaflets drape in a casual manner.

The queen palm is very popular in central and South Florida. The large, graceful leaves help create the tropical look of a coconut or a royal palm in areas too cold to grow those types. The queen palm is native to southern Brazil, Paraguay, and Argentina. At one time, it was known as *Cocos plumosa* and is still sometimes sold as that.

This is a fast-growing palm that reaches 30 to 40 feet tall. Individual plants can be variable. Some have a slender trunk, while others have a thick, stocky trunk. The trunk is smooth and gray with rings. It lacks the green crownshaft (page 157) found on royal palms.

Use the queen palm as a specimen or as a street tree. It looks good when planted in groups. It can also be effectively used near pools or bodies of water.

When The best time to plant is spring or summer.

Where This palm will grow in sun or shade, but sun-grown specimens are usually more robust. It does not grow well in dry, poor soils. Also, avoid planting in areas with very alkaline soils unless you amend the soil with compost or manure first.

How Before planting, amend the hole with organic matter such as compost or manure. In areas with alkaline soils, amend the soil generously with these acidic materials. Plant the palm at the same level that it was growing in the container. Water the palm in well after planting and mulch if desired.

TLC Fertilize 3 to 4 times a year, using a palm fertilizer that contains micronutrients. Manganese deficiency can be a problem in alkaline soils. This palm is not very drought tolerant and looks best with regular watering. Prune to remove dead or dying leaves only. The large clusters of fruit can also be removed without injuring the palm.

Pindo palm (Butia capitata) *is one of the hardiest feather-leafed, trunked palms. It grows well in all parts of Florida.*

PEAK SEASON
Year-round

RELATED SPECIES
Arikury palm, *Syagrus schizophylla,* grows 10 to 15 feet tall. Zone 25 and the warmer areas of 26.

Licuri palm, *S. coronata,* grows 20 to 30 feet tall and has grayish green foliage. Zone 25 and the warmer areas of 26.

Overtop palm, *S. amara,* grows 40 to 50 feet high and has a slender trunk. Zone 25 and the warmest areas of 26.

SIMILAR PALMS
The jelly, or pindo, palm, *Butia capitata,* grows slowly to 10 to 20 feet tall. It has silvery green leaves and bears edible fruit. Zones 25, 26, 28 and 31. Mule palm, *Butiagrus nabonnandii,* is a hybrid of the jelly palm and the queen palm and combines the best traits of both parents.

GARDEN COMPANIONS
Good companions include selloum *(Philodendron bipinnatifidum)*, white bird of paradise *(Strelitzia nicolai)*, hibiscus, Australian tree fern *(Cyathea cooperi)*, lily-of-the-Nile *(Agapanthus)*, dwarf powder puff *(Calliandra emarginata)*, giant elephant's ear *(Alocasia macrorrhiza)*, copperleaf *(Acalypha)*, hedge bamboo *(Bambusa multiplex)*, and banana *(Musa)*.

Ribbon Palm

Livistona decipiens

Thin-trunked ribbon palm resembles the much larger fan palm but is a more manageable size. The fan-shaped leaves are 2 to 5 feet across and borne on spiny stems.

The ribbon palm was once uncommon in Florida but is now being more widely grown, and for good reason. The leaves have deeply divided ribbonlike segments that give the palm a graceful, weeping look. This accounts for the common name. Older ribbon palms have an attractive ringed trunk.

Ribbon palm is a good substitute for the Mexican fan palm *(Washingtonia robusta)* because it doesn't get as tall and out of scale with the average yard. Its shorter height also makes it much less prone to a deadly lightning strike, a common cause of death for fan palms in Florida. The ribbon palm is native to Queensland, Australia.

Ribbon palm grows 30 to 40 feet tall. It is very fast growing until it reaches about 25 feet tall, and then the growth slows.

This palm makes an attractive specimen or street tree.

PEAK SEASON
Looks good all year

RELATED SPECIES
Chinese fan palm, *Livistona chinensis,* grows 30 to 50 feet tall. Zones 25 and 26, and the warmer areas of 28.

Livistona australis grows 30 to 40 feet tall. Zones 25 and 26, and the warmer areas of 28.

Taraw palm, *L. saribus,* grows 20 to 40 feet tall. Zones 25 and 26.

SIMILAR PALMS
Caranday palm, *Copernicia alba,* has a slender trunk that can reach 30 to 40 feet tall. The leaves are a beautiful silvery blue. Roots are very tolerant of either dry or wet soil. Zones 25 and 26.

Mexican fan palm, *Washingtonia robusta,* very quickly grows to 50 to 70 feet, and it is very drought tolerant. Zones 25 and 26, and the warmer areas of 28.

GARDEN COMPANIONS
Combine with fakahatchee grass *(Tripsacum dactyloides),* bird of paradise *(Strelitzia),* cardboard palm *(Zamia furfuracea),* crape myrtle *(Lagerstroemia),* spineless yucca *(Yucca elephantipes),* or pink powder puff *(Calliandra haematocephala).*

ABOVE: *Young specimens of caranday palm show long, narrow segments of fan-shaped leaves.*
BELOW: *Symmetrical, sometimes nearly circular leaves of Chinese fan palm grow to 6 feet wide.*

When Plant any time of the year, but spring or summer is optimal.

Where This palm grows best in full sun or light shade. It is not particular about soil type.

How Before planting, amend the hole with organic matter such as compost or manure. Plant the palm at the same level that it was growing in the container. Water the palm well after planting. Mulch if desired.

TLC Fertilize the palm 3 to 4 times a year, using a palm fertilizer that contains micronutrients. The ribbon palm is drought tolerant but will grow better with regular watering. Prune off old leaves as they yellow or turn brown.

*Warmest areas of zone 28.

Saw Palmetto
Serenoa repens

Long considered a weed or nuisance, the saw palmetto has lately gained new respect and is *The green-leaved form of saw palmetto is accented here by lavender bergamot.* now a valued landscape plant in Florida. It is native to the southeastern United States. There are two forms: one with silvery blue foliage and one with green leaves. The silvery blue form is the one more often seen in cultivation and for sale in nurseries. In the wild, this form is found only along Florida's east coast. The green form, however, is more common in the wild. It often forms vast thickets, especially in the pinelands.

The saw palmetto naturally forms 3- to 6-foot-tall clumps. The trunks often creep along the ground but occasionally grow nearly upright. These upright stems have been known to grow 10 to 15 feet tall, but this height is rare.

Use saw palmetto as a ground cover, a screen, or even a specimen. The silvery blue form looks good near plants with dark green foliage. The flowers produce a high-quality honey, and beekeepers often place their hives near stands of saw palmetto. The fruits are also a source of food for wildlife.

PEAK SEASON

Year-round

SIMILAR PALMS

Lady palm, *Rhapis excelsa,* is a slow-growing clustering-type palm that needs shade. It grows 5 to 8 feet tall and has attractive dark green leaves. Slender lady palm, *R. humilis,* is taller, to about 10 feet, and has lighter green foliage. Zones 25 and 26, and the warmest areas of 28.

Mediterranean fan palm, *Chamaerops humilis,* is a slow-growing, usually clustering palm that grows 5 to 20 feet tall. *C. h. cerifera* is a silver-leafed form from Morocco. Zones 25, 26, 28, and 31.

Needle palm, *Rhapidophyllum hystrix,* grows 3 to 5 feet tall as a cluster or a single-stemmed plant in shade or part sun. Zones 25, 26, 28, and 31.

Paurotis palm, *Acoelorrhaphe wrightii,* forms 10- to 30-foot-tall clumps and needs moist (or even swampy) soil. Zones 25 and 26.

GARDEN COMPANIONS

Good companions include gamma grass *(Tripsacum floridana),* coralbean *(Erythrina herbacea),* sea grape *(Coccoloba),* American beautyberry *(Callicarpa americana),* pink muhly grass *(Muhlenbergia capillaris),* sea oats *(Uniola paniculata),* and wax myrtle *(Myrica cerifera).*

When Plant any time of the year.

Where This palm is very adaptable. It will grow in sun or shade, and it is not particular about whether the soil is wet or dry. Saw palmetto is also very salt tolerant and grows along the dunes.

How Before planting, amend the hole with organic matter such as compost or manure. Plant the palm at the same level that it was growing in the container. Water the palm well after planting and mulch if desired.

TLC Fertilize the palm 3 to 4 times a year, using a palm fertilizer that contains micronutrients. Prune dead leaves from the stems. Thick, suckering palms may be thinned to make individual stems visible and to give the palm a tidier look. Once this palm is established, it is very drought tolerant and needs virtually no care.

RIGHT: *Sharp spines arm Mediterranean fan palm.*
BELOW: *Dark green fronds of lady palm are elegant.*

Vines

Climbing vines have a special charm that goes beyond adding vertical interest to a garden. I think it has to do with the way they reach out to others to form endearing partnerships: if you let me cling to you, I'll make you look beautiful. You see it in the way they embrace arbors, trellises, fences, houses, even the trunks of trees. Vines of nearly every description and color are available for Florida gardeners, and they often exude heavenly fragrances that drift through the evening air.

Vines may seem hopelessly dependent, but I see them as resourceful and tough. After a little help getting started, such as a bit of twine to hold them in place, you'll be reaching for the pruners more often than for scissors and twine ball. Vines are programmed to grow toward the sun.

Vines can hide a multitude of your neighbor's sins, including a boat and trailer, an ugly storage shed, and maybe even an entire house. Even a chain-link fence can be transformed into a stunning flowering wall.

A number of flowering vines also attract resident and migrating butterflies and hum-

mingbirds. The vines with brightly colored, trumpet-shaped flowers are the appropriate candidates to serve both as nectar sources and as food for butterfly larvae.

Vines are easy for even the weekend gardener to maintain. An occasional pruning when they get out-of-bounds is about all they need to perform well and to look their best.

TYPES OF VINES

Vines such as trumpet creeper (page 186) cling to even the slickest surfaces, engaging at every crevice they encounter. It's the *holdfasts*, tendrils

RIGHT: A Florida classic, trumpet honeysuckle covers itself with orange-yellow to red flowers in late spring.
OPPOSITE PAGE: Fragrant flowers of 'Incense' passion vine, a hybrid of Florida's native passion vine, are 5 inches wide.

with adhesive discs at the end, that glue the plant to any surface it touches. When grown along a fence or wall, or trained to drape gracefully over an arbor, the clinging stems help these plants to remain attached to these supports.

Other vines, like trumpet honeysuckle (page 188), send out slender tendrils that curl around a strand of wire, a bamboo pole, a slat in a trellis, or a twig. And vines such as queen's wreath (page 180) and wisteria (page 170) produce vigorous, twining stems that wrap around any kind of support available.

TRAINING VINES

The vision of exotic tropical blooms and twining stems adorned with dark green leaves covering the crisp white lattice of an arbor or gazebo is what many of us Florida gardeners aspire to. The intense heat of the summer day forces us into the refuge of shade, if even for just bit of time, and the shade seems a tad more inviting if it offers fragrant and colorful blossoms.

Furthermore, considering that many Floridians have very limited gardening space, a vine trained over an arbor or trellis may be not only the most practical garden to create, but literally the only kind that will fit in your backyard. If you live in an apartment or condominium with a balcony, there are many attractive vines that you can grow in containers.

American Wisteria
Wisteria frutescens

A favorite throughout temperate regions, wisterias are greatly valued for their large, pendulous flower clusters that bloom in the spring. In the North, the most common wisteria is Chinese wisteria, *Wisteria sinensis,* and you might find this species on sale here. Don't buy it. Here in Florida, it can become very invasive, growing rampantly in natural areas and overwhelming native plants. For the classic look of wisteria in Florida, plant the native American species, *W. frutescens.* Its light purple flowers, borne in 8-inch-long clusters, are just as beautiful and fragrant as the Asian species, but they appear after leaves emerge in spring, not before. And because both leaves and flowers emerge relatively late in spring, they're more likely to avoid getting nipped by late spring frosts in North Florida. More significantly, the plant is much more compact than Asian wisterias, growing to about 30 feet high, and is much less aggressive.

American wisteria is well adapted to Florida gardens.

LEFT: *A particularly dark blue form of American wisteria.*
RIGHT: *The white-flowered variety of American wisteria is 'Nivea'.*

Older, established plants usually develop an interesting, twisted, woody trunk several inches in diameter. On a more practical note, the plant itself is hardy, vigorous, and long-lived.

PEAK SEASON

Spring into midsummer

MY FAVORITES

'Amethyst Falls' has light purple cascading flower clusters.

'Longwood Purple' is a choice selection that has a particularly long blooming period. The blossoms have a musky fragrance.

'Nivea' is white-flowered and blooms earlier than the species.

GARDEN COMPANIONS

Plant with other natives including holly (*Ilex*), cabbage palms, bald cypress, redbud (*Cercis*), dogwood (*Cornus*), fringe tree (*Chionanthus*), loblolly bay (*Gordonia*), red maple, river birch, beautyberry (*Callicarpa*), flame azalea, oakleaf hydrangea (*Hydrangea quercifolia*), sumac (*Rhus*), and sweetspire (*Itea*).

When Install new plants in the fall to establish the roots before the onset of warm weather in the spring.

Where Plant in full sun to part shade in well-drained, rich, organically improved soil.

How Loosen soil to a depth of 10 to 12 inches and work in generous amounts of compost or other organic material. Incorporate a controlled-release fertilizer into the soil before planting. This will usually be the last time you need to fertilize a wisteria. Plant at the same depth that the plant was growing in the container. Water immediately after planting. Provide a sturdy, well-anchored support that can handle the weight of the mature vines.

TLC Consistent watering is especially important during the first 2 years, but even mature plants will wilt in a drought. Keep roots moist but not soggy. Prune side branches back after flowering, always leaving at least 6 leaves per branch. Remove excess branches to improve light penetration and flowering. Wisteria does not have the ability to cling to surfaces. Instead, its stems and side branches twist around supports. If these supports are insufficient, wisteria will eventually crush them.

Bleeding Heart Vine

Clerodendrum

Some plants make me feel good just looking at them, and bleeding heart vine, or *Clerodendrum thomsoniae*, is one of those. Flowers are the most obvious attraction, and those of bleeding heart vine have plenty going for them. A study in color contrast, the pendulous blossoms are white above and lipstick red below. Add to that the leaves: each one is 4 to 7 inches long, dark green, shiny, and distinctly ribbed. There is also the

vine's willingness to grow and flower, twining its way through any available opening and producing its remarkable flowers even when confined to a 6-inch pot. And of course I love the fact that this plant is impossible to grow outdoors almost everywhere but right here in Florida.

Bleeding heart vine will climb to 12 feet high or more, so it's perfect for covering a modest-sized trellis, pergola, or picket fence. To emphasize the color of the blossoms even more, paint the support white.

An evergreen vine, glory-bower is a welcome addition to any garden.

Proving it flowers year-round, flaming glorybower (Clerodendrum splendens) blooms mid-December in South Florida.

PEAK SEASON

Year-round in South Florida; spring through fall elsewhere

MY FAVORITES

Bleeding heart vine, *Clerodendrum thomsoniae*, grows to 12 feet high and blooms summer to fall. 'Delectum' has reddish purple flowers suspended all over the fast-growing vine.

Blue glorybower, *C. ugandense*, grows 10 feet tall and about half as wide. It has glossy dark green leaves and violet-blue flowers.

Flaming glorybower, *C. splendens*, climbs fast to as high as 30 feet, and produces large clusters of brilliant red flowers in winter.

Nodding clerodendrum, *C. wallichii*, is pure white, grows 10 feet tall, and can be trained to grow as a tree.

GARDEN COMPANIONS

Combine with coneflower *(Echinacea)*, goldenrod *(Solidago)*, aster, black-eyed Susan *(Rudbeckia)*, blanket flower *(Gaillardia)*, butterfly weed *(Asclepias)*, tickseed *(Coreopsis)*, gaura, lantana, butterfly bush *(Buddleia)*, firethorn *(Pyracantha)*, holly *(Ilex)*, bottlebrush *(Callistemon)*, and oleander *(Nerium oleander)*.

ABOVE: *Bleeding heart vine,* C. thomsoniae, *has distinctive red and white flowers.* RIGHT: *Flowers of* C. thomsoniae *'Delectum' bleeding heart vine have a vivid red-purple color and notably protruding stamens.*

When Transplant in the early spring before growth begins, or plant container-grown plants anytime.

Where Plant in any well-drained soil that is amended with organic material. This vine is very adaptable to various soil types, except ones that are permanently soggy. Full sun is preferred but partial shade will do. Provide a solid support for the vine.

How Dig a planting hole twice the width of the container and slightly shallower, then dig deeper around the hole's perimeter to leave a firm central core. Remove the root ball from the container and set it on the firm center, making sure the top of the root ball is just a bit higher than the surrounding soil. Then return the soil to the hole and water well.

TLC Prune after flowering, or in spring to clean out any stems damaged by cold weather. By cutting out new growth from the base, you can train glorybower into a small shrub or tree. There are no known pests or diseases.

Bougainvillea

Bougainvillea

For many years, bougainvillea has served as Florida's unofficial floral ambassador. A Brazilian native, it has long been acclaimed as one of the spectacular vines throughout the world, and indeed it does thrive and color landscapes in tropical and subtropical regions everywhere. Whether grown as a large, mounding shrub, rambling up a tree or over an arbor, or cascading from a hanging basket, bougainvillea provides pink, red, orange, white, and yellow blossoms that are among the most colorful flowers in Florida gardens.

Brilliant red bougainvillea flowers show off beautifully against a white fence.

Bougainvillea's vibrant colors actually come not from its small inconspicuous flowers, but from the three large colorful leaves, called *bracts,* that surround them. The dark green leaves of the bougainvillea are shaped like little hearts, and the stiff stems are armed with long, needlelike thorns.

Bougainvillea is a climber by nature, but shrubby kinds or heavily pruned plants make good self-supporting container shrubs for the terrace or patio.

PEAK SEASON

Spring through winter

MY FAVORITES

'Arborea' has lavender bracts and honeysuckle fragrance. Stems are thornless, making it well suited to planting near paths and entryways.

'Barbara Karst' is the most popular cultivar with its vivid fuchsia bracts and strong, full growth habit.

'Imperial Delight' is the best new variety introduced in the last several years. The bracts open a creamy white and soon blush into a rich, vivid pink.

'Lavender Queen' produces larger colorful bracts, and more of them, compared to other varieties.

'Raspberry Ice' is noted for its variegated green and cream leaves. They contrast very well with the bright fuchsia bracts. It is best suited for hanging baskets and small areas.

'Sundown Orange' flowers emerge a deep burnt orange and then mature to a light pink. This cultivar is still new to Florida nurseries and gardens.

GARDEN COMPANIONS

Combine bougainvillea with other tropical plants such as angel's trumpet (*Brugmansia*), *Anthurium*, banana (*Musa*), croton (*Codiaeum variegatum*), butterfly ginger (*Hedychium*), ornamental grasses, and *Spathiphyllum*.

When Plant container-grown plants anytime.

Where Plant in full sun in ordinary, well-drained soil. Where frosts are routine, plant vines in the warmest spot in the garden, such as near a south-facing wall. Plants grown in containers do best in 5- to 10-gallon terra-cotta pots or in hanging baskets that are at least 12 inches in diameter.

How Dig a planting hole twice the width of the bougainvillea's container and about 2 inches shallower than the plant's root ball; then dig deeper around the hole's perimeter (leaving a firm central plateau) and roughen the hole's sides. Set the root ball on the plateau—making certain the top of the root ball is 1 to 2 inches higher than the surrounding soil—and fill in the hole with ordinary garden soil, firming it as you add it. Finally, water the plant well.

TLC Keep shoots tied up so they won't whip around in the wind; the sharp thorns can shred the leaves. Fertilize in spring and summer with a low-nitrogen fertilizer. Water regularly and generously after planting and while plants are growing fast. In winter, watering is less critical, and in midsummer ease off watering to promote flowering. Prune heavily after bloom to shape the plant or to direct growth. Nip back long stems during the growing season to produce more flowering wood.

RIGHT: *'Lavender Queen'*
BELOW: *'Raspberry Ice'*

Crossvine
Bignonia capreolata

Natives such as crossvine grow in almost every Florida climate, and they are a great way to build a more self-sufficient, low-maintenance garden.

Crossvine works well in so many ways. It grows quickly; in a single season it can easily cover a gazebo, whether in full sun or partial shade. Between each pair of 2- to 6-inch-long leaflets is a branching tendril that allows the vine to climb. The common name refers to the fact that a cut stem often shows a dark crosslike mark in its center.

Its beautiful, yellow 2-inch-long tubular flowers, with dark brown on the back side of each petal, come in bundles of 3 to 5 from spring to fall. Hummingbirds love them. In winter, the dark green leaves turn purplish and will drop off if cold persists.

Using fewer pesticides and less water is becoming more important every day in Florida, and when we have a chance to use a native plant that also has a striking appearance, so much the better.

PEAK SEASON

Spring to first frost

MY FAVORITES

'Atrosanguinea' flowers are dark orange-red to purplish red and slightly smaller.

'Dragon Lady' flowers are deep orange-red; the vines are extra vigorous.

'Jekyll' flowers are orange; the vine is cold tolerant.

'Tangerine Beauty' has brilliant, bright orange flowers that have bright yellow throats. The vine is vigorous and can grow to 30 feet.

GARDEN COMPANIONS

Combine with trumpet creeper (Campsis radicans) and you'll have hummingbirds in your garden year-round. Or, plant at the base of an old red cedar skeleton or similar dead tree and it will be reborn by year's end, covered with crossvine.

ABOVE: *Crossvine flowers are 2 inches long and irresistible to hummingbirds.*
RIGHT: *Given minimal training, crossvine will even cover a brick wall.*

When Optimal planting and transplanting time is fall, but you can plant container-grown plants anytime.

Where Plant in full sun or part shade and in ordinary, well-drained garden soil.

How To plant a container-grown plant, dig a planting hole twice the width of the container and slightly shallower, then dig deeper around the hole's perimeter to leave a firm central core. Remove the root ball from the container and set it on the firm center, making sure the top of the root ball is just a bit higher than the surrounding soil. Then return the soil to the hole and water well.

TLC Prune lightly in early spring to stimulate the new growth that will develop flowers. To restrain exuberant growth, cut crossvine back to about half its height in midsummer.

OPPOSITE PAGE: *'Tangerine Beauty' crossvine covers an arched entryway.*

Passion Vine
Passiflora

One of the most enjoyable highlights of gardening in Florida is the ability to grow absolutely fabulous and totally exotic-looking plants in our own backyards. No need to hop on a plane and visit famous gardens for the bizarre and unusual—we've got them here. And tops on this list is passion vine. (And it's a native plant, no less!)

Passion vine spreads its twining vines and tendrils fast, 20 to 30 feet or more in a season or two. Flowers of deep purples and intense reds grow up to 6 inches across on vines that grow so fast you can almost watch them get taller. In addition to the striking flowers, the foliage has many shapes and textures. What's more, the leaves of wild passion vine provide food for the larvae of some of the most beautiful butterflies on the planet. The larvae do little lasting harm to the vigorous plants, and the adult butterflies add a lot of life to the garden.

The "passion" in the name relates the parts of the flower to the passion of Christ: The lacy crown represents a halo or crown of thorns; the five stamens, the five wounds; and the 10 petal-like parts, the 10 faithful apostles. It's a little obscure but if you look closely, you'll see it.

Despite its exotic look, this vine is very easy to grow. Simply plant it in a sunny location and it will, in turn, explode with a riot of color that will make even the most sophisticated gardeners envious.

Exotic flowers on an easy-to-grow plant—passion vine has it all.

The dramatic flowers of native wild passion vine are just as complex and interesting as any exotic. Edible, egg-shaped fruits follow later in the season.

PEAK SEASON

All year in South Florida, spring to fall elsewhere

MY FAVORITES

'Amethyst' is a fast-growing, vigorous hybrid. The flowers are intense purple and the individual petals point backward so the blossoms look like shooting stars.

Blue passion flower, *Passiflora caerulea*, comes in many forms, but my favorite is 'Constance Elliott'. It makes a beautiful, fragrant, white-flowered vine.

Lemon passion flower, *P. citrina*, is the only yellow-flowered passion vine pollinated by hummingbirds. It's a beautiful free-flowering plant that will bloom every month of the year. It prefers slightly acidic organic soil.

Wild passion vine, *P. incarnata*, is a lavender-flowered Florida native. Its leaves are the primary food source of Gulf fritillary and zebra longwing butterflies. I have seen hundreds of zebra longwings roosting at night beneath its cascading stems.

GARDEN COMPANIONS

To encourage butterflies, plant with butterfly weed *(Asclepias)*, butterfly bush *(Buddleia)*, asters, gaura, salvia, ironweed *(Vernonia)*, coneflower *(Echinacea)*, lantana, pentas, and Mexican sunflower *(Tithonia)*.

When Plant in the early spring when nighttime temperatures reach a consistent 55°F (13°C).

Where Plant in full sun in soil that has been enriched with organic matter. Use these vines on trellises, arbors, or walls for their vigor and bright, showy flowers; or plant as a soil-holding bank cover.

How Dig a hole twice the width of the root ball and enhance the entire bed with organic matter to improve flowering. Passion vine roots are very delicate and care must be exercised when spreading them out in the hole. Once planted, the roots should not be disturbed.

TLC The vigorous vines are likely to become overgrown and tangled. To keep them open and prevent buildup of dead inner branches, prune annually after the second year, cutting excess branches back to where they join with another branch. Wait until the nighttime temperatures hit at least 55°F (13°C) before setting container-grown plants outside. If they are set outside too early, they may go dormant and it is difficult to get them growing again.

TOP: *A native of Central America, lemon passion flower blooms spring through winter.* BOTTOM: *'Constance Elliott' is more fragrant than blue passion flower.*

Queen's Wreath
Petrea volubilis

Flowers of queen's wreath come in foot-long clusters several times a year during warm weather, primarily in late summer.

With its cascading dark lavender flowers, queen's wreath resembles wisteria. The big difference is that this vine loves all the heat and sunshine that Florida can throw at it. On the other hand, it's cold tender. Therefore, if you live in the middle to the southern part of the state, where freezing temperatures are rare and summer heat is abundant, plant queen's wreath instead of wisteria.

Queen's wreath flowers appear in late summer. Small and star shaped, the amethyst to deep violet flowers are arranged in 14- to 18-inch-long clusters that create a very dramatic effect. (A form with white flowers is also available, but it's much less showy.) The eye-catching parts of each flower are the five narrow petal-like lobes, called *calyxes*, that surround the flower and hang on long after the darker purple flowers drop. The leaves are 4 to 8 inches long and are notable for their texture that's like a fine sandpaper.

Native to Central and South America, queen's wreath is related to other well-known Florida heat lovers such as verbena and lantana. It can take temperatures into the upper 20s (−2°C) and, once established, it can withstand heavy drought.

Queen's wreath makes an exquisite flowering vine for pergolas, fences, trellises, or porches. It is also very effective in hanging baskets.

When Plant container-grown plants at any time. Transplant in the early fall to establish roots prior to the onset of hot summer weather.

Where Plant in full sun or part shade, although the latter will result in lighter bloom. Warm temperatures and high humidity are essential. Any reasonable soil is okay, although in the alkaline soils common in South Florida, an acidic fertilizer and a layer of mulch will improve growth. Queen's wreath is not tolerant of salty soil.

How Dig a planting hole twice the width of the container and slightly shallower, then dig deeper around the hole's perimeter to create a firm central core. Remove the root ball from the container and set it on the firm center, making sure the top of the root ball is just a bit higher than the surrounding soil. Then return the soil to the hole and water well.

TLC Water plants periodically, and keep lawn grasses away from the root zone; they'll compete with the vine for moisture. Protect young vines from frost. Vines can grow to 40 feet, so give these plants plenty of room and enjoy the show.

PEAK SEASON
Summer to fall

GARDEN COMPANIONS
Combine with banana *(Musa)*, *Ficus*, hibiscus, butterfly ginger *(Hedychium)*, angel's trumpet *(Brugmansia)*, copper leaf *(Acalypha wilkesiana)*, plumeria *(Plumeria rubra)*, princess flower *(Tibouchina)*, palms, and orchid tree *(Bauhinia)*.

LEFT: *The five narrow calyxes persist after the dark purple flower in the center drops.*
RIGHT: *Long flower clusters cover 4- to 9-inch-long, sandpaper-textured leaves.*

Rangoon Creeper
Quisqualis indica

Rangoon creeper is notable for its variously colored flowers on the same plant: They open pure white, then gradually age through pink and finally become red. This is a tropical vine, native to tropical Africa and Asia, and is suitable for the southern half of Florida. Gardeners in the northern half of the state can grow rangoon creeper if they keep it in pots. It will become semidormant during the winter. But as the leaves drop, the cocoa brown bark and strong architectural merit of its twining stems is revealed.

Blooms appear and begin to cover the lush foliage as the weather warms up in late spring. The trumpet-shaped flowers are borne on 2- to 4-inch-long drooping stalks. Flowers are fragrant, too, especially in the evening. Two forms of rangoon creeper are available: one with single and one with double flowers. But the former is easier to propagate and more common.

Rangoon creeper is a strong climber: its main trunk can swell to 4 inches in diameter and its stems are able to grow to 40 feet in height. If you train this vine to a gazebo or

trellis, make sure the structure is strong enough. Despite its potential size, the vine can be trimmed to any size.

If rangoon creeper has one drawback, it's the long (to 1½ inches), sharp spurs on the stems. But when it is grown on a trellis or larger gazebo, they are out of the way and not a concern.

PEAK SEASON
Late spring through fall

GARDEN COMPANIONS
Rangoon creeper combines well with both temperate and tropical plants. In the perennial garden, plant it in the back of the border along loosely draped chains, with roses, lion's mane, butterfly bush (Buddleia), coneflower (Echinacea), daylily (Hemerocallis), and a wide variety of annuals. In the most tropical regions, combine with banana (Musa), butterfly ginger (Hedychium), ornamental grasses, cannas, elephant's ear (Colocasia), bird of paradise (Strelitzia), Spathiphyllum, plumeria (Plumeria rubra), and bleeding heart vine (Clerodendrum).

OPPOSITE PAGE: The double form of Rangoon creeper on a chain-link fence.

When Plant in the fall so the roots have an opportunity to establish themselves before the onset of hot weather.

Where Best blooming occurs when plants receive full sun. This vine will grow well in partial shade, but will produce fewer flowers.

How Dig a planting hole twice the width of the vine's container and about 2 inches shallower than the plant's root ball. Then dig deeper around the hole's perimeter (leaving a firm central plateau) and roughen the hole's sides to encourage the roots to grow into your garden soil. Set the root ball on the plateau—making certain the top of the root ball is 1 to 2 inches higher than the surrounding soil—then fill in the hole, alternating soil and water to eliminate air pockets.

TLC Give Rangoon creeper lots of room and a large, heavy structure on which to grow. Prune in late winter, just before new growth emerges.

*In zones 28 and 31, grow in a container that you can move to a protected place in winter.

Flowering plants are multicolored because individual flowers open white and gradually age to red.

Sky Flower
Thunbergia grandiflora

Why, I don't know, but blue flowers of any kind are difficult to find in the Florida garden. So when I found not only a blue flower—but one on a vine as well—I had to have it for my garden. Sky flower has thick, succulent stems and large light blue flowers that are 5 inches across.

The light blue flowers are perfect for most gardens. Throughout the summer, they look great against the vine's large, broad dark green leaves. When planted with gold, red, and orange flowers in the flower border, the blue flowers tend to cool things down at bit. In semishade, the white species doesn't show off nearly as well as the standard blue form.

Sky flower can grow quite fast, up to 50 feet a year, and in frost-free areas of the state, it blooms year-round. In the Orlando area, it dies back to the ground when temperatures reach the mid 20s (around −4°C), but comes back with vigor when warm weather returns.

PEAK SEASON

In frost-free areas, blooms year-round. In other areas, it blooms late spring through fall.

RELATED SPECIES

Mysore clock vine, *Thunbergia mysorensis,* is a tall climber with spectacular hanging clusters of red flowers that open to reveal yellow interiors.

White sky vine, *T. laurifolia,* looks and behaves the same as the mysore clock vine but produces white flowers. These aren't nearly as dramatic as the light blue form and have a tendency to wash out and disappear in full sun.

GARDEN COMPANIONS

Plant behind other plants such as ornamental grasses, bottlebrush *(Callistemon)*, *Ficus*, orchid tree *(Bauhinia)*, palms, trumpet tree *(Tabebuia)*, angel's trumpet *(Brugmansia)*, bamboo, copperleaf *(Acalypha)*, hibiscus, pineapple guava *(Acca sellowiana)*, plumeria *(Plumeria rubra)*, princess flower *(Tibouchina)*, sago palm, and yellow bells *(Tecoma stans)*.

OPPOSITE PAGE: *Appropriately facing skyward are the azure blue flowers of sky flower.*

When Plant container-grown plants anytime.

Where Blue sky flower enjoys the full, hot sun but can also be planted in part shade. It is ideal for covering a chain-link fence, or wherever you need dense screening; use it to hide service buildings or your neighbor's boat parked in the backyard.

How Dig a planting hole twice the width of the container and about 2 inches shallower than the plant's root ball; then dig deeper around the hole's perimeter (leaving a firm central plateau) and roughen the hole's sides to encourage the roots to grow into your garden soil. Set the root ball on the plateau—making certain the top of the root ball is 1 to 2 inches higher than the surrounding soil—then fill in the hole with soil. Keep well watered to establish a strong root system.

TLC Prune in spring to shape and to remove damaged or dead branches.

TOP: *Funnel-shaped flowers open in loose clusters of several flowers.*
BOTTOM: *Perfectly formed flowers contrast with the dense mass of leaves.*

In zones 28 and 31, grow in a container that you can move to a protected place in winter.

Trumpet Creeper
Campsis radicans

If you want to cover a gazebo with big, brilliant orange flowers and you love hummingbirds, plant trumpet creeper. But keep in mind this vine's single drawback: a tendency to overwhelm everything in its path. It puts out aerial shoots, which is how it manages to scale just about any structure to a height of 30 or 40 feet. The dark green, serrated leaves unfurl in late May. Clusters of trumpet-shaped, 3-inch-long, flame-colored flowers bloom from June through September, followed by attractive woody seedpods that may last all winter.

Hummingbirds love trumpet creeper, and you can assume that if there are any within a 10-mile radius, they'll find your plant.

Trumpet creeper is a native plant here in the Southeast. It's a slow-growing vine, but it's determined. Keep it away from the house—its stems will clog gutters and downspouts, cover up windows, and poke their way through any exposed cracks and crevices.

A dense cover for a fence, arbor, or entry gate is a good use of trumpet creeper.

PEAK SEASON

Blooms late spring through fall

MY FAVORITES

'Crimson Trumpet' flowers are dark red.

'Flamenco' flowers are bright red.

'Flava' flowers are yellow to pale orange.

'Yellow Trumpet' flowers are bright yellow.

RELATED SPECIES

Campsis × tagliabuana 'Madame Galen' has large salmon red flowers on a vine that is more vigorous than other cultivars.

GARDEN COMPANIONS

Combine with other native shrubs and trees such as holly (Ilex), cabbage palms, bald cypress, redbud (Cercis), dogwood (Cornus), fringe tree (Chionanthus), loblolly bay (Gordonia), red maple, river birch, beautyberry (Callicarpa), flame azalea, oakleaf hydrangea (Hydrangea quercifolia), sumac (Rhus), and sweetspire (Itea). Or use perennials like milkweed (Asclepias), tickseed (Coreopsis), lobelia, false indigo (Baptisia), golden-rod (Solidago), blanket flower (Gaillardia), joe-pye weed, and Louisiana iris.

When Plant nursery-grown plants throughout the growing season. Direct-sow seeds in spring or fall.

Where Plant in well-drained soil in full sun to partial shade. Use for large-scale screening.

How Loosen soil to a depth of 10 to 12 inches and work in 2 to 3 inches of compost or other

TOP: *A hybrid with Chinese trumpet creeper, 'Madame Galen' has bright red flowers.*
BOTTOM: *Flowers of 'Flava' are pale yellow, and leaves are light green.*

organic matter. Incorporate a controlled-release fertilizer into the soil. Plant trumpet creeper at the same depth that it was growing in the container. Water immediately after planting.

TLC According to what the vine needs and you desire, prune either before new growth emerges to encourage more flowers and remove winter-damaged wood, or prune later in spring to restrain growth. Or prune both times. Maintain a compact framework of branches to keep the plant in a small space. Old plants sometimes become top-heavy and pull away from the supporting surface. Dig up all pieces of suckering roots that invade nearby gardens. Ants often live on trumpet vine but don't damage the plants.

Trumpet Honeysuckle

Lonicera sempervirens

Trumpet honeysuckle gracefully softens a hard corner and drapes over the top of an iron fence.

Trumpet honeysuckle is a delightful perennial vine, well behaved and graceful, with clusters of brilliant yellow, orange, or red flowers that bloom sporadically all summer and are favorite nectar sources of ruby-throated hummingbirds.

The thick, almost serpentine stems wind around their support as they grow upward. Occasionally a branch will drift away from the support and wave about in the air—tie it in place with twine while it's still young and pliant. Honeysuckle vines become gnarled and rigid over time, which adds to the plant's appeal. The leaves are large, leathery, and round, a fine backdrop for the warm flower colors.

The plant tolerates some shade, but too much shade or poor air circulation will invite fungal problems. The vine also will get ratty looking if it is chronically deprived of adequate moisture or crowded. Given a trellis of its own, an arbor or gate, or even a mailbox, it will more than rise to the occasion. Against the dark metal or rustic stone, the handsome foliage and yellow-orange flowers create a striking display in midsummer.

Be mindful, though, of an imposter—Japanese honeysuckle *(Lonicera japonica)*. This is an invasive vine that chokes out native vegetation, displacing native plants over vast areas, and in the process diminishing the Florida ecosystem.

LEFT: *Close-up of a trumpet honeysuckle flower cluster.*
RIGHT: *The yellow form of trumpet honeysuckle flowers later in spring.*

PEAK SEASON

Late summer through fall

MY FAVORITES

'Alabama Crimson' has bright red flowers.

'Blanche Sandman' produces red flowers with a yellow throat.

'John Clayton' has yellow flowers in spring, followed by a smattering of blossoms through the summer, and brilliant red fruit in the fall.

Lonicera sempervirens sulphurea (or *L. s.* 'Flava') produces totally yellow flowers.

'Magnifica' has 2-inch scarlet red flowers with yellow interiors.

GARDEN COMPANIONS

Combine with other southern natives including holly *(Ilex)*, cabbage palms, bald cypress, redbud *(Cercis)*, dogwood *(Cornus)*, fringe tree *(Chionanthus)*, loblolly bay *(Gordonia)*, red maple, river birch, beautyberry *(Callicarpa)*, flame azalea, oakleaf hydrangea *(Hydrangea quercifolia)*, sumac *(Rhus)*, and sweetspire *(Itea)*. Also use with perennials including milkweed *(Asclepias)*, tickseed *(Coreopsis)*, lobelia, false indigo *(Baptisia)*, golden-rod *(Solidago)*, blanket flower *(Gaillardia)*, joe-pye weed, and Louisiana iris.

When Plant container-grown trumpet honeysuckle anytime.

Where Plant in full sun to part shade in fertile, amended soil that is moist but not soggy.

How Loosen soil to a depth of 10 to 12 inches and work in generous amounts of compost or other organic material. Incorporate a controlled-release fertilizer into the soil before planting. Plant honeysuckle at the same depth that it was growing in the container. Water immediately after planting. Provide a support for the vine's twining stems and guide them to it.

TLC Consistent watering is especially important during the first 2 years, but even mature plants will wilt at the first sign of drought. Apply 2 to 4 inches of shredded bark, composted leaves, or wood-chip mulch around plants as soon as the ground warms in spring and replenish as necessary throughout the growing season. Fertilize in spring with a 10-10-10 fertilizer or an organic equivalent sprinkled around the base of the plants and watered in well. Prune after flowering to maintain shape. Next year's flowers will bloom on new wood. Regular washing with the garden hose will help keep aphids from becoming a serious problem.

Ground Covers

Ground covers are dependable plants that you can count on to blanket the soil with dense foliage, adding beauty and variety to the landscape and suppressing weeds at the same time. Lawn grass is the best-known ground cover, unsurpassed as a surface to walk or play on. But in areas where foot traffic is infrequent and on sites inhospitable to lawn grasses—in the shade under large trees or on hot, steep banks, for example—there are many other ground covers that offer the neatness and uniformity of a lawn for much less effort.

These plants run the gamut of foliage textures and colors, and many are noted for their bright flowers as well. Height varies too. Some are low mats, while others are knee-high or even taller. Some ground covers spread by underground runners or root on top of the ground as they grow. Others form clumps and should be planted close together to produce a tight cover.

PLANTING GROUND COVERS

Throughout most of Florida, the best time to plant ground covers is in fall. Temperatures are mild then, and the rains will help the plants off to a good start. In northern Florida where winters are colder, planting in early spring is okay, though fall is still preferred.

Although ground covers are tough, they will grow and spread more quickly if you prepare the planting area carefully. Dig out weeds, amend the soil with compost or well-rotted manure, and broadcast a complete fertilizer over the area (follow package directions for amounts). Work in amendments and fertilizer with a shovel or tiller, and then rake to level the soil.

RIGHT: *Varieties of bromeliads* (Neoregelia) *line a shaded pathway.*
OPPOSITE PAGE: *Variegated periwinkle is a hardy and long-lived ground cover that excels in the shade of trees.*

SPACING GROUND-COVER PLANTS

How much spacing to allow between ground-cover plants depends on the particular plant and, to some extent, on how quickly you want the growth to cover the area. When planting ground covers from small pots or flats, set the plants in holes just deep enough for and slightly wider than the root ball. To plant from gallon containers, dig a hole that is slightly deeper around the perimeter to accommodate the loosened roots, leaving a plateau of undisturbed soil in the middle. The root ball rests on the plateau, with the crown (where the roots and top growth meet) of each plant remaining slightly above the soil surface to prevent rot.

When planting on a slope where erosion is likely, set plants in staggered rows. Make an individual terrace or level area for each plant and create a basin or low spot behind it to catch water.

After planting, water the plants thoroughly. As they become established over the next several weeks, water every few days, keeping the soil moist but not soggy.

To help maintain even soil moisture and to prevent weed seeds from growing, spread a 2- to 4-inch-thick layer of an organic mulch between the young plants, taking care not to cover the plants' crowns.

WEEDS

One of the primary reasons for planting a ground cover is to control weeds, but don't expect to be freed from weeding right away. Replenishing the mulch around plants as it decomposes will aid in weed control. For serious weed problems, you may be able to use a selective herbicide—one that will kill weeds but not your ground cover.

191

Algerian Ivy

Hedera canariensis

At the mention of ivy, images of large, imposing brick buildings draped with vertical carpets of green often come to mind. That's Boston ivy. Here in Florida, it's different. We use two other ivies: English ivy *(Hedera helix)* and Algerian ivy *(H. canariensis).* And for starters, neither should ever grow on buildings.

'Variegata' Algerian ivy and peace lily (Spathiphyllum) brighten a shaded corner.

English ivy grows well in the northern part of the state. The heat and humidity from around midstate and south are just too much for it. But even where it does grow well, it is likely to become an invasive nuisance, so I don't recommend planting it.

That's where Algerian ivy steps in. Its large, disease-free leaves and less exuberant habit make it a suitable ivy alternative for the Florida landscape. Algerian ivy is great in partial to deep shade, in areas of the garden where ordinary lawn grass is difficult to grow.

PEAK SEASON
Year-round

MY FAVORITES

'Canary Cream' leaves are 3 inches wide and blotched with white.

'Ravensholst' leaves are an extra large 4 to 6 inches wide, and very dark green.

'Variegata' (also sold as 'Gloire de Marengo') leaves are 1½ to 2½ inches across. They are a mixture of cream, gray, and green, but many will revert to solid green as the plant ages.

GARDEN COMPANIONS

Algerian ivy is perfect for large shady areas and looks good with azaleas, camellias, Japanese aucuba, cleyera, fatsia, and dogwood (Cornus).

ABOVE: *A lustrous green bed of Algerian ivy flanks steps of cut stone.*
BELOW LEFT: *Close-up of cream-splotched leaves of 'Variegata'.*

When Plant in the fall, if possible, so plants have an entire season of mild weather to root. A spring planting can work if some additional irrigation is provided during dry spells.

Where Plant in partial to deep shade, in well-drained soil. Plant ivy in those areas where nothing else will grow, such as where lawn struggles to grow in shade, or where exposed tree roots wreak havoc with your lawn mower.

How Before planting, amend soil with compost and a controlled-release fertilizer. Plant from pots, plugs, or six-packs. Space plants 8 to 12 inches apart, closer for faster coverage and on slopes and banks. You can take cuttings of ivy anytime and place them directly into well-prepared garden soil. Or, root several stems together in a pot for planting out into the garden later.

TLC Use an edging tool on a weekly basis to prevent ivy from escaping into areas of the garden where it is unwanted. Other than that, it requires no special care.

Asiatic Jasmine
Trachelospermum asiaticum

The small leaves of Asiatic jasmine knit together to form a tight and neat evergreen ground cover. Fragrant, pinwheel-shaped flowers come in spring.

Asiatic jasmine is one of those great plants for today's environmentally friendly gardens. It fits into just about any landscape and looks neat, trim, and attractive in the process.

This evergreen trailing vine serves admirably as a ground cover. Small (nickel-sized), creamy yellow blossoms come in late spring and last into early summer; bees like the flowers. The leaves are 1 to 2 inches long and, on many varieties, are striped with creamy white markings. Once established, this vine forms an impenetrable mat of good-looking foliage.

Asiatic jasmine handles poor soils very well and can tolerate short periods of drought. It performs well even in harsh environments such as traffic medians or coastal areas where salt spray is common.

You can train Asiatic jasmine to cover or spill over a wall, or to climb a trellis or pergola. But it really excels as a ground cover. For instance, I've seen it used very successfully to replace lawn where the walk-on surface wasn't really needed, reducing the need for water, fertilizers, and pesticides.

When Plant in the fall, if possible, so plants have an entire season of mild temperatures to root.

Where Choose a location that receives full sun to full shade, in well-drained soil. Plant it where it cannot reach other plants: it might grow into and climb over them.

How The recommended spacing is 12-inch centers between plants in 4-inch pots, and 18-inch centers for 1-gallon pots.

TLC Once established, Asiatic jasmine can withstand tough environments. Lack of water and blistering sun are typical of the conditions in which it thrives. Enhance either of the above, and it will establish itself at shocking speed. To maintain a neat appearance, give Asiatic jasmine a "haircut" in early spring with the lawn mower (use the collection bag) set on its highest setting.

LEFT: *The tight, carpetlike nap of Asiatic jasmine creates a green band down the center of a brick drive.*
BELOW: *A low and narrow planting of Asiatic jasmine bridges paving and shrubs.*

PEAK SEASON

Flowers in late spring. Evergreen and attractive all year.

MY FAVORITES

'Bronze' puts out new growth that is markedly copper bronze but ultimately turns dark green.

'Elegant' has tiny dark green leaves.

'Flowerwood Tricolor' has handsome foliage mottled with green and white; new growth emerges bronze.

'Sakida Hashura' has tiny leaves. New foliage is pure white and later changes to a mottled green and white in partial shade. It is very slow growing.

RELATED SPECIES

Asiatic jasmine is easily confused with Confederate, or star, jasmine (*Trachelospermum jasminoides*), which is hardier and grows taller.

GARDEN COMPANIONS

Plant Asiatic jasmine adjacent to sidewalks, or in similar locations where it will be unable to invade other plants. It can choke and overwhelm them with its vigor.

Beach Sunflower
Helianthus debilis debilis

Dark green and sprawling, beach sunflower grows in and stabilizes coastal sand, making an attractive base for a grove of coconut palms.

Here is one of those great Florida plants that can grow in just about any sunny location. There are two forms of beach sunflower. One is upright and the other is prostrate. The prostrate form, *Helianthus debilis debilis*, is the one you want for a ground cover. It's native to both of Florida's coastlines, so is an obvious candidate for dune stabilization or a ground cover

adjacent to beach paths and boardwalks. But it grows well inland too, needing little more than full sun and well-drained soil. The other form, sometimes called cucumber leaf sunflower, *H. d. cucumerifolius,* grows up to 5 feet tall, has variable yellow to creamy white flowers, and is native along the northern Gulf Coast of Florida and west to Texas. Both are irresistible to a wide variety of native and migrating butterflies!

Beach sunflower is a spreading plant that grows to about 2 feet tall. It has glossy, dark green heart-shaped leaves, and during the hottest summer months it is covered with 3-inch yellow flowers, each one with a dark eye. A vigorous grower, it will produce a new plant and begin to grow wherever it touches the ground.

There is nothing prettier than the sight of a sunny Florida beach dune covered in the pale yellow flowers of the beach sunflower. Look for this plant at nurseries and garden centers that offer native plants. Plant it, and you won't be disappointed.

PEAK SEASON

Summer through first frost

MY FAVORITES

The prostrate form of beach sun-flower is an easy-to-grow ground cover that will fill in and look good where few other plants can.

GARDEN COMPANIONS

Plant where you want masses of color. Under sasanqua camellias, crape myrtle *(Lagerstroemia)*, fringe tree *(Chionanthus)*, dogwood *(Cornus)*, magnolia, redbud *(Cercis)*, cassia, coral tree, chaste tree *(Vitex)*, angel's trumpet *(Brugmansia)*, princess flower *(Tibouchina)*, and yellow bells *(Tecoma)*, it provides color and foliage contrast.

ABOVE: *Miniature versions of full-size sunflowers, the blossoms of beach sunflower appear intermittently through the summer.*

BELOW LEFT: *Brightly colored flowers attractively contrast with beach sunflower's glossy green leaves.*

When Fall is the ideal planting time, but planting any time of the year can be successful.

Where Plant in full sun or dappled shade. After planting, keep the soil moist until the roots are established in the sur-rounding soil. Use beach sunflower in mass plantings to create a ground cover, or wherever you want a wild or natural look.

How Plant in well-prepared soil enriched with plenty of organic matter. Propagate by rooting cuttings in fall.

TLC Provide a modest amount of fertilizer a few times a year and one plant will grow to cover a 10- by 10-foot area in a single season. Otherwise, beach sunflower requires no spe-cial care other than lots of sun and a little water now and then.

Bromeliads

Aechmia, Guzmania, and *Neoregelia*

Well known as indoor and gift plants everywhere, bromeliads are among the most useful landscape plants for gardeners in Florida. Several serve very well as ground covers.

Among the bromeliads are plants of widely divergent sizes, leaves, and flowers. Most common are those with thick, broad leaves that form a funnel-shaped rosette, called a *tank*, which holds water. Many bromeliads also develop beautiful flowering stalks. The best-known bromeliad is the pineapple.

Some bromeliads can hold several gallons of water in their tank and can provide homes for various creatures, including salamanders, snails, beetles, mosquito larvae, and frogs and their tadpoles. The animals that die there decompose and nourish the plant.

The bromeliad family contains a wide range of plants, including some very un-pineapple-like members such as Spanish moss (which is neither Spanish nor a moss). Here in Florida, we're lucky to be able to use bromeliads in our landscapes.

A ground cover of bromeliads (Neoregelia macwilliamsii) suits tropical and subtropical gardens.

LEFT: *Banded leaves of Aechmea provide color contrasts in an otherwise green garden.*
RIGHT: *A common houseplant, Guzmania serves as a reliable ground cover in Florida.*

PEAK SEASON

Year-round

MY FAVORITES

Blushing bromeliad (*Neoregelia carolinae*) is an impressive foliage plant. 'Martin' has green and white leaves that turn crimson at the center of the plant at flowering time. *N. macwilliamsii* has light green leaves that are shorter and blunt-tipped; top leaves turn mostly bright red at flowering time.

Living vase plants (*Guzmania*) have flower spikes that grow out of the center of the plant with durable, intensely colored leaves, called *bracts*.

Tank plants (*Aechmea*) are trouble-free, reliable plants that serve well as ground covers. Funnel-shaped *A. fasciata* is readily available. 'Foster's Favorite' is an upright variety with wine red leaves and pendant spikes of coral red, pear-shaped berries tipped with midnight blue flowers.

GARDEN COMPANIONS

Bromeliads add an air of the tropics to any outdoor garden. Plant with other bromeliads that have different shapes, sizes, and colors. For an easy tropical look, plant them with elephant's ear (*Colocasia*), ornamental grasses, viper, butterfly ginger (*Hedychium*), banana (*Musa*), clump-forming bamboo, tropical fruit trees, palms, and bird of paradise (*Strelitzia*).

When The best time to plant a bromeliad ground cover is in the spring, when temperatures are getting warmer.

Where All of these ground-cover bromeliads need filtered light and well-drained soil.

How To establish a ground-cover planting, set plants about 12 inches apart, and at the same depth that they grew in their nursery pots. Amend soil with a very porous, fast-draining soil mix, such as the kind used to grow cactus in pots.

TLC Bromeliads are slow-growing and long-lived landscape plants. Water plants thoroughly when you do water, but allow the soil to dry before watering again; they're prone to root rot if the soil stays soggy. You may hear of a weevil that is threatening Florida bromeliads, but the ones I've recommended here are largely immune. Although the central plant dies after flowering, it produces offsets, or *pups*. Separate these from the main plant and replant them, or leave them in place and allow the clump to slowly expand.

As landscape annuals in zones 28 and 31.

Carpet Bugle
Ajuga reptans

Plants for shady gardens are often the most difficult to locate, given all the variables involved, such as exactly how much shade and whether it's from taller plants or buildings, or whether the soil is wet or dry. So if your landscape includes a shaded area where you'd like a good-looking, low-growing plant, carpet bugle just might be the plant for you. Use it in the deepest shade or in the very front of the border in a perennial garden.

Carpet bugle spreads quickly by sending out runners that grow new plants. (Where conditions are right, it can invade a lawn!) It hugs the ground, rarely growing taller than 2 or 3 inches, though spikes bearing many flowers will reach up to 6 inches. Within a season or two, carpet bugle will form a dense foliage carpet.

The evergreen foliage has different textures and colors, depending on the selection. The flowers, which bloom late spring through summer, come in an assortment of colors ranging from deepest purple-blue to polar white.

Although it prefers a moist, richly amended soil in part shade, carpet bugle can withstand ordinary soil, including clay, and will also tolerate drought remarkably well.

Blue flower spikes rise above spreading carpet bugle foliage in spring.

PEAK SEASON

Flowers appear spring into summer; leaves are evergreen.

MY FAVORITES

'Bronze Beauty' has bright blue flowers and metallic bronze foliage.

'Burgundy Glow' has multicolored evergreen foliage with wine red splashes. Upright spires of deep blue flowers appear in spring. This plant soon "knits" together to form a low carpet of cream-edged leaves.

'Catlin's Giant' is one of the largest-growing varieties, forming a vigorous mound of deep bronzy red spinach-like leaves and purple-blue flowers.

'Chocolate Chip' is a new natural dwarf variety (2 to 3 inches tall) that covers its miniature, spreading, chocolate-colored foliage with shiny, lacy blue flowers.

'Metallica Crispa' has tight, crisp-leafed rosettes of crinkled, bronzy purple leaves and cobalt blue flowers.

GARDEN COMPANIONS

In North Florida, spring-flowering bulbs emerging through the dense mat of carpet bugle foliage look lovely. In zone 26, plant with other shade-loving plants like azaleas, toad lily (*Tricyrtus*), *Carex* 'Sparkler', *Selaginella*, and flax lily (*Dianella*).

TOP LEFT: *'Burgundy Glow'*
TOP RIGHT: *'Catlin's Giant'*
RIGHT: *'Bronze Beauty'*

When Plant in fall or early spring.

Where Plant in full to partial shade. Try carpet bugle in the front of a perennial border or as an edging plant.

How Before planting, enrich the soil with organic matter. Plant from pots, flats, or plugs, setting plants at the same level that they grew in their nursery containers and spacing them about 6 to 10 inches apart. Water well and lightly fertilize.

TLC Carpet bugle is a very easy plant to grow, provided it is shaded. It can tolerate drought for short periods. Mow or trim off old flower spikes. Separate clumps in fall every 3 to 4 years to invigorate the planting.

Coontie

Zamia pumila

Coontie's slow growth and rugged constitution make it both low maintenance and long-lived, even in challenging situations.

Coontie is a native of South Florida, and, as such, is the only surviving North American representative of an ancient group of seed-producing plants, the cycads. If you don't know of them, cycads are remarkable plants for having survived on earth longer than most others, for 300 million years or so. Dinosaurs likely browsed on them! Don't let coontie's fernlike look give you the wrong impression. This is one tough plant that is extremely well adapted to Florida.

The 2- to 4-foot-long leaves grow from a rosette at the top of a trunk that is often underground, or mostly so. Leaflets are dark green and leathery. Plants are either male or female, and the latter produces russet green, 5- to 6-inch-long cones in summer. Later, the cones open to reveal several dozen bright orange seeds that are roughly the size of grapes. After many years, plants can grow to 4 or 5 feet high and wide, but coontie is very slow growing, so half that size is more typical.

Years ago, Native Americans (and later, the European settlers) would grind the roots to use as a substitute for wheat flour. But don't experiment carelessly: coontie is very poisonous if not handled properly. In South Florida, the leaves of coontie are an important food for the larvae of the endangered atala butterfly.

If you have a shady area that can accommodate it, coontie is tough to beat.

When Fall is the best time to plant, but anytime is okay.

Where Plant coontie in full to part shade and in any Florida soil. Space plants 2 to 3 feet apart. The leaves are very tolerant of salt spray, so planting near the coast (although not in beach sand) is an option. Use it in mass plantings to cover large areas, or try it in containers.

How Plant from 1- or 2-gallon containers. Before planting, amend soil with compost. Set plants at the same depth that they grew in their containers and space them 3 to 4 feet apart. Use the closer spacing for a quicker cover, and the more generous one to avoid overcrowding in the future. Mulch between plants to stop weeds and conserve moisture. To grow plants from seeds, remove the bright orange pulp and crack the hard shell around the seed. Half-bury seeds on their side, and they'll germinate in about 3 weeks. Or, propagate by offsets, or by division (if there is more than one crown). Do not transplant from wild populations.

TLC Prune only to remove dead or dying leaves.

LEFT: *Close-up of coontie frond suggests the leathery quality of the leaflets.*
BELOW: *Compared with coontie, cardboard palm makes a less dense ground cover, and its leaflets are broader.*

PEAK SEASON
Year-round

RELATED SPECIES
Cardboard palm, *Zamia furfuracea*, grows about 3 feet high and twice as wide from an underground trunk, similar to coontie.

GARDEN COMPANIONS
Plant coontie with other shade-loving plants, including azaleas, Florida anise tree *(Illicium)*, camellia, holly *(Ilex)*, aucuba, Oregon grape holly *(Mahonia)*, heavenly bamboo *(Nandina)*, sweet olive *(Osmanthus)*, summersweet *(Clethra)*, and leucothoe *(Agarista)*.

Lawn Grasses

Large enough to spread a blanket but small enough to be quick and easy to care for, small lawns are a practical choice in Florida.

The classic lawn—lush, green, and crisply mowed—has long been a basic landscaping element. Today, however, water conservation is an important issue everywhere, and attention has naturally focused on the huge amount of water needed to keep lawns alive and green.

But despite their requirements, lawns do have their good side—they help filter pollutants, prevent the erosion of our topsoil, and increase real estate market value (this is, in itself, a measure of the importance of an attractive lawn).

The trick to growing lawn grass in Florida is using enough fertilizer and pest control to keep the lawn looking good, but not so much that our drinking water is sacrificed. One key to finding this balance is selecting a type of grass that is well adapted to our climate—obviously, it will then look better with less maintenance.

Another key consideration is the size of the lawn. There's no sense in planting lawn from property line to property line: You'll save time and water and reduce pollution by making a lawn area small. Keeping it fairly level makes good sense too; it minimizes runoff and makes mowing safer. For that matter, a simple geometric shape is easier to mow and easier to irrigate, reducing the amount of water wasted on paving.

Finally, be sure you prepare and plant the site carefully, and maintain the lawn properly.

When Plant bahiagrass, bermudagrass, centipedegrass, and zoysiagrass from seed in spring. The latter three can also be grown from sprigs, plugs, or sod anytime, provided water and warm weather are available. Plant St. Augustinegrass anytime from plugs or sod.

Where With the exception of 'Seville' St. Augustinegrass, most Florida lawn grasses prefer full, hot sun. If the area is shaded by trees or tall buildings, consider a shade-tolerant ground cover instead. Lawns also need well-drained soil that has a slightly acidic pH.

How Proper site preparation is essential. Remove any existing sod with a sod cutter, and have the soil's pH tested. Spread a 3- to 4-inch layer of an organic amendment, such as commercial compost, and then till the site to a depth of about 8 inches. Apply a fertilizer and any other materials recommended by the soil test lab to adjust the pH, such as limestone. Till again, rake the area smooth, water, and then let the soil settle for a few days before planting.

TLC Every lawn grass grows at a different rate and requires a different frequency of mowing and level of soil fertility. Generally, as more water and fertilizer are applied to the lawn, mowing and pest control needs also increase. If shade or tree roots are problems in your yard, consider planting shade-loving ground covers like ivy or mondo grass. Cutting grass too short stresses the plants, leading to disease, weeds, and insect infestations. Letting grass grow taller results in deeper roots, better drought resistance, and healthier plants.

Compared with other lawn grasses, St. Augustine is more shade tolerant.

PEAK SEASON

Warm, sunny months

MY FAVORITES

Bahiagrass *(Paspalum notatum)* has a medium to coarse texture and good resistance to nematodes. 'Pensacola' is more cold tolerant and is somewhat more attractive.

Bermudagrass *(Cynodon dactylon)* has fine to medium texture. It is seen most often on golf courses and athletic fields. Bermuda hybrids, such as 'Tifgreen', 'Tiflawn', and 'Tifway', are available as sod only.

Centipedegrass *(Eremochloa ophiuroides)* is grown in North Florida, but unfortunately doesn't stand up to wear well. It has low-maintenance requirements and medium texture.

St. Augustinegrass *(Stenotaphrum secundatum)* features a coarse texture, ease of maintenance, and good nematode tolerance. Top varieties are 'Floratam', 'DelMar', 'Floralawn', 'Jade', and shade-tolerant 'Seville'.

Zoysiagrass *(Zoysia matrella)* has narrow, wiry blades and drought-tolerant roots. It's sold as sod, sprigs, and plugs. 'Empress' and 'Empire' are good sod varieties. You can plant 'Zen 300' and 'Zenith' from seed.

GARDEN COMPANIONS

Lawn grass offsets flower and shrub beds perfectly.

Mondo Grass

Ophiopogon

Deep to partial shade, exposed tree roots, and limited irrigation are perfect reasons to grow the southern gardener's favorite ground cover: mondo grass. Its thin, grasslike, dark green blades grow to 12 inches tall. A few new selections grow to only 3 inches high and never need mowing, making them the perfect shade-tolerant, low-maintenance substitute for lawn grass. Mondo grass makes flowers too. Blossoms come in white and various shades of purple and, in some cases, are quite showy and long-lasting in arrangements. Don't confuse mondo grass with liriope *(Liriope muscari)*; the leaves of mondo grass are narrower.

Mondo grass (sometimes called monkey grass) can take a little foot traffic, and, once established, it can withstand full sun. It is also attractive as a border along paths, between stepping-stones, in flower beds, or in rock gardens. It grows well along streams and around garden ponds.

This plant solves so many common landscape problems, and with such apparent ease, that it's worth consideration by every gardener and landscaper. If there's shade, chances are mondo grass will grow well.

Just like a lawn grass, mondo grass creeps between and beyond flagstone pavers, and looks both natural and neat.

When If possible, plant container plants in fall, though any time of the year is okay. After a planting has matured, divide it by cutting 1½-inch clumps, or plugs, out of the original planting.

Where Mondo grass grows just about anywhere it has deep to part shade and well-drained soil. Once well established, most varieties (except black mondo grass) can withstand full sun. Plant along paths, between flower beds and lawn, among rock groupings, or along streams and around garden pools. It competes well with the roots of other plants; try it (either in the ground or in large containers) under bamboo or to cover bare soil at the base of trees or shrubs.

TOP: *Mondo grass forms a dense mat in the shade beneath a pair of trees.*
BOTTOM: *Black mondo grass is an easy way to add a unique color to your garden.*

How Plant from pots, flats, or plugs, spacing plants 6 to 9 inches apart. Water well, and lightly fertilize with a controlled-release complete fertilizer or organic equivalent about a month after planting. To increase, divide in early spring before new growth starts.

TLC Plantings can become ragged and brown with neglect. To keep mondo grass looking neat, go over it every 2 or 3 years with the lawn mower set on the highest setting in the early spring before the new growth begins to emerge. Plants don't need heavy feeding. Protect from snails and slugs.

PEAK SEASON
Year-round good looks

MY FAVORITES
'Gyroku-ryu' (also sold as 'Kyoto Dwarf') is the most diminutive form, growing only 1½ inches tall. It's sometimes used in containers, even around bonsai trees.

'Kijimafukiduma' (also sold as 'Silver Mist') grows to 10 inches tall. It has stark white and green vertical stripes on the leaves.

'Nanus' is very short (only 3 inches high) and very slow growing.

'Torafu' is a white and green variegated form with unusual horizontal striping. It grows about 4 inches high.

RELATED SPECIES
Ophiopogon planiscapis 'Nigrescens' is known as black mondo grass. It grows to 10 inches tall and looks good combined with variegated plants.

GARDEN COMPANIONS
Plant with other shade-loving plants like azaleas, camellias, dogwood *(Cornus)*, redbud *(Cercis)*, and oakleaf hydrangea *(Hydrangea quercifolia)*. A favorite combination of mine is toad lily *(Tricyrtus)* emerging from a blanket of green mondo grass.

Peacock Ginger

Kaempferia pulchra mansonii

If Florida gardeners ever desire a catalog plant, it is likely to be that holy grail of shade-tolerant ground covers—the hosta. Unfortunately for us, hostas won't grow in the warmer areas of the Sunshine State. So we plant peacock ginger instead. It comes as close to hosta as is possible in our hot climate. And, given their foliage textures and vivid colors, peacock gingers are welcome addition.

Peacock gingers have seen a resurgence in the last 10 years, and many remarkable selections are now available. Nearly all are short, 6-inch-tall plants that have dark green leaves with various silver, bronze, or burgundy patterns. In addition to the flat, ground-hugging leaves, peacock gingers also have small lavender or white flowers held underneath the foliage.

K. p. mansonii is like having two plants in one. In spring, it has distinctive green and silver leaf markings that later fade to solid green. It spreads so rapidly, it is the best species for covering large shady areas.

Peacock gingers are hot-weather plants and begin to turn yellow when fall nighttime temperatures settle in around 50°F (10°C). Shortly after, the plants will become completely dormant and disappear from sight. (Mark their locations when you can so you don't dig them up by mistake in winter.) They'll resprout in spring, but not until days are reliably 85°F (29°C).

PEAK SEASON

Late spring through summer

MY FAVORITES

'Satin Checks' is very similar to the species, but has dark green leaves, with a bronze checkerboard pattern throughout the leaf.

RELATED SPECIES

Kaempferia gilbertii '3-D' may be the showiest, and slowest-growing, peacock ginger. It grows to only 4 inches tall with narrow green leaves edged in creamy white.

K. loatica 'Shazzam' has attractive silver, light green, and dark green feathered patterns on the leaves.

GARDEN COMPANIONS

Shade is essential for growing peacock gingers, and other plants that share the same habits include hidden gingers *(Curcuma), Calathea,* oakleaf hydrangea *(Hydrangea quercifolia),* Oregon grape *(Mahonia),* begonia, bat plant *(Tacca),* banana *(Musa), Plectranthus, Clerodendrum,* sweet olive *(Osmanthus),* camellia, gardenia, and lady palm *(Rhapis).*

OPPOSITE PAGE: *Deeply veined and pleated leaves of peacock ginger,* Kaempferia pulchra mansonii, *are an iridescent green.*

When Set out inexpensive small plants in the fall and let them grow a good root system before warm weather returns in the spring. Planting in spring provides too little time for roots to establish enough to support top growth.

Where Plant peacock ginger in deep to partial shade and in rich, well-prepared soil. Dappled morning sun is acceptable, but keep away from afternoon sun.

How Set out plants from 4-inch pots in individual holes, or preferably in a prepared bed. Cultivate the soil about 6 inches deep and amend with compost and a controlled-release fertilizer. Plant 8 to 10 inches apart. Water well and consistently during the first season.

TOP: *Unfurling leaves of peacock ginger.*
BOTTOM: *Young leaves of* K. p. mansonii *are marked with a silver pattern.*

TLC Peacock ginger is virtually maintenance free. Allow it to spread to cover large areas. Remove fading leaves in the fall only after they can be gently pulled from the underground stem. Plants rarely need to be divided, and they have no pests of note.

Periwinkle

Vinca major

It seems as if periwinkle has been around forever, and for good reason. It survives long after the house is gone, sometimes the only remaining sign of a former homestead.

Periwinkle looks good, is easy to grow, and, as its longevity testifies, is resilient far beyond expectation. It has spreading or arching wiry green stems, clothed in pairs of shiny leaves. Stems may root at their joints or even at their tips when they touch moist soil; each newly rooted part is then another plant, ready to send out additional stems. Encouraged with moisture, periwinkle grows fast, to the point of invasiveness.

The dark green and narrowly oval leaves grow about ¾ to 1 inch long and are spaced fairly close together. Ultimately, plants create a 4- to 6-inch-high carpet of stems and leaves in sun or full shade, against which the blossoms stage their show.

Bloom time comes in early spring, when the foliage cover is adorned with single, phloxlike flowers of a medium-light lilac blue—the color known as periwinkle blue.

Periwinkle is very tolerant of various types of soils, competes well with tree roots, and readily absorbs and covers fallen leaves.

LEFT: *The center of 'Maculata' leaves are a lighter shade of green.*
RIGHT: *'Variegata' leaves are edged in white.*

PEAK SEASON

Early through late spring

MY FAVORITES

'Alba' has white flowers.

'Maculata' flowers are dark blue but with golden green centers.

'Oxyloba' has deep purple flowers.

'Ralph Sugert' leaves have very broad white edges.

'Sterling Silver' leaves have white edges.

'Variegata' (also known as 'Elegantissima') has creamy edged leaves.

'WoJo's Gem' has cream-edged leaves and light green centers.

RELATED SPECIES

Vinca minor has smaller leaves (to ½ inch long) and dime-sized lilac- or white-colored flowers.

GARDEN COMPANIONS

Plant beneath trees, especially ones that produce leaf litter that the periwinkle can "swallow." Good smaller trees include redbud (*Cercis*), dogwood (*Cornus*), *Magnolia* 'Little Gem', mango, and sweet olive (*Osmanthus*). Larger trees that combine well include river birch, Chinese pistache, jacaranda, sassafras, and cherries.

When Fall is preferred, but well-rooted plants can be set out in spring if you provide adequate water the first summer.

Where Plant periwinkle in any soil, in sun or shade. Plants establish most quickly with at least 6 hours of sun per day. Plant it where it has room to spread out; it can be too aggressive for a small garden.

How Set out plants from pots, spacing them about 1½ feet apart, or closer for faster coverage. I have planted periwinkle on 8-inch centers in the spring and had nearly complete coverage of the ground by that same fall.

TLC Water newly planted periwinkle for the first two summers and fertilize lightly with a controlled-release fertilizer or organic equivalent. Whenever plantings mound too high or become layered with old stems, shear or mow them in late summer to stimulate new growth from the ground level. Lightly fertilize after a severe renovation of the planting to encourage strong new growth.

Fruit Trees

Florida's climate, more than any other in the United States, allows you to grow tropical fruits right in your own backyard. The warm ocean water that surrounds the southern tip of Florida creates a climate that is ideal for many tropical fruits, and subtropical fruits thrive farther north.

Many new Florida gardeners may be just discovering the variety of fruits we can grow here, but most of these edibles have been delicacies in other cultures for many generations. Carambola has been popular in Malaysia for centuries, and the papaya was a staple throughout South America long before Columbus docked in the New World.

In addition to producing fruit, many of these trees also make handsome landscape plants. Bananas (page 214), with their large leaves, are appropriate additions to many Florida gardens. You can choose from species and varieties of different sizes, as well as ones that produce edible or inedible fruits. Some banana plants only reach 5 feet tall at maturity; others can grow to more than 20 feet tall. Some varieties taste like bananas from the store, while others can taste like peanut butter or ice cream.

Carambola (page 216), or star fruit, produces yellow ribbed fruits throughout the year. Even if it didn't produce a tasty, sweet-tart fruit, the small leaves and vase-shaped growth habit would make it an attractive shrub or small tree for almost any backyard. And the same can be said about mangoes. The glossy leathery leaves and the dense shade the trees provide make them a welcome addition to many South Florida gardens.

Fresh figs (page 220) or jaboticabas (page 222), picked and popped right into your mouth, are two of the best reasons to grow your own fruit, not to mention juicing a bowl of oranges for the family breakfast early in the morning. Beyond that, when you grow your own fruits, you know where they've been and how they've been treated, a small but welcome reassurance.

OPPOSITE PAGE: *Ripening clusters of bananas, called hands, hang downward on a stalk but curve upward.*
TOP RIGHT: *'Brown Turkey' fig is one of the best for Florida.*
CENTER RIGHT: *'Minneola' tangelo is known for its prominent "neck."*
BOTTOM RIGHT: *Plain-looking sapodilla has delectable flesh inside.*

None of the tropical and subtropical fruits described here are difficult to grow, provided they are in soil that drains well and they get plenty of water. Initially, of course, new fruit trees need regular watering to get them established in Florida soils. Later, after they have been growing for a year or two, you can water them less often, once every 7 to 10 days. Healthy and well-watered plants will also have fewer insect or disease problems.

Growing up in Ohio, I could only imagine eating a freshly picked banana or being able to grow an orange tree in my own backyard. Since then, I have learned that growing exotic tropical fruits is neither exotic nor difficult, and my apple-oriented palate has been transformed to one that includes citrus, mangoes, and loquats. Given our sunny, hot days and warm nights, you can grow a wide variety of tropical and subtropical fruits here that will produce an abundant harvest. Whether you're new to Florida or a native, I encourage you to give them a try.

Banana

Musa

Growing bananas in the backyard is what gardeners in northern climates can only dream about. Imagine being able to walk out into the yard in the morning in your sandals, pick a fresh banana, and slice it on your cornflakes. The only thing that could top that would be to have a glass of fresh-squeezed juice made from oranges right off the tree, which, by the way, is growing next to the banana. That's living in Florida.

Bananas enjoy the hot, humid conditions that central and South Florida can provide. If you live farther north, don't despair. Many varieties grow well in containers. That's the good news. The bad news is that bananas can't stand cold weather and at temperatures below 32°F (0°C), they may be irreversibly harmed. In addition to frost-free weather, bananas need acidic, well-drained soil that has been thoroughly amended with organic matter. They don't like flooded soil, even for only a few hours.

'Koae' produces large bunches of bananas that are excellent cooked or fresh.

PEAK SEASON

Summer and fall

MY FAVORITES

'Dwarf Cavendish' and 'Giant Cavendish' both produce very high-quality edible bananas. The former grows 5 feet tall; the latter grows to 8 feet.

'Goldfinger' is a notably disease- and wind-resistant 12-foot-tall plant. It produces a 6-inch-long stubby banana with excellent flavor.

'Koae' (or 'Ae Ae', pronounced "eye eye") grows quickly to 18 feet in height. If possible site it in a location that offers partial shade and wind protection. It is notable for its very attractive variegated leaves and fruits.

'Orinoco' produces high-quality, 8- to 12-inch-long bananas. It grows 12 to 15 feet tall. 'Dwarf Orinoco' is the same but half the height.

GARDEN COMPANIONS

Create a grove by planting bananas with other tropical fruits such as jaboticaba, citrus, papaya, guava, and carambola.

ABOVE LEFT: 'Dwarf Orinoco' is ideal in smaller gardens, or even in containers. ABOVE RIGHT: Worldwide, 'Giant Cavendish' is the most important commercial banana.

When Plant container-grown bananas anytime.

Where Choose a location in full sun (except for 'Koae') that has well-drained, highly organic soil. If drainage is poor, plant in elevated beds. Bananas will not grow in soils that are high in salts. Ideally, the planting site should be flat.

How Plant the rhizomes just below the soil surface, water thoroughly, and mulch.

TLC Fertilize with a high-nitrogen fertilizer (a nitrogen-phosphorus-potassium, or NPK, ratio of 10-2-22 or similar) at the rate recommended on the package. As soon as a shoot, called a *sucker*, begins to grow, make the first application. Follow up with applications of the same fertilizer, at twice the rate, every 4 to 6 weeks through the growing season. Do not fertilize if the banana is not actively growing. There are virtually no pests that cause extensive damage to bananas. The most common problem is tattering of the leaves due to wind. Cut off damaged leaves that hang down the trunk as needed.

Carambola, Star Fruit

Averrhoa carambola

Carambolas are slow-growing shrubs or small trees that reach 30 feet in height. Small clusters of lilac-colored flowers, about ¼ inch wide, grow along the stems. The showy, oblong fruits, which are produced sporadically throughout the warm months of the year, have thin, waxy, orange-yellow skin and juicy, crisp, yellow flesh when fully ripe. Slices cut in cross sections have the form of a star, hence carambola's other common name. The fruit ranges from very sour to mildly sweet. Eat ripe carambolas out-of-hand, sliced, or in salads, or use them as a garnish.

Cultivated in Southeast Asia and Malaysia for many centuries, carambolas are believed to have originated in Ceylon. Home gardeners have grown the tree for many decades in Florida, but now commercial orchards are established here. Once mature, the tree produces more fruit than one household can possibly eat. For backyard gardeners, star fruit is one of the easiest tropical fruits to grow.

'Arkin' is a sweet type; its crunchy flesh is somewhat less tangy than tart varieties.

PEAK SEASON

Summer months for harvest

MY FAVORITES

There are two main types of carambolas: the smaller, tart, more flavorful ones, and the milder, sweet types.

Sweet

'Arkin' is the best mild type for Florida. It has very low acid and sugar content.

'Fwang Tung' will ripen to light yellow but is mild enough to eat green.

'Kary' is sweeter, more colorful, and juicier than 'Arkin', but less crunchy.

Tart

'Golden Star' is a unique tart variety that will become sweet if allowed to ripen to golden yellow on the tree.

GARDEN COMPANIONS

Most other subtropical and tropical plants will combine well with carambola.

ABOVE: 'Kary' is sweet, very juicy, and particularly colorful.
BELOW LEFT: Very mild 'Fwang Tung' is tasty at the green stage.

When Fall is the best time to plant.

Where Plant in full sun and any well-drained soil. Carambola grows faster and bears more heavily in rich, well-drained loam. Leaves may yellow on plants growing in limestone soil. Mature carambolas can tolerate temperatures to 27°F (–3°C) for short periods. In Florida, the tree grows well in sheltered sites as far north as St. Petersburg on the west coast and Daytona Beach on the east coast.

How Dig a planting hole twice the width of the container and slightly shallower than the root ball, then dig deeper around the hole's perimeter to create a firm central plateau. Set the root ball on the plateau, making sure the root ball's surface is higher than the surrounding soil; backfill and water.

TLC Use a fertilizer that contains nearly equal amounts of NPK (such as 6-6-6) plus magnesium (Mg), 3 to 4 times per year. Plants are relatively pest free, but sometimes the fruits are attacked by fruit flies.

*Warmer areas of zone 26.

Citrus

Citrus

If Florida is known for one fruit, it would have to be citrus. One of the many things we can be grateful for

Remnants of former citrus groves survive and produce for many years around homes.

as Florida gardeners is the great diversity of fresh citrus we can grow right in our back-yards. Oranges, grapefruits, lemons, limes, and mandarins (also known as tangerines)—you can grow all the common supermarket citrus here. You can also grow some of the more unusual ones, such as kumquats, blood oranges, grapefruit-pummelo hybrids, and mandarin hybrids, which are also quite tasty.

All citrus are evergreen shrubs or small trees. The leaves are an attractive, bright, glossy green, and the intoxicating fragrance of the white flowers is well known. Citrus plants are very versatile in the garden. Grow them as specimen plants, in groves of any size, in containers, or even as espaliers, trained flat against a wall or fence.

When The best time to plant citrus is late winter or early spring.

Where Plant in full sun.

How Remove any fruit on the tree at planting time. Dig a hole that's twice the diameter of the root ball and mix in a controlled-release fertilizer. Position the tree so the juncture of the stem and the root ball is 3 inches above the soil's surface. Finish by building a watering basin around the tree that extends beyond the spread of the branches to concentrate water at the root zone.

TLC Citrus trees, especially young ones, need plenty of water during periods of little or no rainfall. Remove weeds and sod from the area under the tree canopy to reduce competition for water and nutrients. Fertilize 5 or 6 times a year with an balanced-ratio NPK fertilizer (such as 8-8-8) that includes magnesium.

Warmer areas of zone 26.

TOP LEFT: *'Minneola' tangelo is a 'Dancy' tangerine and 'Duncan' grapefruit cross.*
TOP RIGHT: *'Eureka' lemon is one of the two standard supermarket lemons.*
BOTTOM LEFT: *'Dancy' tangerine is seedy but exceptionally flavorful.*
BOTTOM RIGHT: *Tart and cold-hardy calamondin makes a good container plant.*

PEAK SEASON

Flowers in spring; harvesttime varies.

MY FAVORITES

Grapefruit

'Duncan' fruits have white flesh and many seeds. Harvest December to March.

'Flame' produces a large fruit that has sweet, red flesh and no seeds. Harvest from December to March.

Sweet oranges

'Ambersweet' produces small fruits in November and December.

'Hamlin' produces small fruits with few seeds from October to January.

Tangerine

'Dancy' is very sweet and seedy. Harvest October to December.

Other citrus

Calamondins are very ornamental and fruits make good marmalade. Peak harvest is November to April.

'Eureka' produces a high-quality supermarket-type lemon. Harvest September to November.

'Key' lime makes a medium-sized, thorny shrub that produces very flavorful fruits year-round.

GARDEN COMPANIONS

Other plants that complement citrus include trumpet tree (*Tabebuia*), coral tree (*Erythrina*), frangipani (*Plumeria*), and angel's trumpet (*Brugmansia*).

Fig
Ficus carica

Eating fresh figs is one of those rare pleasures everyone should experience. Fig trees not only make a trouble-free addition to your garden of edible plants, they make a handsome landscape shrub as well.

Edible figs grow well throughout Florida. In North Florida, a cold snap down to about 15°F (−9°C) will burn the plant back to the ground, but it will return in spring. Elsewhere, it makes a low-branching tree that, over the years, becomes gnarled and picturesque. It grows 15 to 30 feet tall and about as wide. The bright green, rough-textured leaves have three to five lobes, that, combined with the strong trunk and branch pattern, make the fig a top-notch ornamental tree.

Figs are very easy to grow, provided you select the correct variety for Florida. Older varieties had an open "eye" at the end of the fruit to allow pollinators to enter. But this opening allowed water and other insects to get in too, which often damaged the fruit. Newer closed-eye varieties have solved the problem of fruits splitting and rotting in Florida.

Figs may be trained as trees, or as large, irregular shrubs like this one.

PEAK SEASON

Fall for harvest

MY FAVORITES

'Brown Turkey' is best if you live where periodic freezes threaten because it will fruit the summer after being frozen to the ground. Fruits have purplish brown skin and pinkish amber flesh. Other names for this variety include 'Black Spanish', 'Brunswick', 'Everbearing', 'Harrison', 'Ramsey', 'Lee's Perpetual', and 'San Pedro'.

'Celeste' is the most widely grown fig in Florida. It's fairly cold hardy, but if it is damaged by frost, it will take two summers before it fruits again. Fruits are bronzy with a violet tinge on the outside, and a rosy amber color on the inside. This fig is also known as 'Blue Celeste', 'Celestial', 'Little Brown', and 'Sugar'.

GARDEN COMPANIONS

Figs are very adaptable. Plant as a landscape tree, or in a vegetable or fruit garden. Figs combine well with fruit trees such as loquat, guava, carambola, and persimmon.

When Plant a container-grown fig tree in spring; plant a bare-root tree during the dormant season.

Where Choose a site in full sun to part shade with plenty of water and well-drained soil. In North Florida, plant figs near a south wall, or train them against one, so they can benefit from the reflected heat.

ABOVE: *Harvest ripe figs once they're slightly soft and beginning to bend at the neck.*
BELOW LEFT: *A ready-to-harvest brownish purple fruit of 'Brown Turkey'.*

How Plant container-grown trees by digging a hole twice the width of the container and slightly shallower, then dig deeper around the hole's perimeter to create a firm central plateau. Set the root ball on the plateau, making sure the root ball's surface is just a bit higher than the surrounding soil. Then return the soil to the hole and water well. Before planting a bare-root tree, soak the roots to refresh them. Dig a hole that's at least twice as wide as the roots, and spread them over a cone of soil in the center, making sure the juncture of the roots and stem is slightly above the level of the surrounding soil. Backfill and water well.

TLC Cut the branches back halfway or more after planting. Prune lightly each winter, cutting out dead and crossing branches. Avoid deep cultivation, which may damage surface roots. Do not use high-nitrogen fertilizers that will stimulate growth at the expense of fruit. Apply a 2-inch mulch layer to conserve water, moderate the soil temperatures, and reduce nematode damage. Figs are not usually browsed by deer.

221

Jaboticaba

Myrciaria cauliflora

Every gardener needs at least one unusual plant to show off, and in the Florida garden, jaboticaba fills the bill perfectly. Native to central South America, it grows to a large, roundheaded shrub or a small tree with evergreen leaves. The purple fruits are ¾ to 1½ inches in diameter and are very similar in appearance, size, and flavor to muscadine grapes (page 248). But remarkably, the fruits are borne on the trunk and the larger branches, instead of on the smallest branches, as with most fruit trees. A tree loaded with mature fruit makes quite an unusual sight.

Jaboticaba's smooth, light brown bark flakes off in patches. The dark green leaves are long and thin and give the tree a very fine texture. Unpruned, it can reach 25 feet in height, with tight, compact branching at the top. The tree is hardy to 25°F (−4°C).

White flowers with prominent yellow stamens cover the trunk and the larger branches during warm weather. Most varieties produce multiple bumper crops in a year. The fruits can be eaten right off the tree or used in wine and jellies.

The only downside to this tree is that it can be hard to find. But once you do locate one and you have enjoyed it for a few seasons, I think you'll agree that jaboticaba is one of Florida's very special fruit trees.

White flowers with prominent yellow stamens appear on the trunk at the same time as the mature fruit.

PEAK SEASON

Summerlong harvest season

MY FAVORITES

'Paulista' fruits are relatively large, thick-skinned, and tasty, but this variety typically produces only one mature crop per summer.

'Ponhema' fruits are best for jams and jellies. The tree is very productive, but the fruits are only really edible once fully ripe.

'Sabara' is the variety that's most popular in South America. A prolific tree, its fruits are relatively small, sweet, and thin-skinned.

GARDEN COMPANIONS

Fit a plant into your landscape where you can, or combine with other tropical fruit and nut trees, including mangoes, macadamia, citrus, carambola, papaya, lychee, sapodilla, soursop, and tamarind.

OPPOSITE PAGE: *Rather than bearing fruits on younger, smaller branches and stems like most fruit trees, jaboticaba fruits are borne directly on the trunk and the larger branches.*

When Plant container-grown trees any time of the year.

Where Jaboticaba performs best in full sun or part shade in well-drained soils with an average pH. The two most common situations that preclude planting a jaboticaba are salt-laden air and poorly drained soil.

How Dig a hole roughly three-fourths the depth of the plant's root ball and twice as wide. Place the plant in the hole, making sure the juncture of the stem and the root ball are slightly above the level of the surrounding soil (1 to 2 inches in well-drained soil). Water as needed to maintain good soil moisture and to prevent wilting.

TLC Use a mulch to maintain even soil moisture, and water as needed to prevent the soil from drying out. You can shear plants to form a dense hedge.

Warmer areas of zone 26.

Loquat
Eriobotrya japonica

Loquat trees make attractive and low-maintenance ornamentals, trained as either a small tree or large shrub. Apricot-like fruits are a bonus.

Flavorful fruits that ripen in early spring, large, bold leaves, and a plant that's very easy to grow and live with are the virtues of loquat.

Each orange-yellow, slightly fuzzy fruit is about the size and shape of a small hen's egg. A central cavity contains one or more seeds. The fruits come in clusters of 4 to 10, and when ripe, they're firm and juicy, with a flavor that varies between tart and sweet. Most people just enjoy them fresh from the tree, but if you're ambitious, they are excellent canned or made into jelly. Or, combine peeled and seeded fruits with sliced banana, orange sections, and grated coconut.

Loquat trees grow 15 to 25 feet tall and about as broad. Toothed leaves grow 8 to 12 inches long. They are hairy when young but become smooth, leathery, and dark green as they mature. The white, very fragrant flowers are borne in clusters at the branch tips, mostly in early spring.

Most trees bear fruit regularly and well, even if they are far from another loquat tree; cross-pollination isn't needed. After just a few years, you can expect a tree to bear 100 pounds of fruit in a typical year.

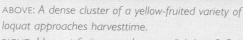

ABOVE: *A dense cluster of a yellow-fruited variety of loquat approaches harvesttime.*
RIGHT: *Harvest fruits once they are slightly soft. Snip them off individually to avoid damaging them.*

PEAK SEASON

Flowers in early spring; fruits appear in late summer.

MY FAVORITES

'Advance' has late-ripening, pear-shaped, yellow fruits with excellent flavor. The tree is a natural dwarf that grows to a little over 5 feet and is disease resistant.

'Champagne' has large, pear-shaped fruits with deep yellow, thick skin. The flesh is soft, juicy, and sweet. The leaves are long, narrow, and pointed.

'Premier' has large, oval-shaped, salmon orange fruits with large white dots. The fruits ripen late; the flesh is juicy, with four or five seeds per fruit.

'Tanaka' is the cold hardiest of the group. It has large, round fruits that are orange-yellow in color. The flesh is brownish orange and juicy.

'Wolfe' bears slightly pear-shaped, pale yellow fruits on a tree that can grow to 25 feet tall. The flesh is very sweet if the fruits are permitted to ripen on the tree.

GARDEN COMPANIONS

Loquats can be planted with other fruit trees (citrus, guava, mango, and carambola) or with landscape plants, including gardenia, pineapple guava (Feijoa), anise tree (Illicium), nandina, azaleas, and sweet olive (Osmanthus).

When The best time to plant, or transplant, is late fall, but any time of year is okay for loquats grown in nursery containers.

Where Loquats are adapted to sub-tropical and tropical climates and have survived temperatures to 12°F (−11°C). Loquats can tolerate a variety of soils ranging from heavy clay to sandy loam, but they require good drainage.

How When planting, dig a hole roughly three-fourths the depth of the plant's root ball and twice as wide. Place the plant in the hole, making sure the juncture of the stem and root ball are slightly above the level of the surrounding soil (1 to 2 inches in well-drained soil). Water as needed to maintain good soil moisture and to prevent wilting. Set loquats 20 feet apart for fruiting and 10 feet apart when used as an evergreen hedge.

TLC For best harvest, fertilize monthly with a complete fertilizer and maintain adequate soil moisture. Loquats have very shallow roots, so avoid planting or cultivating beneath them. To harvest larger but fewer fruits, thin them after they set.

Fruits less reliably north of Jacksonville.

Mango
Mangifera indica

Internationally, mangoes win the title of "the most popular and most sought-after fruit" hands down, and only citrus gives them much of a contest here in Florida.

The mango originated in eastern India and Burma and has been cultivated, praised, and even revered in its homeland since ancient times. Buddhist monks are believed to have carried mangoes on voyages to Malaya and eastern Asia in the fourth and fifth centuries B.C. By all accounts, the mango is as valued today as it was then.

Medium-sized evergreen trees, mangoes become 30 to 50 feet tall in Florida, spreading about half as wide. The long, leathery leaves are a shiny dark green to deep burgundy when young, gradually turning a dull dark green. Leaves drop from the tree all year.

The flowers are small and numerous, ranging from yellow to red, and are borne in long sprays. Of the hundreds of flowers, only a few will set fruit, and none require cross-pollination from another tree.

In Florida, fruits ripen in mid- to late summer. They dangle from the ends of long stalks, producing a dramatic display as they hang outside the foliage canopy. They are ready to pick when they pull easily from the tree. Each fruit is up to 6 inches long and shaped somewhat like a kidney bean. The color of the skin varies by variety from greenish yellow to orange and red. The flesh is more or less fibrous or stringy, depending on the variety; little fiber is one of the key indicators of an improved variety.

One of the world's favorite mangoes, 'Keitt' is a Florida selection that is noted for its sweet, fiberless flesh. The tree is productive and disease resistant. Fruits ripen August to October.

PEAK SEASON

Late summer is harvest season.

MY FAVORITES

'Keitt' bears one of the largest fruits of the common varieties—nearly 2 pounds. Its yellow-green skin makes it less popular in the United States, but the golden yellow flesh is fiberless and full flavored.

'Kent' has medium-sized, nearly round fruits that are about 1¼ pounds. The skin is attractively blushed with red; the flesh is fiberless and very flavorful.

'Tommy Atkins' is the most common mango in North America. It's medium sized (about 1 pound). It has an attractive skin and low-fiber flesh.

GARDEN COMPANIONS

Combine mangoes with colorful exotic flowers such as butterfly ginger (Hedychium), angel's trumpet (Brugmansia), frangipani (Plumeria), bird of paradise (Strelitzia), or princess flower (Tibouchina), or with foliage plants, including elephant's ear (Colocasia), banana (Musa), or bamboo.

LEFT: *Harvest once the fruit softens slightly and the skin reaches the characteristic color for that variety.*
RIGHT: *Good-looking 'Van Dyke' has a flavor that's both spicy and sweet, and flesh that is fiber free.*

When The best time to plant is in early fall. But as long as you can supply the necessary water to establish the roots, you can plant container-grown trees anytime.

Where Mango trees are not too particular as to soil type, providing they have good drainage. They grow very well in sand, gravel, and even in South Florida's limestone. The amount of rainfall is not as critical as *when* the rain occurs. The best climate for mango delivers 30 to 100 inches of rain in the summer followed by 8 months that are relatively dry.

How When planting, dig a hole roughly three-fourths the depth of the tree's root ball and twice as wide. Place the plant in the hole, making sure the juncture of the stem and root ball are slightly above the level of the surrounding soil (1 to 2 inches in well-drained soil).

TLC Wherever frost is a possibility, provide overhead cover to protect the tree the first 2 years. Fertilize only after spring bloom, using a high-nitrogen fertilizer such as 15-10-10 for the first three years. Then shift to one that is higher in phosphate and potash, such as 5-10-10. Apply fertilizer 3 times a year at the rate of 1 pound per year of tree age. Scale, mealybugs, and mites are occasional pests.

Southern extremes of zone 26.

Papaya
Carica papaya

The yellow fruits at the base of the cluster are ready to harvest.

Commonly considered trees, papayas are actually tall perennials with a relatively soft and hollow stem. These fast-growing, short-lived plants produce perhaps the favorite breakfast fruit of people in tropical regions around the world. Botanists believe the plant is native to southern Mexico and Central America, but now the papaya is well known and widely grown throughout the tropics and subtropics.

Two types of papayas are grown in Florida: Hawaiian and Mexican. The 10-inch-long fruits of the Hawaiian type are most common in grocery stores. They weigh about 1 pound and are yellow when ripe. Their flesh is either bright orange or pink, and there are small black seeds in the center. Fruits of Mexican papayas weigh up to 10 pounds and have yellow, orange, or pink flesh. Both kinds are delicious, but the Hawaiian type is smaller and easier to manage, and I prefer their more intense flavor. The varieties recommended here are all Hawaiian.

Hawaiian papayas grow about 10 feet tall, and they are unbranched. Large, palmlike, 2-foot-wide leaves form a sort of umbrella at the top that varies between 3 and 6 feet in spread, depending on the plant's age. All papaya fruits and leaves contain papain, an enzyme that helps digestion and is used in a variety of products from beer to chewing gum. Given the right South Florida conditions, papayas are easy to grow and a great pleasure to harvest and enjoy.

When Plant papayas in spring.

Where Papayas need full sun and a fertile, well-drained, slightly acidic soil. They need warm temperatures and a frost-free environment, but can often withstand light freezes. (If possible, cover plants with an old blanket on frost nights.) For best fruiting, plant three plants.

How When planting, dig a hole roughly three-fourths the depth of the tree's root ball and twice as wide. Place the plant in the hole, making sure the juncture of the stem and root ball are slightly above the level of the surrounding soil (1 to 2 inches in well-drained soil). To start seeds indoors in winter, remove them from a fruit and wash and dry them. Plant in potting soil and place in a warm location; germination takes 2 to 5 weeks. Transplant to the garden carefully, taking care not to damage the young roots.

TLC Keep soil moist in hot weather and dry in cool weather. Start young plants with ½ pound of 10-10-10 shortly after planting. Repeat twice monthly, gradually increasing to 1½ pounds until the plants are 8 months old. Continue with that amount monthly. Harvest fruits when most of the skin is yellow-green. Avoid touching the stem's milky sap; it sometimes causes dermatitis.

Warmer areas of zone 26.

PEAK SEASON

Late spring through late fall is harvest season.

MY FAVORITES

'Solo' has round fruits that weigh in at 1 to 2 pounds each. The skin is smooth; the reddish orange flesh is firm and very sweet.

'Sunset' ('Sunset Solo') has small to medium-sized, pear-shaped fruits with orange-red skin and flesh. They are very sweet. This is a high-yielding commercial dwarf variety.

'Vista Solo' fruits are 5 inches wide and up to 18 inches long. The skin is yellow and the flesh orange to orange-yellow. A compact 'Solo' type, this variety produces high-quality fruit that needs hot weather to become sweet.

GARDEN COMPANIONS

Papayas are truly tropical in appearance and look best when planted with other tropical-looking plants, such as banana *(Musa)*, bottlebrush *(Callistemon)*, empress tree *(Paulownia)*, palms, trumpet tree *(Tabebuia)*, bougainvillea, grevillea, yellow bells *(Tecoma)*, butterfly ginger *(Hedychium)*, canna, and crinum.

LEFT: *'Solo' papayas mature under the umbrella-like canopy of leaves.*
RIGHT: *Near-ripe fruits will ripen off the tree, but dark green fruits will not. Leave fruits on the tree until skin is yellow-green.*

Persimmon
Diospyros kaki

Astringent 'Hachiya' persimmons are very soft, very sweet, and almost custardlike when ripe.

Two kinds of persimmons grow in Florida: the native American and the Asian. The native species is larger and more cold hardy, but the Asian type bears the larger and far more desirable fruit, so it is the one I am recommending. At one time, there were large commercial orchards of these trees throughout the state.

Asian persimmons grow 30 feet tall (or more) and at least as wide. They have a handsome branching pattern and are one of the most ornamental fruit trees. Leathery, 6- to 7-inch-long leaves are light green when new, but they mature to dark green. Persimmons are one of Florida's most colorful trees in fall: Leaves turn vivid yellow, orange, or red. After they drop, brilliant orange-scarlet 3- to 4-inch fruits decorate the tree for weeks and will persist into winter if not harvested. Without pollination, the persimmon sets seedless fruit; pollinated trees often produce more abundant crops, however.

Varieties of Asian persimmons are either astringent or nonastringent. The astringent type is tart until it's soft-ripe, at which point the fruits become very sweet. Pick them while firm; they'll ripen off the tree. Nonastringent types are hard and mildly sweet when ripe, but their flavor improves if the fruits are allowed to soften slightly off the tree. In North and central Florida, the nonastringent types are best; in South Florida, the astringent types are a better choice.

When The best time to plant is fall, but you can plant container-grown trees anytime.

Where Plant in full sun and in any well-drained soil.

How When planting, dig a hole roughly three-fourths the depth of the tree's root ball and twice as wide. Place the plant in the hole, making sure that the juncture of the stem and root ball sits 1 to 2 inches above the level of the surrounding soil. Backfill the hole and water well.

PEAK SEASON
Fall for leaf color and harvest

MY FAVORITES
Astringent
'Hachiya' fruits are large with an oblong-conical shape, glossy, deep orange skin, and dark yellow flesh. They are excellent for drying.

'Tanenashi' bears medium-sized, conical fruits with orange-red skin and very sweet yellow flesh.

Nonastringent
'Fuyu' is the size of a baseball but flattened on the stem end like some tomatoes. Overall, it's the most popular persimmon in Florida.

'Hana Fuyu' is a good persimmon for the home garden. It has slightly larger fruits than most varieties, and they have few blemishes.

'Hanagosho' is a large tree with a vigorous upright habit and strong branches. The somewhat flattened fruits are very sweet and attractive.

'Izu' bears medium-sized, round fruits on a tree about half the standard size. The fruits ripen early.

GARDEN COMPANIONS
Combine with loquats, peaches, or plums. As a landscape tree, plant persimmons with Southern Indica azaleas, privet (Ligustrum), chaste tree (Vitex), pineapple guava (Feijoa), and holly (Ilex).

ABOVE: *Astringent persimmons soften once temperatures cool in fall.* BELOW: *Harvest nonastringent 'Fuyu' once they show their mature color.*

*Cooler areas of zone 26.

TLC Prune trees when they are young to establish a good framework; thereafter, prune only to remove dead wood, shape the tree, or open up a dense interior. Remove any suckers that grow from below the graft union. Fertilize 3 times a year: in late winter when still dormant, in June, and in late summer.

Sapodilla
Manikara zapota

A Florida selection, the skin of 'Prolific' is a rough brown that becomes nearly smooth at maturity. Inside, flesh is red-tan, moderately fragrant, and tasty.

An attractive, long-lived, and large evergreen tree that is a native of Mexico and Central America, sapodilla also produces one of the most flavorful and delectable tropical fruits of Florida.

Sapodilla fruits are nearly round and 2 to 4 inches in diameter. Brown and not particularly appealing from the outside, their yellow to reddish brown flesh is very pleasantly fragrant, sweet, and flavored something like a peach or pear topped with crunchy brown sugar. Normally enjoyed out of hand, the fruits can also be made into a mousse-like dessert. They can be seedless or may contain shiny black seeds.

The ripe fruits are brown and soft. If brown but still firm, ripen them by washing them to remove any milky sap on them, and place them at room temperature. They'll soften after a few days. You can also remove the ripe pulp and freeze it.

The tree is strong and wind resistant, an important consideration here where strong winds and hurricanes pass through regularly. Where native, trees reach 100 feet tall, but in gardens, the typical height is one quarter of that. The stiff, pointed, dark green leaves are 2 to 5 inches long and clustered at the ends of shoots. Small off-white flowers appear off and on throughout the year. They are pollinated by insects and bats. The milky sap that is exuded by all tree parts is a latex, known as *chicle*, which is used to make chewing gum.

PEAK SEASON

May to September for harvest

MY FAVORITES

'Brown Sugar' produces small, 2- to 2½-inch-long, nearly round fruits. The pale brown, slightly granular flesh is fragrant, juicy, and very sweet.

'Prolific' bears 2½- to 3½-inch fruits. The light reddish tan flesh is smooth and sweet.

'Russel' fruits are large (4 inches in diameter), and the red-brown flesh has a rich, sweet flavor.

'Tikal' fruits are more elliptical than round. They ripen very early and have excellent flavor.

COMPANION PLANTS

A variety of tropical plants combine well with sapodilla. Consider butterfly ginger (Hedychium), elephant's ear (Colocasia), banana (Musa), angel's trumpet (Brugmansia), frangipani (Plumeria), princess flower (Tibouchina), bamboo, and bird of paradise (Strelitzia).

ABOVE: Aptly named 'Brown Sugar' has very sweet, fragrant, and slightly grainy flesh.
BELOW LEFT: Early-ripening 'Tikal' is noted for its excellent flavor.

When Plant in late spring, just prior to the wet season. Or if irrigation is available, plant any time of year.

Where Sapodillas grow well throughout South Florida as far north as Tampa. Young trees may be killed or injured at freezing temperatures, but mature trees can withstand 26°F (–3°C) for a few hours with only minor damage. Trees are very tolerant of strong and salt-laden winds. Plant where the tree will receive full sun; any well-drained soil is okay, even salty and occasionally dry ones.

How Dig a hole roughly three-fourths the depth of the tree's root ball and twice as wide. Set the tree slightly higher (1 to 2 inches) than it grew in the pot, and backfill with the excavated soil. Water well. Finish by building a berm of soil around the tree that extends beyond the spread of the branches to concentrate water at the root zone.

TLC Water new trees every 2 weeks during dry spells. Mature trees are usually not watered at all, though doing so will increase fruit production. Fertilize new trees every 3 months with a 6-2-6 or similar fertilizer. Fruits are ready to pick if they separate from the stem without leaking latex. Store fully ripe fruits for a month in the freezer.

*Warmest areas of zone 26.

233

Edibles

Growing fruits and vegetables has always been a passion of mine, and apparently it is becoming more important to many people in nearly all walks of life. When you grow your own food, you know exactly how it has been treated. Needless to say, when you shop at most markets, you have no idea where the produce is from, not to mention how it was treated.

If you're new to food gardening, start small. An area of just 100 square feet can yield a great bounty.

List the fruits and vegetables your family enjoys, and then determine how much room each kind requires. If space is limited, grow plants that give a good yield for the area they occupy. Beans (page 236), muscadine grapes (page 248), and tomatoes (page 254), for example, can overwhelm you with their bounty. At the other extreme are melons, corn, and some other kinds of squash, which all require a great deal of space relative to their yield.

Also consider that most food plants need at least 6 hours of full sun each day. To avoid both shade and root competition, locate a vegetable patch away from trees and large shrubs. It may also be important to choose a spot protected from cold winds in the spring and hot, dry winds in summer. Watering and other routine tasks are easier on a level site; if only sloping land is available, try to find a south- or southeast-facing slope to take full advantage of the sun.

Vegetables are designated as either warm season or cool season, depending on the weather they need for best growth. Warm-season vegetables, such as peppers and tomatoes, are summer crops that are planted in late spring, and cool-season crops like lettuce (page 246) are planted in early spring or fall.

RIGHT: *Green and red lettuce, radishes, and onions fill a garden bed.* OPPOSITE PAGE: *Fresh-picked home-grown blackberries provide an explosion of sweet-tart flavor.*

But in South Florida, it's not so simple. There, summer heat is too much even for many warm-weather crops, and winters are warm enough for them to continue growing. In this region, home gardeners plant many of the traditional "summer" crops in early fall and harvest them through the winter.

PLANTING FOOD GARDENS

Start with careful soil preparation; you'll be repaid with faster growth and a substantially larger harvest. Remove any weeds from the plot and spread the soil with a 3- to 4-inch layer of compost or well-rotted manure. If you're planting a wide bed, scatter a complete fertilizer over the area. Work in amendments and fertilizer by hand or with a rotary tiller, and then rake the area smooth. If you're planting in rows, apply fertilizer in furrows alongside the rows after planting. In both cases, follow

package directions for the amounts. If your soil is poor or doesn't drain well, you may elect to grow vegetables in raised beds filled with a mixture of compost and good topsoil.

You can start vegetables either by planting seeds outdoors in the garden or by setting out transplants you have started yourself or purchased from a nursery. Vegetables that require a long growing season—peppers and tomatoes, for example—need many more days of consistently warm temperatures before they produce fruit, and so are best set out as transplants. Other vegetables, including broccoli (page 242), cabbage (page 244), and lettuce (page 246), need less time; they can be seeded directly or transplanted. Still other vegetables, notably beans, carrots, corn, and peas, grow fast and don't transplant well. These vegetables are best grown from seed that you sow directly in the garden.

Beans, Green and Lima

'Kentucky Wonder' pole bean is the best green (snap) bean to grow in Florida.

Can there be anything better than going out to the vegetable garden just after the sun has risen, picking a handful of fresh green or wax (yellow-pod) beans, and eating them as you survey the garden for chores to do that day? Okay, strawberries are better, but the point is, there is pure pleasure in the act of early-morning grazing in your own garden.

Green beans are a popular warm-season crop, and they grow well in well-drained soil with plenty of sunlight. Hundreds of bean varieties are sold for the home garden. Don't know beans about them? No matter. All fall into one of these three groups—snap, shell (or shelly or shelling), or dry—signifying the growth stage at which they taste best. *Snap beans* are eaten pod and all; *shell beans* are shelled and the seeds are eaten when young and fresh; *dry beans* are left to harden on the plant (and then store for months or years). You can eat some varieties at more than one stage.

You'll also need to consider the growth habits of the varieties you choose: beans are available as "bush" or "pole." *Bush beans* stand erect without support, so they require the least amount of work. They tend to ripen all at once, so succession plantings are a good idea to extend the harvest. Green bush beans were formerly called "string beans" because of a fiber that developed along the back seam of the pod. Plant breeders have reduced these fibers through selection and these green beans are now also referred to as snap beans.

Pole beans grow tall, to 10 feet, and need a structure on which to grow. They are slower to mature but picking stimulates the plants to produce more, so you get two to three times as many beans in the same space and the harvest extends over a longer period of time. Lima beans are a type of shell bean. They are available as either bush or pole types.

PEAK SEASON

Late winter through late fall in warmer areas of the state; May through October in cooler areas.

MY FAVORITES

Bush

'Bush Blue Lake' and 'Contender' are the two overall best for Florida's climate and soils. Other bush beans that grow well here include: 'Cherokee Wax', the best yellow-pod bean and the best of the shelling types; 'October Glory', edible young as shelling or later as dry beans; 'Purple Bush', with purple pods that turn green after cooking; and 'Roma II', an Italian flat-pod bean that's good in soups. 'Fordhook 242' is the preferred bush lima bean for this region.

Pole

'Kentucky Wonder' is the best snap variety, with 'Dade' and 'Blue Lake' as close seconds. 'Florida Butter' works well as a pole lima bean.

GARDEN COMPANIONS

Plant beans with other warm-season vegetables, such as tomatoes, cantaloupe, collards, okra, eggplant, cucumbers, and peppers.

When Plant beans in zones 25 and 26 in the late summer and again in the late winter. Sow seeds outdoors when the soil temperature is 55°F (13°C) or higher, or a week or two after the threat of frost has passed. Seeds rot in cold, wet soil. To extend the harvest of bush beans, sow successive crops every 2 weeks up to 12 weeks before the first expected fall frost. Beans of all kinds enjoy heat and are intolerant of frost.

Where Beans need a warm, sunny location and light soil that is well drained and rich in organic matter. Avoid saline soils. Place pole beans along the north side of the garden where they won't shade other sun-loving vegetables.

How Cultivate the garden soil to a depth of 6 to 7 inches and plant seeds 1 inch deep, 5 to 6 inches apart. Plant bush types in rows 3 feet apart. Pole beans need some sort of support, such as string, a trellis, or tepee-style poles, which should be set in place before seeds are planted. To make a tepee, lash five tall bamboo stakes together at the top with twine.

TLC Beans need an even supply of water—about 1 inch a week. Thin seedlings of bush types to 5 to 6 inches apart, pole beans 6 to 8 inches apart. After plants have their second set of leaves, mulch to conserve moisture and control weeds. Beans have the ability to "fix" nitrogen (take the nitrogen from the air between soil particles and convert to a plant-usable form), so avoid adding fertilizers high in nitrogen or plants will produce too much leaf growth at the expense of beans. Harvest snap beans when the pods swell but before seeds begin to form. Harvest beans for fresh eating frequently to keep the plants productive. Harvest shell beans when pods are plump and bright green. Harvest dry beans after pods have dried on the plant. To avoid spreading diseases, never work around beans when the foliage is wet.

Purple beans lose their color when cooked but look good on the plant.

Blackberries

Blackberries have always grown well in Florida, and several new varieties make growing them in the Sunshine State even easier.

Blackberry plants are categorized as either erect or trailing, with various degrees of both in between. Erect types have stiff stems and grow about 4 to 6 feet in height. Trailing kinds, known as dewberries or boysenberries, have cascading stems that need the support of a trellis.

The stems (called *canes*) of most blackberries are very thorny. This has always been a problem when picking and working with blackberries, and is enough to discourage many gardeners. But the University of Arkansas' introduction of a thornless variety, 'Apache', has solved that problem, and it has been followed by other thornless cultivars.

All blackberries fruit in summer. Trailing types ripen earlier; the berries are smaller and the clusters of fruit are more open than those of erect or semierect types.

Many of our favorite childhood memories are related to food, and fresh blackberry jam atop a thick slice of freshly baked bread is one that is hard to forget.

This semierect-type blackberry is restrained by cables strung between posts.

ABOVE: *'Arapaho' is a thornless, erect type of blackberry.*
RIGHT: *'Chester' is a semierect, heavy-bearing blackberry.*

PEAK SEASON

May and June

MY FAVORITES

Thornless

'Apache' fruits are glossy black, blocky, and conical. Canes are more erect than other thornless varieties so don't require a trellis. 'Arapaho' and 'Navajo' are very similar. Both have smaller fruits than 'Apache', but 'Navajo' fruit quality is particularly high. 'Chester' is semierect, and very cold hardy.

Thorny

'Chickasaw' produces the most and the sweetest blackberries, so it is the only one to plant if you're willing to deal with the thorns. Canes are upright.

GARDEN COMPANIONS

Plant blackberries towards the back of a vegetable garden, or wherever they'll have space. To expand your fresh fruit options consider combining blackberries with fruits such as peaches, nectarines, pears, blueberries, grapes, and peaches.

When Plant December through February. If purchased bare-root, plant as soon as possible. If you must wait, keep roots moist but not wet until planted. Store one or two plants in the refrigerator for short periods, or for many plants, bury the roots briefly in a shallow trench until planting time. Plant container-grown plants anytime.

Where Plant blackberries in full sun, in mildly acidic and well-drained soil. Avoid cold pockets—blackberry flowers can be killed at 28°F (2°C).

How Clip back the roots to about 6 inches long and spread out in the hole. Set plants 3 to 4 feet apart. Gradually fill the hole with regular garden soil, alternating soil and water to eliminate air pockets. Keep well watered during the first year.

TLC After the first year, prune the main canes to 36 inches in height to initiate new cane development from below. Blackberries produce berries on canes that formed the previous year.

Cooler areas of zone 31.

Blueberries

In full spring bloom, a rabbiteye blueberry is nearly as showy as any azalea or rhododendron.

Gardeners throughout Florida can grow blueberries. Not only do they produce the famous and tasty fruits, but the plants also put on a year-round show: in late winter they have delicate white or pink flowers; the late spring–early summer fruit is an attractive sky-blue; and the fall foliage adds red and yellow to the landscape. Blueberries are truly outstanding all-season landscape plants.

Two types of blueberries grow well here: southern highbush blueberries (which are hybrids of the northern highbush blueberry and an evergreen blueberry from Texas) and the rabbiteye blueberry from here in the Southeast. The southern highbush cultivars that are commonly grown in Florida are well adapted to areas south of Ocala and north of Sebring.

Rabbiteyes are the traditional blueberries of the South. They're big plants, growing 12 to 15 feet tall over an 8- to 10-foot area. They are easier to grow than southern highbush types and are more drought tolerant. Rabbiteye blueberries grow well in areas of Florida that have winters as cold as, or colder than, Ocala.

Two plants per person will produce all the fresh blueberries the average gardener can enjoy, with enough left over for a wealth of blueberry cobblers, muffins, pies, and pancakes.

LEFT: *Closeup of the small but numerous flowers of the rabbiteye blueberry.*
RIGHT: *The harvest of rabbiteye blueberries extends through midsummer.*

PEAK SEASON

The harvest season for rabbiteye blueberries extends from May to July, depending on the cultivar. The harvest season for highbush blueberries is April through May, depending on the cultivar.

MY FAVORITES

Southern highbush

'Emerald' is by far the best for areas from Ocala to Sebring. On rich, highly organic soil, this plant will produce heavy crops.

'Jewel' grows well in mild-winter regions, is very early ripening, and has very high berry quality.

'Millennia' is one of the most widely planted varieties in north-central Florida. It has medium to high vigor and a spreading, rather than an upright, growth habit.

Rabbiteye

'Beckyblue', 'Bonita', and 'Climax' are three early-season cultivars that are widely grown in Florida. Equally good but later-ripening cultivars include 'Brightwell', 'Powderblue', 'Tifblue', and 'Woodard'.

GARDEN COMPANIONS

Blueberries are typically used in the landscape as hedges for screening, but they can also be used in cluster plantings or as single specimen plants.

When Plant bare-root or container-grown blueberries from mid-December to mid-February.

Where Blueberries require a very acidic (pH of 4.0 to 5.5) and well-drained soil that is high in organic matter. Allow at least a 7- by 7-foot space for rabbiteyes and a 4- by 4-foot space for southern highbush blueberries. Plant where they will get at least 8 hours of full sun.

How Add peat moss and pelletized or powdered sulfur to the planting hole to increase soil acidity. Add a 3-inch layer of pine bark mulch in a 3-foot circle around the main stem to moderate soil temperature and to increase the organic content of the soil. Plant different cultivars of each type (rabbiteye with rabbiteye and southern highbush with southern highbush) to ensure proper flower pollination and subsequent fruit production as well as to lengthen the harvest season.

TLC Blueberries respond best to frequent, light fertilization. Keep the soil around blueberries moist during fruit set and while the berries are maturing.

Cooler areas of zone 31.

Broccoli

Broccoli is relatively easy to grow and homegrown is immeasurably better than the tough, bland offerings at the supermarket. Broccoli is a member of the mustard family, which includes cabbage, Brussels sprouts, kale, and collards. It develops best during cool seasons of the year. The broccoli head is actually an undeveloped flower head that you cut from the central stem just before the head begins to bloom. Later, if water and fertilizer are maintained, side shoots next to where the main flower grew will produce smaller but equally tasty florets. When it comes to nutritional value, broccoli tops the list. It is rich in vitamins, high in fiber, and low in calories. Broccoli is said to contain as much calcium, gram for gram, as milk.

Harvest broccoli sprouts before the tiny yellow flowers open; these sprouts of 'Purple Sprouting' broccoli are ready for cutting.

PEAK SEASON

Enjoy broccoli in Florida during the cooler months—October through April. Broccoli can withstand freezing temperatures down to 25°F (4°C).

MY FAVORITES

'Waltham 29', 'Packman', and 'Green Comet' have all been around for some time and grow well in a variety of soils. 'Spartan Early', 'Atlantic', 'Green Sprouting', 'Purple Sprouting', 'Italian Green Sprouting', 'DeCicco', and 'Green Duke' also perform well in Florida's cool winter temperatures.

RELATED VEGETABLES

'Minaret' romanesco cauliflower has a delightful mild flavor that many prefer to the more familiar broccoli. It has chartreuse-colored pointed buds.

GARDEN COMPANIONS

Plant with other cold-tolerant vegetables, such as carrots, cauliflower, collards, onions, kohlrabi, and cabbage, and with herbs such as thyme, cilantro, and rosemary.

TOP RIGHT: *A romanesco-type cauliflower with its attractive chartreuse head.*
BOTTOM RIGHT: *This standard broccoli variety is ready to harvest.*

When Plant seeds directly in the garden. Or, buy or grow your own transplants. Start seedlings in late September, and time planting so that vigorous young plants are ready to set out in late fall once daytime temperatures are consistently below 75°F (24°C).

Where For best results, plant in well-prepared, well-drained soil. Broccoli requires at least 6 hours of full sun.

How Sow seeds directly into the garden ¼ inch deep in early fall and thin to 18 inches apart. Water the transplants well after planting and keep the soil moist during the growing season.

TLC Mulch between rows of broccoli with newspaper and cover it with leaves or straw to reduce competing weeds.

Cabbage

Cabbage is a cold-hardy, easy-to-grow vegetable that does especially well in the cool, mild winters of Florida. Head shape varies from the standard round type to flattened or pointed. Green is the most common color, but red and purple are also grown here. Most varieties have smooth leaves, but there are savoy types that have striking crinkled leaves. Harvest times vary, but most cabbages require 50 to 60 days from when they are transplanted into the garden. Harvest when the head forms and while it is firm. Chinese cabbage forms dense heads that may be very upright and tall. The leaves are slightly wrinkled and thinner than the leaves of regular cabbage, with wide, crisp midribs.

Large leaves surround the dense head of cabbage forming at the plant's center.

PEAK SEASON

Fall to spring

MY FAVORITES

'Chieftan Savoy' was an All-America Selections winner in 1938, and it is still a great cabbage for Florida. The 4- to 5-pound heads have densely crinkled leaves with a very mild flavor that improves after a frost.

'Copenhagen Early' is a good early variety that produces uniform, globe-shaped, 6-inch heads that are firm and solid, weighing 3 to 4 pounds.

'Early Jersey Wakefield' is a compact cabbage with a unique conical head; it is particularly suited for small gardens.

'Red Acre' is the earliest red cabbage to mature in Florida. Its globe-shaped, compact heads weigh only 2 pounds.

GARDEN COMPANIONS

Plant cabbage with other cold-tolerant vegetables, such as kohlrabi, collards, onions, cauliflower, bok choi, mustard, and carrots, and with herbs such as thyme and cilantro.

TOP RIGHT: *Nearly mature plants of 'Red Acre' develop in a raised bed.*
BOTTOM RIGHT: *Savoy types of cabbage are notable for their crinkled leaves.*

When Plant cabbage by sowing seeds where you want plants to grow, or by setting out transplants 18 inches apart. Plant when the weather is cool, generally November through January. Successive plantings 30 to 40 days apart will guarantee a long harvest season.

Where Plant in full sun in any well-drained soil. Cabbages prefer a soil that will retain moisture but is not soggy.

How This shallow-rooted crop requires moderate amounts of fertilizer. Apply fertilizer with nitrogen about 3 or 4 weeks after transplanting and 4 to 6 weeks after sowing seeds. Cabbages prefer a firm soil, so don't cultivate the soil immediately prior to planting.

TLC To prevent pest infestations, never plant cabbages in the same place 2 years in a row.

Lettuce

Cool weather, sunshine, and water are all you need to grow lettuce. In Floridian terms, plant in fall as temperatures drop, plant again in late winter, expect little through midsummer, and resume planting in fall. Lettuces with bright red leaves, freckled leaves, and bright green leaves are commonplace in backyards all over Florida.

Flourishing bed of lettuce in early spring includes romaine (foreground), and a red leaf lettuce (center). They're separated by a row of dwarf basil.

For the sake of convenience, the different kinds of lettuce are grouped into four distinct classes: butterhead, head, leaf, and romaine. *Butterhead* types have loose heads and are available with either crunchy or tender leaves. They can be harvested all at once like any head lettuce or you can pick single leaves, as with leaf types. *Head lettuce* is by far the most common kind on American dinner tables, but is less favored by home gardeners for its more exacting growing needs, and because whole heads are harvested at once. In contrast, *leaf lettuce* forms a loose, open head. It's very popular in home gardens, as the tender leaves are harvested as needed, not all at once. *Romaine lettuce* grows upright with broad, crunchy leaves that you can harvest as needed.

Lettuce seeds germinate quickly and the plants grow fast, making it easy to ensure a steady supply. You can harvest in only 45 to 75 days from seeds sown directly in the garden. Lettuce is so easy to grow and has so few problems that it's a good way to introduce children to gardening. Considering how much lettuce most of us eat, it makes good sense to find room in your garden to grow your own.

PEAK SEASON
Fall to spring

MY FAVORITES
Butterhead
'Buttercrunch' is a small, fast-maturing lettuce, with very green outer leaves and a small, crisp center; 'Deer's Tongue' leaves are tongue shaped and light green; and 'Tom Thumb' is very small, pale to medium green.

Head
'Great Lakes' is the best one for Florida. It's a classic iceberg type. Start it early, in fertile soil, and watch for slugs. Don't be discouraged if perfect heads don't develop; they require good timing on your part and good weather.

Leaf
'Black Seeded Simpson' is the classic fast-growing loose-leaf type; 'Oak Leaf' and 'Red Salad Bowl' have deeply cut, tender leaves; and 'Red Sails' has red, ruffled leaves.

Romaine
'Parris Island Cos' has been around for years and remains one of the best; 'Valmaine' and 'Dark Green Cos' are similar, with equally good flavor.

GARDEN COMPANIONS
Grow lettuce with cool-weather vegetables, such as carrots, broccoli, turnips, mustard, collards, kohlrabi, onions, cauliflower, and cabbage.

When Direct-sow small amounts of lettuce seed in 2-week intervals as cool weather approaches in fall, and 6 weeks before warm spring weather arrives. The intervals will ensure you have fresh, tender lettuce in the garden during the entire growing season. Lettuce grows best at temperatures between 60° to 65°F (15° to 18°C) and will go to seed (called *bolting*), once temperatures exceed 80°F (27°C).

Where Plant lettuce in full sun in well-drained soil. The bright greens and reds of lettuce are very attractive and a good addition to flower borders and container plantings.

How Add plenty of organic matter to the soil and rake it smooth before sowing seeds or setting out plants. (If slugs are a problem in your area, however, a great deal of organic matter will encourage them; be ready with bait.) Scatter the small seeds on the surface and press them lightly into the soil, but don't cover them. They need light to germinate. Sow seeds directly into the garden 4 to 5 inches apart in short rows 12 inches apart, or start seeds in seed flats and transplant into the garden after the third set of true leaves appear. Thin seedlings to allow others to grow to their full potential.

TLC Lettuce is susceptible to heavy frost, so cover when cold or freezing temperatures are expected.

LEFT: *Named for the shape of its leaf, 'Deer's Tongue' is a succulent butterhead lettuce.*
RIGHT: *'Red Salad Bowl' is an oak leaf–type that adds color to both garden and salad bowl.*

Muscadine Grapes
Vitis rotundifolia

The most famous grapes in the world, including table grapes like 'Thompson Seedless' as well as the classic wine grapes, are all European. But despite all their good qualities, they won't grow in Florida. Here the grape of choice is the native muscadine. It thrives in our long and hot summers, is immune or resistant to the pests that destroy other kinds of grapes, and produces a very tasty grape.

Typically, muscadine vines bear large, ¾-inch-diameter grapes with 4 to 10 fruits per cluster and as many as 25 clusters per mature plant. Fruit color is usually dark but may be green, gold, red, pink, purple, blue, or black. (The bronze-fruited kinds are called *scuppernongs*, for North Carolina's Scuppernong River, where a particularly desirable variety was found and propagated 200 years ago.) The skin of all muscadines is tough and inedible, but slips off easily. Inside the sweet pulp are five seeds. With some varieties, you need to plant a pollinating vine; for others, you don't. Be sure to ask before you buy.

Wild muscadines have a pronounced musky flavor, but most modern varieties have little of this. Coincidentally, the fruit tastes a great deal like a jaboticaba (page 224). Notably, muscadine grapes contain high levels of resveratrol, a natural plant compound that's beneficial to health.

Sweet and flavorful, perfect for jams, jellies, and dessert wines, and good for you too: Muscadines are a southern specialty that you should not miss.

Trellised muscadine vines glow on a foggy spring morning.

PEAK SEASON

Fall

MY FAVORITES

'Fry' is a bronze grape that is large and very sweet. It comes in very large clusters, and is the most popular muscadine in Florida. Needs a pollinating vine.

'Nesbitt' is black, medium sized, and high yielding. Self-fertile.

'Southern Home' is a black-fruited hybrid with a lot of muscadine character. Somewhat less productive than others, but ornamental. Self-fertile.

'Summit' is an outstanding fresh market bronze selection for the home garden. The number of grapes and this variety's resistance to disease is better than with 'Fry', but the individual grapes are a little smaller. Needs a pollinating vine.

GARDEN COMPANIONS

Plant grapevines with other fruits, including blueberries, blackberries, nectarines, plums, peaches, and pears.

ABOVE: *The classic purple-black muscadine grape.*
BELOW LEFT: *A bronze, speckled scuppernong type of muscadine grape.*

When Plant container-grown plants in early spring; bare-root plants in late winter.

Where Choose a location where plants will receive full sun; even partial shade will reduce the grape harvest. Almost any soil is fine, but plants will benefit from well-drained, slightly acidic soil. Soils with an impervious hardpan layer and soils that are high in calcium will not support muscadines.

How Start with 1-year-old container-grown plants, or, in late winter, bare-root plants. Make holes large enough to spread the roots without crowding. Plant muscadines 15 feet apart. Set them at the same depth that they grew in the nursery. Water as you backfill, and pack soil firmly as you fill the hole. Mulch with compost or shredded leaves to retain moisture around the newly set vines. Set two horizontal wires above plants to train them. Make the first 3 feet high and the second 6 feet high, and train the shoots along them.

TLC In well-drained soil, you cannot overwater. Keep the soil moist and fertilize 4 times a year. Remove weeds to reduce competition for water and nutrients. Prune annually to prevent vines from becoming too tangled and to maintain a supply of new fruiting wood.

249

Onions

Onions have been a part of human diets for a very long time. The wild plants from which all our

The pom-pom flower heads of bunching onions serve well in the flower border.

varieties descend originated in the Middle East, and the ancient Egyptians were known to have grown onions along the Nile River. Indeed, onions are one of the oldest vegetables in continuous cultivation. Brought to Florida by the Spanish, onions are today one of the most important vegetable crops here.

Onion classification can be a bit confusing. All are members of the genus *Allium*. Bunching onions (or scallions) are grown from seed and then chopped into salads or eaten raw, green tops and all. The common, or bulb, onion is the most important type commercially. These onions are usually planted as transplants or as *sets* (tiny, immature bulbs) and harvested after the green tops have withered. (You can also harvest them early and use in the same way as bunching onions.) Bulbing onions are further grouped according to the season in which their bulbs form: short-day onions form bulbs in spring and long-day onions form bulbs in summer. In Florida, short-day onions are best.

When Set out transplants November through December, or sow seeds in September or October.

Where Plant onion transplants or seeds in full sun and in well-drained fertile soil.

How Space onion rows 14 to 18 inches apart, and space plants 4 to 6 inches apart. When planting transplants, trim foliage back by about half after planting. Sow seeds ¼ inch deep. To reduce onion maggots, change the location of your onion crop year to year, and cover young crops with a floating row cover.

TLC Onions can generally withstand light to heavy frosts, but hard freezes will damage them. Control weeds. They compete with onions for light, nutrients, water, and space; they may also harbor insects and diseases. Onions are heavy feeders and require more fertilizer than is used traditionally in most other vegetable crops. For large bulbs, work ¼ cup of 10-10-10 fertilizer per 10 feet of row before planting; repeat after the first 4 to 6 weeks, and again as bulbs are forming. Determine harvest time by pinching the necks of the growing onions. If stiff, the onions are not ready; if soft and limber, then harvest.

RIGHT: *Ready-to-harvest bulb of 'Candy'.*
BELOW: *A bed of bulbing onions nears harvest and storage.*

PEAK SEASON
Spring

MY FAVORITES
Bunching onions
'Lisbon' is by far the best for Florida. Tops remain fresh and crisp well after harvest.

'Red Baron' is bright red up to the lower portion of the leaves.

Bulbing onions
'Candy' delivers extra-sweet and mild flavor in a 3- to 4-inch globe-shaped bulb.

'Copra' is the best storage onion available. Its extra-hard medium-sized bulbs will provide you with onions for cooking until you plant again the following season.

'Mars' stores well and will provide your salads with color all spring and summer. This variety combines earliness and large size and is ideally grown from transplants. At maturity, it has beautiful red color both inside and out.

GARDEN COMPANIONS
Plant onions with other cool-weather vegetables, such as carrots, cauliflower, collards, kohlrabi, and cabbage, and with herbs such as thyme and cilantro.

Strawberries

When asked what their favorite berry is, chances are most folks will say the strawberry. These plump, bright red, juicy little morsels are grown commercially throughout Florida and are easy to grow in backyard gardens as well.

Strawberries at peak bloom in early spring promise an abundant harvest to come.

Strawberries are perennials, but in Florida we treat them as annuals. We plant them from October to mid-November, when they establish strong roots. Later, as a result of the cool nights and short days in midwinter, the plants produce flowers. A month or so later when we're into spring, these flowers begin producing fruits that are soon ready for picking. When warmer weather begins, the flower production stops and the strawberries begin to put out runners to produce new little plants. As hard as it may be to do, you must pull these plants from the garden. The tiny plants, called *runners*, often contain harmful diseases and should not be left to produce next year's plants.

Strawberries are well suited to small gardens. If you don't have room to grow them in mounded rows as farmers do, plant them in raised beds, tubs on a sunny patio, window boxes, hanging baskets, or decorative strawberry pots. You can even grow them as a ground cover.

When Plant certified disease-free plants from October 1 to November 15.

Where Plant in well-drained soil that is moist but not wet. Strawberries can grow just about anywhere in Florida but in muck soil. Full sun is a must for heavy fruit production.

How Soak roots for a half hour or until rehydrated. Dig a hole to accommodate the roots just to the crown (where the roots and stems meet), positioning each plant so its crown is slightly above the soil level. Space plants 15 to 18 inches apart, in rows about 4 feet apart.

TLC Strawberries prefer a mulch to maintain adequate soil moisture. Thin black plastic works best because it doesn't harbor diseases; pine straw or coastal hay works well also.

PEAK SEASON

Spring

MY FAVORITES

'Florida 90' is an older variety. The large, vigorous plants yield large, red, pointed fruits heavily over a long period of time.

'Florida Belle' is a good variety for Florida gardeners because of its disease resistance. The plants are upright and the large fruits are blunt and conical.

'Tioga' makes very large and vigorous plants with big, dark green, glossy leaves and very large, firm fruits.

GARDEN COMPANIONS

Plant strawberries with other cold-hardy vegetables, including broccoli, cauliflower, cabbage, beets, Swiss chard, kohlrabi, lettuce, and onions.

TOP RIGHT: *A ripe strawberry that is ready to harvest.*
BOTTOM RIGHT: *Don't kid yourself—home-grown strawberries really are better.*

Tomatoes

A single cherry tomato plant is productive enough to provide plenty of sweet fruits for grazing gardeners and their friends.

Granted, commercially grown tomatoes are an important agricultural crop in Florida, but nothing can compare to a tomato picked right off the vine in your own backyard. Tomatoes are the most popular home garden crop, and for good reason.

Bush (determinate) types get to a certain size and stop growing, then produce tomatoes for a 10-day period. *Vining* (indeterminate) types are a little more rampant; they continue to grow and produce until the frost kills them. They need staking and lots of space, but many gardeners feel that the varieties they offer are worth it.

One reason we love tomatoes is because they are so easy to grow so many different ways. Grow them in the ground the traditional way, or in containers, in hanging baskets, in a greenhouse, or hydroponically.

For best quality, harvest tomatoes when fully red-ripe. In anticipation of foul or cold weather, pick tomatoes when they are pink and ripen in the house in a well-ventilated place at room temperature.

Tomatoes are quite attractive, especially when you include a few of the multicolored ones. Colors range from white to yellow to red to purple to almost black, and fruits may even be variegated or striped.

PEAK SEASON
Summer and fall

MY FAVORITES

'Better Boy' is a top variety nationally and here in Florida. It has good resistance to many diseases and nematodes.

'Bonnie Best' produces medium-sized fruits. The plants adapt well to being grown in cages. This variety performs best in North Florida.

'Manalucie' is an old commercial staking variety with large red fruit and resistance to many of the diseases that plague tomatoes throughout the state.

Other large-fruited varieties 'Floramerica', 'Celebrity', and 'Flora-Dade' are good determinate, large-fruited varieties.

Other small-fruited varieties 'Red Cherry', 'Sweet Chelsea', and 'Sweet 100' are all excellent small-fruited indeterminant varieties. Determinate varieties include: 'Floragold', 'Patio', and 'Roma'.

GARDEN COMPANIONS
Plant tomatoes with other warm-season vegetables, such as beans, corn, cucumbers, eggplants, okra, peppers, and squash.

TOP RIGHT: *'Floragold' is a small-fruited tomato that does well in Florida.*
BOTTOM RIGHT: *Tomatoes come in various sizes, shapes, and colors.*

When In North Florida, plant transplants in the spring after frost has passed. Time later plantings so that fruits mature in fall prior to frost. In South Florida, plant in early fall so that plants mature and fruits ripen in late winter.

Where Tomatoes need sun and consistently moist soil that is fertile and rich in organic matter. Compact bush types grow well in large containers.

How Loosen soil to a depth of 10 to 12 inches and work in 2 to 3 inches of compost or other organic matter. Space staked or caged plants 3 feet apart. Snip off lower leaves and set plants deep so that only the top three or four leaves are above the soil line. This will encourage roots to develop along the stem of the plant.

TLC Water plants thoroughly once a week. Provide light applications of fertilizer or compost throughout the growing season. Stake or cage plants to keep the fruits off the ground, increase air circulation around plants, and reduce the chance of infection from soilborne diseases. Certain roundworms, called nematodes, suck water and nutrients out of the roots. If these are in your soil, grow tomatoes in 5-gallon containers filled with artificial soil mix and placed on a sheet of plastic.

255

Seasonal Chores

Of all the seasons in Florida, fall is the finest. The scorching heat and high humidity release their hold, and temperatures are milder. Moreover, the afternoon rains return, and a wider selection of plants is available at garden centers.

Fall

DIVIDE AND REPLANT CROWDED PERENNIALS. After digging the clump out of the soil, push two spading forks back to back through the clump and gently pull the handles apart. Repeat this procedure as needed to reach the right-sized clump. Plant and water immediately. Fall is the perfect time to plant new perennials (page 58), and garden centers usually offer a great selection at this time of year.

OPPOSITE: *Brilliant orange fall leaf color precedes the ripening of persimmon fruit, which later hangs on the bare trees like colorful ornaments.*

HARVEST AND PLANT PAPAYAS. Fruits are ready when they begin to turn yellow and get soft. In North Florida, sow seedlings in small containers to grow through the winter for spring planting.

PLANT BULBS. The soil is warm and the air is cool, perfect conditions for planting bulbs of all sorts. Consider African iris, amaryllis, blackberry lily, blood lily, calla, clivia, crinum, elephant's ear, gladiolus, lily-of-the-Nile, Louisiana iris, walking iris, spider lily, and rain lilies.

PLANT HERBS. Fall is the season for herbs in Florida. Just about everything you've read about in gardening magazines can be grown now, including chives, garlic chives, dill, oregano, lemon balm, fennel, rosemary, lemon grass, cilantro, salad burnet, lavender, Mexican tarragon, thyme, and chervil.

PLANT PERMANENT LANDSCAPE PLANTS. Now is the time to plant new trees, shrubs, vines, perennials, and ground covers. Take your landscape plan to the garden center and prioritize those areas in your garden that will require the most work. Consider planting shrubs to attract migratory birds, which begin arriving this month.

PLANT ROSES. Fall is the best season for planting roses. Choose only roses grafted on certified *Rosa fortuniana* rootstock. Roses grown on either 'Dr. Huey' rootstock or *Rosa multiflora,* both of which are used in the northern United States, seldom live more than 3 to 4 years in Florida gardens. But roses on *R. fortuniana* rootstock will be healthier and more vigorous and will live for decades.

PLANT VEGETABLES. Plant the cool-season vegetables: broccoli, beets, kale, cabbage, carrots, cauliflower, kohlrabi,

PLANTING A CONTAINER PLANT

Place the container on its side and roll it on the ground while tapping it to loosen the roots. Upend the container and slide the plant out. Cut off any badly coiled roots.

1 Dig a planting hole at least twice as wide as the root ball and slightly shallower, and spread the roots out over a central plateau of firm soil. Adjust the plant until it sits an inch or so above the surrounding soil.

2 Backfill the hole with the unamended soil that you dug from the hole. (Amending the soil will only encourage the roots to circle around the plant instead of probing outward in search of nutrients.)

3 Mound the soil to create a ridge around the plant to direct water to the roots. The trunk should not be directly exposed to water or it may rot. Irrigate gently.

1

2

3

mustard, onions, peas, ruta-bagas, spinach, and turnips. Leave space in your garden for planting small rows of lettuce every 3 to 4 weeks for fresh harvests. Till plenty of organic matter into the soil to prepare for planting strawberries after mid-October.

SOW FLOWER SEEDS. Prepare now and you will reap rewards during winter. Plant cool-season annuals such as calendula, pansies, snapdragons, sweet peas, alyssum, dianthus, lobelia, nasturtiums, scabiosa, strawflowers, petunia, stock, and flowering kale.

WATER CONTAINER PLANTS. Reprogram automatic watering systems when the weather cools. Plants in terra-cotta pots need more water than plants grown in plastic or glazed ceramic pots.

MAKE COMPOST. Leaves that fall to the ground in North Florida can be added to the compost pile. If possible, run them through a shredder or

HOW TO STAKE VARIOUS PLANTS

Support thin-stemmed, bushy perennials with a grid (top left) or stakes and string (bottom left). Tie tall plants to a bamboo stake (right).

mow over them to increase the surface area so they decompose faster.

STARVE YOUR BOUGAINVILLEA. If you want your bougainvillea to bloom next summer, stop fertilizing and watering now and begin again in spring.

WATCH FOR CATERPILLARS. Gardeners aren't the only ones working out in the garden during the fall months. Fall is a period when caterpillar populations soar. Use an organic biological spray or a drench of the organic insecticide Bt (Dipel) for best control.

PLANTING A ROSE OR OTHER BARE-ROOT SHRUB

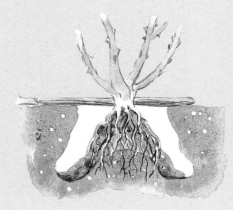

1 Make a firm cone of soil in a planting hole wide enough to fit the roots. Spread the roots over the cone, positioning the plant at the same depth that (or slightly higher than) it was growing in the field. Use a shovel handle or yardstick to check the depth.

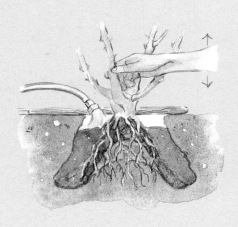

2 Hold the plant upright as you firm soil around its roots. When backfilling is almost complete, add water. This settles the soil around the roots, eliminating any air pockets. If the plant settles below the level of the surrounding soil, gently pull it to the proper level while the soil is saturated, and firm it in place with soil.

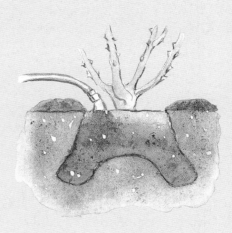

3 Finish filling the hole with soil, then water again. Take care not to overwater while the plant is still dormant, because soggy soil may inhibit the formation of new roots. When the growing season begins, build up a ridge of soil around the planting site to form a basin that will keep water from running off; water the plant whenever the top 2 inches of soil are dry.

Winter

CONTINUE PLANTING ANNUALS AND HERBS. Choose between alyssum, flowering kale, pansies, petunias, snapdragons, and ultrafragrant stock. Plant cool-season herbs—fennel, garlic chives, lemon balm, lemon grass, Mexican tarragon, parsley, rosemary, thyme, and sage—until the onset of hot weather.

FERTILIZE MANGO TREES. Once blossoms begin to open in December, apply 4-0-9 fertilizer evenly under the canopies of the trees and water well. Follow up with a liquid foliar spray in late February. Fertilize other tropical and subtropical fruit trees in January or early February.

HARVEST CITRUS. In November, harvest 'Navel', 'Parson Brown', and 'Hamlin' oranges, 'Orlando' tangelo, 'Dancy' and 'Robinson' tangerines, and grapefruit. In December, continue harvesting November's sweet oranges and pick 'Pineapple'

orange, tangelos, 'Temple' and 'Dancy' tangerines, and grapefruit. Keep weeds away from the base of citrus trunks to help avoid bark disease.

HARVEST VEGETABLES. Winter's moderately warm days and cool evenings provide the perfect weather for many vegetables to thrive. Vegetables harvested during the winter season include beets, broccoli, cabbage, carrots, cauliflower, collards, lettuce, mustard, onions, peas, potatoes, radishes, rutabaga, spinach, and turnips.

PLANT CAMELLIAS. Nearly all Florida gardeners have room for a camellia or two. Use them as a specimen in the landscape or as informal hedges.

PLANT SPRING AND SUMMER BULBS. Most of Florida doesn't get cold enough for tulips, daffodils, and hyacinths. But there's a wealth of heat-tolerant bulbs that do thrive here. African iris, amaryllis, crinum, daylilies, gloriosa lily, hurricane lily, lily-of-the-Nile, spider lily, rain lily, and walking iris are a few of the bulbs to plant now for stunning summer blooms. If moles or voles chew through your bulbs as they look for grubs and worms, place a handful of pea gravel in each hole to make them change course.

PLANT TREES AND SHRUBS. Early winter is not too late to plant trees and shrubs. While plants' demands for water and nutrients are lower during winter months, the soil is still warm. Newly installed plants will produce many new roots in the inviting soil and later, as soil cools, plants will gently go dormant. In spring, when the demand for water increases, the roots will have grown appreciably, and they can readily supply moisture to the stems and leaves without undo stress on the entire plant.

PROTECT PLANTS FROM FROST. If frost threatens, cover tender plants with old blankets or quilts. Cover larger plants with blankets and provide supplemental heat by burning a 150-watt floodlight inside the enclosure. A lightweight spun fabric called "freeze cloth" is available at garden centers and can protect cold-sensitive plants for little cost. Be certain to remove the covers the following morning after the air temperature rises above 35°F (2°C).

PRUNE, FERTILIZE, AND MULCH ROSES. Remove all the leaves from rose plants during late February pruning and rake up any old leaves to reduce black spot disease. Then apply a 16–4–8 fertilizer that includes minor elements, and spray the denuded bushes

Many herbs are ornamental, and these blooming chives are an example. This four-tiered planting begins with boxwood in back, and ends with sage, then thyme.

with horticultural or neem oil to eliminate insects hiding in cracks and crevices. Place a fresh layer of mulch (see pages 264 and 265) around each plant or over the entire flower bed. Keep the plants moist and the roses will be in full bloom in 9 to 10 weeks.

SOW FLOWER SEEDS. In late January, begin sowing summer flowers in plastic seed trays. Plant seeds of asters, bachelor's buttons, cosmos, dianthus, marigolds, periwinkle, portulaca, salvia, statice, strawflowers, and verbenas for brilliant spring and summer color.

SOW SEEDS OF HERBS. Only a few herbs, notably basil, dill, and chives, are sown directly into the garden now. Others,

Purple bromeliads contrast green plants and limestone pavers. Ferns, Cuban petticoat palm (left), and gumbo limbo tree (center right) are prominent.

such as catnip, fennel, garlic, horehound, lemon balm, marjoram, oregano, parsley, sage, tarragon and thyme, are better sown in small trays or individual pots indoors.

263

Spring

AVOID CYPRESS MULCH. It doesn't decompose, so cypress mulch creates a mat that prevents water, nutrients, and air from reaching plants' roots. Moreover, cypress trees are clear-cut from essential wetlands solely for mulch, and this clear-cutting creates an opening for invasive trees like Brazilian pepper.

CARE FOR CITRUS TREES. Citrus trees need 1 inch of water every week in well-drained soil. As the new spring growth appears, so do aphids and spider mites. Control these pests on citrus with sprays of either neem or horticultural oil. Don't mulch: it promotes root rot and encourages shallow roots. Fertilize every 6 to 8 weeks with an 8-3-9 or 8-2-10 fertilizer that includes at least 3 percent magnesium.

KEEP LAWNS WATERED. The spring months are normally the driest of the year in Florida. When St. Augustine grass turns blue-green, or if footprints remain in the lawn for 10 minutes or more, it is time to water. Bahiagrass can go completely dormant in dry weather and then green up when rains begin again.

PLANT PERENNIALS. Gardening can be hot work when summer arrives and perennials can provide lots of color without a lot of effort. Now is the time to plant them. Surefire perennials for the garden include blanket flower, firespike salvia, periwinkle, black-eyed Susan, goldenrod, ornamental grasses, and butterfly weed.

PLANT TREES. Most tree seedlings are grown in plastic nursery containers and can be planted at any time of year. Consider trees acclimated to the Florida climate, including natives such as bald cypress, live oak, shumard oak, magnolia, red cedar, and winged elm.

PLANT TROPICAL AND SUBTROPICAL PLANTS. In central and southern areas of Florida, set out plants such as banana,

264

Brazilian plume flower, flowering ginger, passion vine, queen's wreath, and Texas olive trees.

PLANT VINES. With so many Florida homes being built on small lots, gardeners throughout the state are beginning to grow vertically. Trellises, arbors, gazebos, and even chain-link fences offer wonderful opportunities for a wide array of flowering vines for both sunny and shady areas. Prolific vines include blue sky vine, petrea (in southern zones), passion

vine, Dutchman's pipe, Rangoon creeper, and honeysuckle.

PLANT WARM-SEASON VEGETABLES. Early spring is the best time to plant beans, cantaloupes, corn, cucumbers, eggplants, okra, southern peas, squash, and sweet potatoes. Set out transplants of peppers and tomatoes by early or mid-March.

PRUNE AZALEAS. In central and North Florida, spring is the best time to prune these shrubs. Trim right after plants bloom without fear of removing next year's flowers; avoid pruning after the Fourth of July.

REFRESH MULCH. Before the hot weather arrives, replenish the mulch around trees and shrubs. Use eucalyptus chips, pine bark, straw, or recycled wooden pallets (sold as red- or brown-colored "environmental" mulch).

WATCH FOR CHINCH BUGS. Look for these pests (they have an "X" on their backs) by looking closely where a suspicious brown spot in the lawn meets the healthy green grass. If chinch bugs are the problem, supply adequate moisture to your lawn to increase its tolerance to feeding damage and to promote the beneficial fungi that attack chinch bugs. Also, minimize nitrogen fertilization to slow chinch bug reproduction.

SOW FLOWER SEEDS. Easy-to-grow annuals for spring sowing include ageratum, amaranth, celosia, coleus, cosmos, gomphrena, marigolds, melampodium, moss rose, salvia, sunflowers, and zinnia.

Summer

CHECK AUTOMATIC SPRINKLERS.

If you haven't done so already, turn your sprinkler system on manually during the day and check to make certain everything is working before the weather gets too hot and steamy. Water deeply to direct the roots deep into the ground where they will have less exposure to the scorching sun. Water container plants regularly.

CONSIDER NATIVE PLANTS.

Some Florida gardeners may consider native plants to be "scruffy" and unattractive. But native plants are acclimated to Florida's summer heat and humidity and its rainfall patterns, so they are very drought tolerant. Consider visiting nurseries with a good selection of native plants and see which ones could fit into your garden design.

GREEN UP A YELLOW LAWN.

Lawns often look pale this time of year. Rather than adding nitrogen fertilizer, which makes the grass grow taller, apply an iron fertilizer. The grass will green up in a matter of a day or two without additional growth.

PLANT HEAT-TOLERANT ANNUALS.

Only the toughest of annuals will survive the intense heat of a Florida summer. Transplants to set out now include celosia, coleus, gomphrena, impatiens, marigold, moss rose, salvia, vinca, wax begonia, and zinnia. Be certain to water well right after sowing and then every day for the first 7 to 10 days.

PLANT HEAT-LOVING VEGETABLES.

Now is the time to plant heat lovers, including cherry tomatoes, collards, eggplant, Malabar spinach, okra, southern peas, sweet potatoes, and yard-long beans.

LEFT: *'Peter Pan Red' zinnia is combined here with 'Victoria' mealycup sage.*
RIGHT: *Ripe 'Camp Joy' cherry tomatoes glisten with morning dew.*

SOLARIZE VEGETABLE GARDEN SOILS. Till the garden area to fluff up the soil and then water well. Cover the entire area with a sheet of clear plastic and seal the edges. The intense heat will bake the nematodes (microscopic worms) to death, reduce the number of disease organisms, and eliminate most weeds.

MANAGE ROSE BLACK SPOT AND PESTS. Summer is the prime season for black spot disease and spider mites. Wash spider mites and aphids off the leaves with a strong stream of water. For black spot, 4 teaspoons of baking soda and a few drops of dishwashing liquid in 1 gallon of water sprayed or sprinkled on the rose leaves every 10 days has shown good results. Or spray Orthenex (an insect and disease control) every 7 to 10 days. If problems persist, consider replacing

Combined with ferns and fibrous begonias, 'White Christmas' caladium brightens a shaded corner of a garden.

plants with disease-resistant varieties in the fall; check with the local botanical garden or a good garden center for recommendations.

WATER CITRUS TREES. Don't forget to water citrus trees. Soak the root zone with at least 1 inch of water every 7 to 10 days.

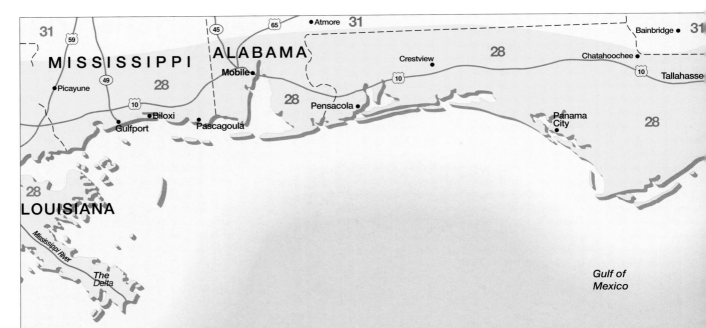

A plant's performance is governed by the total climate: length of growing season, timing and amount of rainfall, winter lows, summer highs, and humidity. Sunset's climate zone maps take all these factors into account—unlike the familiar hardiness zone maps devised by the U.S. Department of Agriculture, which divide the United States and Canada into zones based strictly on winter lows. Below are brief descriptions of the four zones found in Florida.

Zone 25, South Florida and the Keys. Zone 25 boasts the mildest climate in the continental United States. In the mainland part of the region, winters are often frost free, though temperatures do occasionally dip below freezing (lows range from 25° to 40°F/–4° to 4°C). The Florida Keys, at zone 25's southern tip, are truly frost free; on Key West, the lowest temperature on record is 41°F/5°C.

The warmth and high humidity here rule out certain slightly tender plants that grow well in other parts of the South and up the East Coast—camellias, for example.

Zone 26, Central and Interior Florida. Gardeners in zone 26 enjoy two horticultural worlds. They can grow many of the tropical trees and shrubs that thrive in neighboring zone 25; they also succeed with many plants that flourish in the cooler winter climates to the north.

Winter brings some frosts, but not many—typically about a dozen up in Daytona Beach, six in Orlando and Tampa, perhaps one in Fort Myers or West Palm Beach. Lows range

from 15°F/–9°C at the north end of the zone to 27° to 30°F/ –3 ° to –1°C at the south end. However, the region does experience the occasional severe freeze that kills many plants. Humidity is always high. Rainfall is heaviest in summer and early autumn, with annual averages varying from 46 inches in the north to 60 inches in the south.

Zone 28, Northern Florida and the Gulf Coast. Zone 28 is America's prime location for camellias and azaleas. Most of zone 28 produces especially big, productive camellia and azalea plants—so big that they usually need pruning to control size. Winters are often entirely or nearly frost free, but every 5 to 10 years, masses of arctic air (down to 20°F/–7°C or even lower) move down the continent and damage or kill many subtropical plants.

Zone 31, Interior Plains of the Gulf Coast and the Coastal Southeastern States. The typical last spring freezes come between February 27 and March 19, and autumn's first freeze usually arrives between November 7 and December 3. During the hot, humid summers, average highs are all in the high 80s or low 90s (low 30s C); in winter, record lows measure from 0° to 7°F/–18° to –14°C. Average annual rainfall measures 44 to 54 inches. Camellias and azaleas perform splendidly in zone 31, as do various flowering dogwoods and magnolias—including the South's showy trademark tree, *Magnolia grandiflora*.

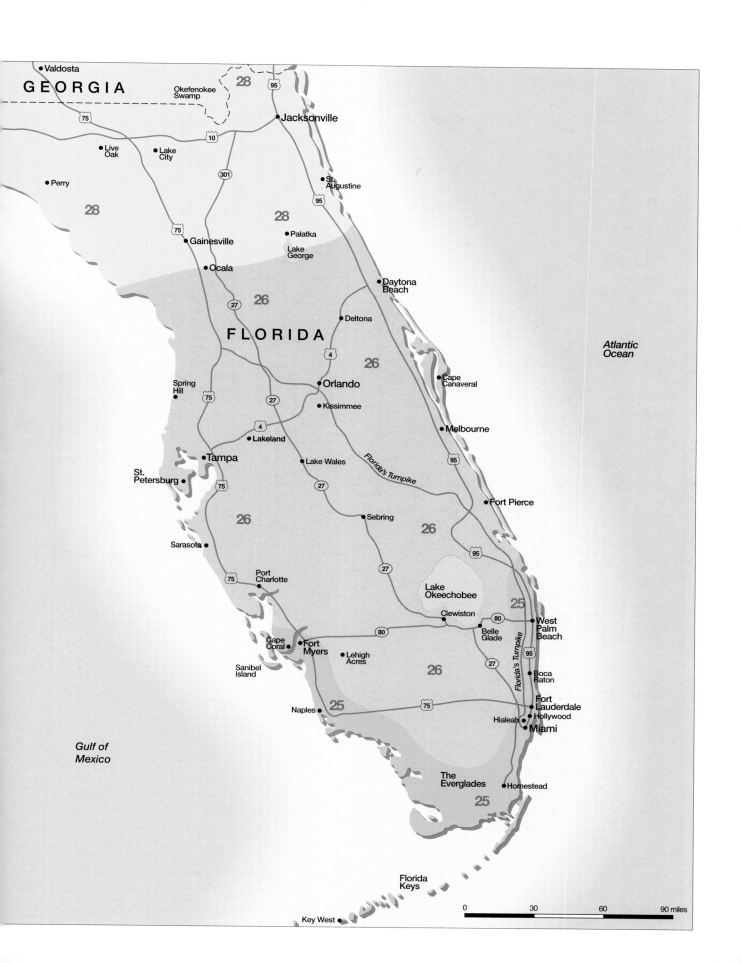

GEORGIA

• Valdosta

Okefenokee
Swamp

28

95

75

• Jacksonville

10

• Live
Oak

• Lake
City

301

• Perry

28

75

• Gainesville

28

• Palatka

95

• St.
Augustine

26

• Ocala

Lake
George

27

• Daytona
Beach

FLORIDA

• Deltona

4

26

Spring
Hill •

75

Orlando

27

• Cape
Canaveral

• Kissimmee

4

26

• Lakeland

• Melbourne

• Tampa

• Lake Wales

Florida's Turnpike

95

St.
Petersburg •

75

27

26

• Sebring

26

• Fort Pierce

Sarasota •

95

75

Port
Charlotte •

Lake
Okeechobee

25

27

Clewiston •

80

West
Palm
Beach

Cape
Coral •

• Fort
Myers

80

Belle
Glade •

Florida's Turnpike

95

Sanibel
Island

• Lehigh
Acres

26

27

• Boca
Raton

25

75

Fort
Lauderdale

Naples •

Hialeah •

• Hollywood

• Miami

Gulf of
Mexico

The
Everglades

• Homestead

25

Florida
Keys

Atlantic
Ocean

0   30   60   90 miles

Key West •

Index

Pages listed in *italics* include photographs.